CAMBRIDGE

CB081797

# EMPOWER

## SECOND EDITION

## STUDENT'S BOOK WITH DIGITAL PACK

A1

STARTER

Adrian Doff, Craig Thaine
Herbert Puchta, Jeff Stranks, Peter Lewis-Jones
with Rachel Godfrey

**EMPOWER SECOND EDITION** is a six-level general English course for adult and young adult learners, taking students from beginner to advanced level (CEFR A1 to C1). *Empower Second Edition* combines course content from Cambridge University Press with validated assessment from the experts at Cambridge Assessment English.

*Empower Second Edition's* unique mix of engaging classroom materials and reliable assessment enables learners to make consistent and measurable progress.

## Content you love. Assessment you can trust.

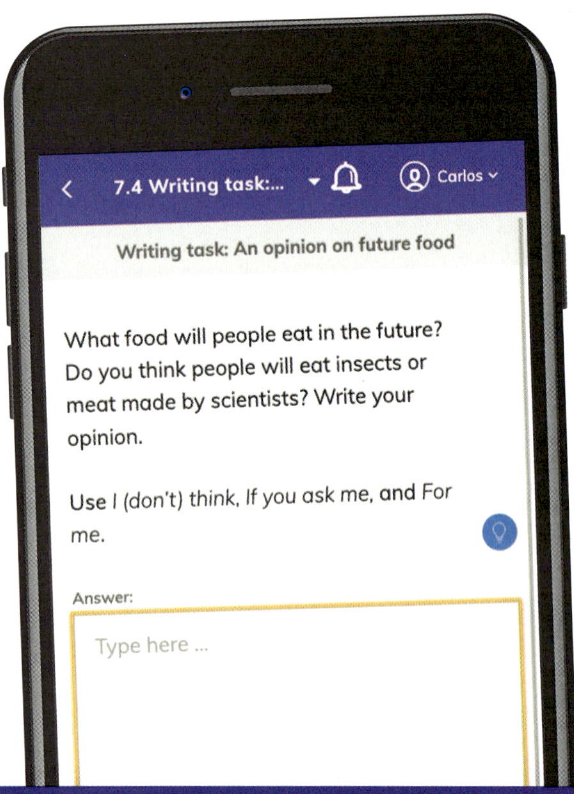


## Better Learning with *Empower Second Edition*

Better Learning is our simple approach where **insights** we've gained from research have helped shape **content** that drives **results**.

# Learner engagement

## 1 Content that informs and motivates

**Insights**
Sustained motivation is key to successful language learning and skills development.

**Content**
Clear learning goals, thought-provoking images, texts and speaking activities, plus video content to arouse curiosity.

**Results**
Content that surprises, entertains and provokes an emotional response, helping teachers to deliver motivating and memorable lessons.

8A I WAS ON TOUR WITH MY BAND

Learn to talk about past events
G Past simple: *be*
V Past time expressions

1 READING

a Look at the events in pictures a–d. Choose one you like and one you don't like. Tell a partner. Say why.

a a party
b a sports game
c a concert
d a meeting

b Read about Cara, Antonio and Ava. Which events in 1a do they talk about?

c Read the texts again. Which cities does each person talk about?

d Talk about Cara, Antonio and Ava's lives with a partner. Who would you like to meet? Why?

My name's Cara. I'm a photographer. I was in New York three days ago for work and then I was in Dublin yesterday at a meeting about newspaper photography. Life's busy right now!

'Yesterday I was in Dublin.'

'I was at a game in Bristol. It was the Final!'

The people in our team …
My name's Antonio Marotto. I'm the doctor for our team. It's a great job – I really like helping our players. I often go away with the team. We were in Newcastle two weeks ago for a game and we were in Bristol last week. It's fun to travel with the team.

Ava on the road …
Hi everyone, it's Ava. Last week I was on tour with my band in Europe – three cities in five days. We were in Munich on Wednesday and then we were in Vienna on Thursday. But Saturday was the best night. We were in Milan and about 1,000 people were at our concert.

'In this photo we were in Milan.'

64

UNIT 8

2 GRAMMAR Past simple: *be* positive

a Complete the table. Find examples of the past simple of *be* in the texts about Cara, Antonio and Ava.

| + | |
|---|---|
| I [1] ______ | we [3] ______ |
| you were | you were |
| he/she/it [2] ______ | they were |

b 08.01 Pronunciation Listen to sentences 1–4. Are *was* and *were* stressed? Practise saying the sentences.

1 We were in Munich.
2 I was in Madrid.
3 We were in Newcastle.
4 I was in New York.

c Now go to Grammar Focus 8A Part 1 on p. 128.

d Write sentences about where you were:
- this morning
- last night
- yesterday afternoon

e Compare your sentences in 2d with a partner. Were you in the same places?

Chan and I were at the supermarket yesterday afternoon.

3 VOCABULARY Past time expressions

a Today is Friday of week 3. Put the number of sentences 1–4 in the correct place on the timeline.

week 1 | week 2 | week 3
Monday Tuesday Wednesday Thursday Friday

1 We were in Munich on Wednesday.
2 We were in Madrid two weeks ago.
3 … we were in Bristol last week.
4 I was in Dublin yesterday.

b Look at the underlined words in 3a. Replace them with words in the box.

months this morning Saturday year

c Now go to Vocabulary Focus 8A on p. 149.

d Work in pairs.
Student A: Say a past time expression.
Student B: Say where a person you know was.
Then swap roles.

last weekend
My parents were in London last weekend.
two years ago
My friend Marco was in Thailand two years ago.

4 LISTENING AND GRAMMAR Past simple: *be* negative and questions

a 08.06 Review the texts about Cara, Antonio and Ava again. Then listen to them talking to friends. Write the correct name for each conversation.

Conversation 1 ______
Conversation 2 ______
Conversation 3 ______

b 08.06 Match events 1–3 with adjectives a–c. Listen again and check.

1 the meeting — a exciting
2 the game — b interesting
3 the concert — c fun

c 08.07 Listen to Conversation 1 again. Complete the conversation with the words in the box.

was (x2) were (x2) wasn't

WILL ______ you at work yesterday?
CARA Yes, I ______, but I ______ here in the office.
WILL Where ______ you?
CARA I was at a meeting in Dublin.
WILL Oh, ______ it interesting?
CARA Yes, it was really interesting.

d Now go to Grammar Focus 8A Part 2 on p. 128.

e 08.11 Complete the conversation with *was*, *were*, *wasn't* or *weren't*. Listen and check.

A You ______ at work yesterday.
B No, it ______ a holiday for me.
A Nice. ______ you at home all day?
B No, I ______. I ______ in town in the morning and then I ______ at a party last night.
A ______ the party good?
B Yes, it ______ a lot of fun.

f Practise the conversation in 4e with a partner. Change some of the information.

I was at a football match in the morning and then at the cinema last night.
Was the film good?

5 SPEAKING

Communication 8A Student A: Go to p. 113. Student B: Go to p. 111. Student C: Go to p. 115.

65

## 2 Personalised and relevant

**Insights**
Language learners benefit from frequent opportunities to personalise their responses.

**Content**
Personalisation tasks in every unit make the target language more meaningful to the individual learner.

**Results**
Personal responses make learning more memorable and inclusive, with all students participating in spontaneous spoken interaction.

> *There are so many adjectives to describe such a wonderful series, but in my opinion it's very reliable, practical and modern.*

**Zenaide Brianez, Director of Studies, Instituto da Língua Inglesa, Brazil**

# Measurable progress

## 1 Assessment you can trust

### Insights

Tests developed and validated by Cambridge Assessment English, the world leaders in language assessment, to ensure they are accurate and meaningful.

### Content

End-of-unit tests, mid- and end-of-course competency tests and personalised CEFR test report forms provide reliable information on progress with language skills.

### Results

Teachers can see learners' progress at a glance, and learners can see measurable progress, which leads to greater motivation.

Results of an impact study showing % improvement of Reading levels, based on global *Empower* students' scores over one year.

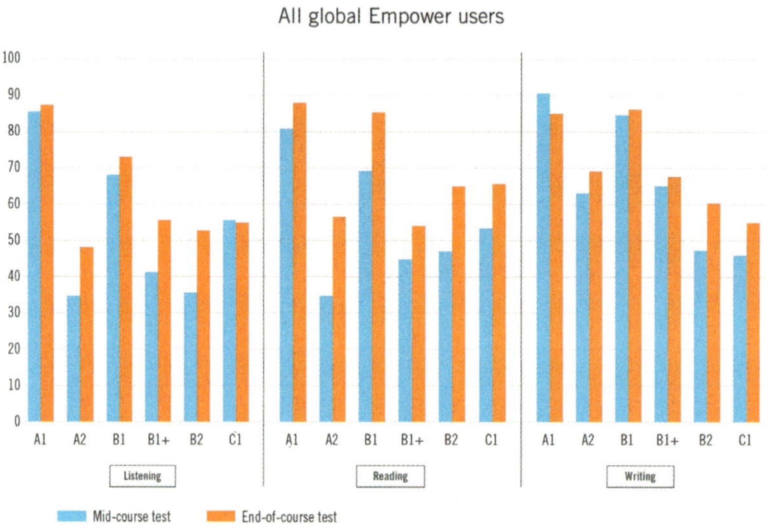


*Average score for listening, reading, and writing in the mid-course test and end-of-course test. Based on global students' scores from August 2016 to July 2017.*

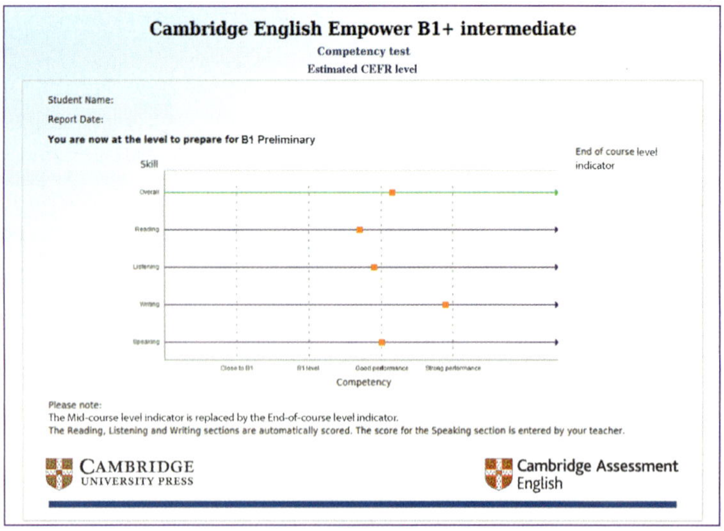

**Cambridge English Empower B1+ intermediate**

Competency test

Estimated CEFR level

Student Name:

Report Date:

**You are now at the level to prepare for B1 Preliminary**

Skill

End of course level indicator

Competency

Please note:

The Mid-course level indicator is replaced by the End-of-course level indicator.

The Reading, Listening and Writing sections are automatically scored. The score for the Speaking section is entered by your teacher.

CAMBRIDGE UNIVERSITY PRESS

Cambridge Assessment English

> *"We started using the tests provided with Empower and our students started showing better results from this point until now."*

**Kristina Ivanova, Director of Foreign Language Training Centre, ITMO University, Saint Petersburg, Russia**

## 2 Evidence of impact

### Insights

Schools and colleges need to show that they are evaluating the effectiveness of their language programmes.

### Content

*Empower* (First edition) impact studies have been carried out in various countries, including Russia, Brazil, Turkey and the UK, to provide evidence of positive impact and progress.

### Results

Colleges and universities have demonstrated a significant improvement in language level between the mid- and end-of-course tests, as well as a high level of teacher satisfaction with *Empower*.

# Manageable learning

## 1 Mobile friendly

**Insights**
Learners expect online content to be mobile friendly but also flexible and easy to use on any digital device.

**Content**
*Empower Second Edition* provides easy access to Cambridge One: Digital Workbook content that works on any device and includes practice activities with audio.

**Results**
Cambridge One: Digital Workbook content is easy to access anywhere, and produces meaningful and actionable data so teachers can track their students' progress and adapt their lesson accordingly.

*"I had been studying English for 10 years before university and I didn't succeed. But now with Empower I know my level of English has changed."*

**Nikita, *Empower* Student, ITMO University, Saint Petersburg, Russia**

## 2 Corpus-informed

**Insights**
Corpora can provide valuable information about the language items learners are able to learn successfully at each CEFR level.

**Content**
Two powerful resources – Cambridge Corpus and English Profile – informed the development of the *Empower* course syllabus and the writing of the materials.

**Results**
Learners are presented with the target language they are able to incorporate and use at the right point in their learning journey. They are not overwhelmed with unrealistic learning expectations.

# Rich in practice

## 1 Language in use

**Insights**
It is essential that learners are offered frequent and manageable opportunities to practice the language they have been focusing on.

**Content**
Throughout the *Empower Second Edition* Student's Book, learners are offered a wide variety of practice activities, plenty of controlled practice and frequent opportunities for communicative spoken practice.

**Results**
Meaningful practice makes new language more memorable and leads to more efficient progress in language acquisition.

8B HE SAW A BEAR

Learn to describe events in the past
G Past simple: positive
V Free time activities

1 READING

a Look at pictures 1–3 below. Match the pictures to the animal names. Where do they usually live? What do you know about them?

___ deer ___ bear ___ hippo

b Read the stories below. Write the story titles next to the sentences.
1 Hippos were on a rugby field. ______
2 Three deer were in a woman's flat. ______
3 A bear was in a man's garden. ______

c Read the stories again. Complete the information.

| | Where? | When? | Animal activity? |
|---|---|---|---|
| Andrew from Utah | at home | | |
| Ben from South Africa | | evening | |
| A woman from Indiana | | | jump |

d Talk about the questions.
1 Which story do you like?
2 Which animals sometimes come into houses in your country?
cat dog bird snake
3 What do you do if a wild animal comes into your house?

WILD STORIES!

1 CURIOUS CREATURE
Andrew Singer from Utah was at home in his house on a farm. One evening he was in the kitchen and he heard something strange in the garden, so he looked out of the window. He saw a bear in the garden. The bear walked around the garden and looked in the windows of the house. It tried to open the kitchen door and Andrew was really scared. It wasn't possible for the bear to get in, so it went away. Andrew thinks the bear was hungry, but it's not a good idea to give bears food.

2 SURPRISE VISITORS
A woman from Indiana had a ground floor flat with a garden. In the evening, she went into her living room and watched TV. She heard something in her bedroom, so she went to look. She saw three deer near her bed. They came into the living room and jumped on her sofa, then they went into the bathroom. The woman called the police and they came to catch the deer. She had an exciting night with her three new friends!

3 READY TO PLAY
Ben Kruger from South Africa loves playing rugby. He has a business in Limpopo, a city in the north of South Africa. One night after work, he went to a rugby field nearby. It was dark and he saw something on the field. It was large, but it wasn't a person – it was a hippopotamus (hippo)! Then he saw another hippo and then another – there were a lot of them. The hippos ate some grass and then went away. Ben thinks the hippos were from a river near the rugby field.

66

UNIT 8

2 GRAMMAR Past simple: positive

a 08.12 Read the stories again and find the past simple forms of the verbs in the table. Listen and check.

| A | | B | |
|---|---|---|---|
| Verb | Past form | Verb | Past form |
| look | looked | have | had |
| watch | | hear | |
| call | | eat | |
| jump | | see | |
| walk | | go | |
| try | | come | |

b Answer the questions about the table in 2a.
1 What do we add to the verbs in A to make the past form?
2 Do the verbs in B all change in the same way or in different ways?

c Sound and spelling /t/ and /d/
1 08.13 Listen and practise these sounds.
1 /t/ talked 2 /d/ lived
2 08.14 Listen to the past forms in the box. Which -ed endings sound … ?
• more like /t/ • more like /d/
looked watched called tried walked played finished
3 Practise saying the words.

d Cover the table in 2a. Test a partner.
Student A: Say a verb.
Student B: Say the past form.
Then swap roles.

e Now go to Grammar Focus 8B on p. 128.

f Complete the sentences so they are true for you.
1 Yesterday I called ______ (a person)
2 Last month I saw ______ (a TV programme)
3 Last weekend I went to ______ (a place)
4 Last night I ate ______ (food)
Tell your partner about your sentences.

3 LISTENING AND VOCABULARY Free time activities

a 08.17 Listen to three conversations about the three stories. In each conversation, some information is incorrect. What is the wrong information?
1 ______
2 ______
3 ______

b 08.18 Listen to the sentences from the conversations. Use the correct verb in the box.

read (x2) talked went had watched heard

1 I just ______ to a café.
2 I ______ a large coffee.
3 And I ______ the newspaper.
4 I ______ this funny story.
5 I ______ this story on a podcast.
6 I ______ to my friend Katie last night.
7 She ______ the video online.

c Match verbs 1 to 6 with a word or phrase in the box to make more past simple phrases.

a book to my parents home dinner a film for a walk breakfast a song on the radio to my friend

1 went ______, ______
2 had ______, ______
3 read ______
4 heard ______
5 talked ______, ______
6 watched ______

d 08.19 Listen to Emily talk about the things she did yesterday. Put pictures a–e in the correct order.

e 08.19 Complete what Emily says with phrases from 3c. Then listen again and check.
Yesterday I [1]______ at about 9:00, and then I went to a café and had coffee with my friend Karen. After that, I went to work and was there all day. I [2]______ with my brother and then I [3]______ and called my parents. I [4]______ Rosie in Brazil on Skype. After that, I [5]______ online and then I went to bed and [6]______ before going to sleep.

f Now go to Vocabulary Focus 8B on p. 150.

g Complete the sentences about free time activities.
1 When I was a child, I ______
2 After work / school, I often ______
3 On weekends, I like to ______

h Tell other students your sentences in 3g. What free time activities were/are popular … ?
a when everyone was a child
b after work / school
c at the weekend

4 SPEAKING

Communication 8B Student A: Go to p. 113. Student B: Go to p. 111.

67

## 2 Beyond the classroom

"There are plenty of opportunities for personalisation."

**Elena Pro, Teacher, EOI de San Fernando de Henares, Spain**

**Insights**
Progress with language learning often requires work outside of the classroom, and different teaching models require different approaches.

**Content**
*Empower Second Edition* is available with a print workbook, online practice documentary-style videos that expose learners to real-world English, plus additional resources with extra ideas and fun activities.

**Results**
This choice of additional resources helps teachers to find the most effective ways to motivate their students both inside and outside the classroom.

# Unit overview

### Unit Opener

**Getting started page** – Clear learning objectives to give an immediate sense of purpose.

### Lessons A and B

**Grammar and Vocabulary** – Input and practice of core grammar and vocabulary, plus a mix of skills.

**Digital Workbook (online, mobile):** Grammar and Vocabulary

### Lesson C

**Everyday English** – Functional language in common, everyday situations.

**Digital Workbook (online, mobile):** Listening, Speaking, Reading and Writing

### Unit Progress Test

### Review

Extra practice of grammar, vocabulary and pronunciation. Also a 'Review your progress' section for students to reflect on the unit.

### Mid- / End-of-course test

### Additional practice

Further practice is available for outside of the class with these components.

***Digital Workbook (online, mobile)***

***Workbook (printed)***

## Components

### Resources – Available on cambridgeone.org

- Audio
- Video
- Unit Progress Tests (Print)
- Unit Progress Tests (Online)
- Mid- and end-of-course assessment (Print)
- Mid- and end-of-course assessment (Online)
- Digital Workbook (Online)
- Photocopiable Grammar, Vocabulary and Pronunciation worksheets

# CONTENTS

# CLASSROOM LANGUAGE

00.02 Listen and read.

## CAN DO OBJECTIVES

- Say your name and country
- Talk about people you know
- Meet and greet new people

# UNIT 1

# HELLO!

## GETTING STARTED

**a** Look at the picture. What countries' flags do you see?

**b** What other countries do you know in English?

# 1A I'M FROM MEXICO

Learn to say your name and country

**G** *be: I / you / we*

**V** Countries

## 1 READING AND GRAMMAR
### *be: I / you / we* positive and questions

**a** 01.01 Listen. Then say *Hi, I'm …* or *Hello, I'm …* and say your name.

**b** 01.02 Read and listen to conversations 1–3. Match the conversations with groups of people a–c in the picture below.

**c** Complete the sentences in the table.

| I/we | you |
|---|---|
| I ______ Camila. (= *I am* …)<br>We ______ from Spain.<br>(= *we are* …) | ______ you from the UK?<br>How ______ you? |

**d** Now go to Grammar Focus 1A Part 1 on p. 116.

**e** **Sound and spelling** *I'm, we're*

1 01.06 Listen to the sound of *I'm* and *we're*.
a I am  b I'm  c we are  d we're

2 Practise saying *I'm* and *we're*.

**f** Practise the conversations in 1b.

1 Work in pairs. Practise Conversation 1.
2 Work in groups of three. Practise Conversation 2.
3 Work with a new partner. Practise Conversation 3.

**g** Practise the conversations in 1b again. Use your own name.

**1**
**V** Hi, I'm Vilma. What's your name?
**C** I'm Camila.
**V** Hi, Camila. Nice to meet you.

**2**
**H** Hello, I'm Harumi.
**K** Hi, I'm Katia.
**P** And I'm Pablo. Hi.
**H** Are you from the UK?
**P** No, we're from Spain.

**3**
**L** Hi, Berkay. How are you?
**B** Hi, Li. I'm fine. How are you?
**L** Fine, thanks.

## 2 LISTENING AND GRAMMAR *be: I / you / we negative*

**a** 01.07 Read and listen to the conversation. Choose the correct answers.

**KELLY** Are you Berkay?
**BERKAY** Yes, I am.
**KELLY** Hi, I'm Kelly.
**BERKAY** Oh, hi. Are you a student here?
**KELLY** No, I'm not a student. I'm your teacher!
**BERKAY** Oh … sorry.

1 Berkay is:
**a** a student. **b** a teacher.
2 Kelly is:
**a** a student. **b** a teacher.

**b** Complete the sentences in the table.

| Positive (+) | Negative (–) |
|---|---|
| I'm a student. (= *I am*)<br>We ______ from the UK. (= *we are*) | I'm ______ a student. (= *I am not*)<br>We aren't from the UK. (= *we are not*) |

**c** Now go to Grammar Focus 1A Part 2 on p. 116.

**d** Read the sentences. Make them true for you.

1 I'm a student.
2 We're teachers.
3 I'm from the UK.
4 I'm Laura.
5 We're from Tokyo.

**e** Tell a partner your sentences in 2d. Are they the same?

## 3 VOCABULARY AND READING Countries

**a** 01.09 Match the countries in the box with maps 1–8. Listen and check.

the United Kingdom / the UK  China  the United States / the USA  Spain  Japan  Turkey  Brazil  Mexico

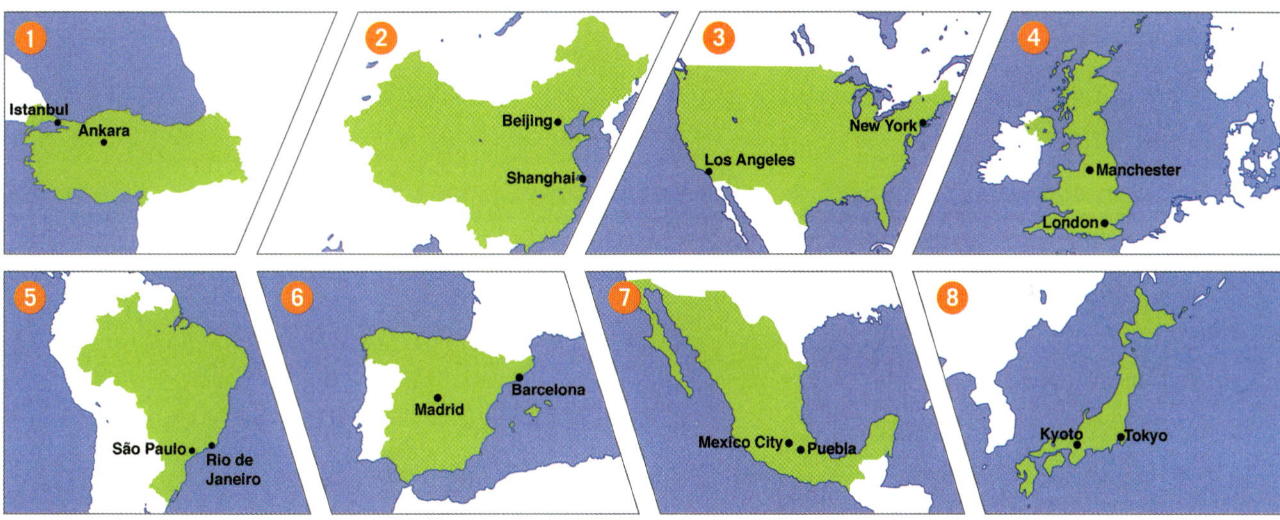


**b** 01.10 Complete the sentences with the correct country. Listen and check.

### OUR GROUP

Vilma 17:02
I'm Vilma. I'm from Rio de Janeiro, in ¹________.

Pablo 17:02
Hi, I'm Pablo. I'm from ²_______. I'm from Barcelona.

Camila 17:03
Hello. I'm from Puebla, in ³_______, and my name's Camila.

Li 17:03
Hi, I'm Li. I'm from Beijing, in ⁴_______. But I'm not in Beijing now. I'm a student in Shanghai.

Harumi 17:03
My name's Harumi. I'm from Tokyo, in ⁵_______.

Michael 17:03
I'm Michael. I'm from ⁶_______. I'm a teacher in London.

Berkay 17:03
I'm from Istanbul, in ⁷_______, and my name's Berkay.

Kelly 17:03
Hello. I'm a teacher, and my name's Kelly.
I'm from New York, in ⁸_______.

**c** Now go to Vocabulary Focus 1A on p. 136.

**d** Choose a city and a country in 3a. Write it on a piece of paper.

*Puebla, Mexico*

**e** Give your piece of paper to the teacher and take a new one. Try to find the student with the information on your piece of paper.

Are you from Puebla?
No, I'm not. I'm from Mexico City.

## 4 SPEAKING

**Communication 1A**

Student A: Go to p. 104.
Student B: Go to p. 106.

# 1B HE'S ITALIAN

**Learn to talk about people you know**

**G** *be: he / she / they*

**V** Nationalities

## 1 VOCABULARY Nationalities

**a** Do you know the people in pictures a–h? Ask your partner.

Do you know Serena and Venus Williams?

**b** Match the nationalities with pictures a–h.

A|mer|i|can Chi|nese Mex|i|can I|tal|ian
Span|ish Brit|ish Jap|a|nese Bra|zil|ian

**c** 01.12 **Pronunciation** Listen to the words in 1b. How many syllables are in each word?
A|mer|i|can = 4 syllables

**d** 01.13 Listen and notice the stressed syllable.

**e** 01.12 Listen to the words in 1b again. Underline the stressed syllables. Then listen and repeat.

**f** Now go to Vocabulary Focus 1B on p. 136.

a

Ricky Rubio – basketball player

b

Shohei Ohtani – baseball player

c

Serena and Venus Williams – tennis players

d

Fabio Fognini – tennis player

e

Neymar - football player

f

Heather Watson – tennis player

g

Zhu Ting – volleyball player

h

Javier Hernández and Guillermo Ochoa – football players

## 2 GRAMMAR *be*: *he* / *she* / *they* positive

**a** 01.15 Match 1–3 with a–c. Listen and check.

1 Heather Watson is a tennis player.
2 Shohei Ohtani is a baseball player.
3 Serena and Venus Williams are tennis players.

a He's Japanese.
b They're American.
c She's British.

**b** Complete the table.

| + | |
|---|---|
| she is … | she's … |
| he is … | [1] ______ … |
| they are … | [2] ______ … |

**c** Now go to Grammar Focus 1B Part 1 on p. 116.

**d** Write two sentences about the people below.

1 Ricky Rubio
2 Zhu Ting
3 Javier Hernández and Guillermo Ochoa

**e** Tell a partner your sentences in 2d. Are they the same?

## 3 LISTENING

**a** 01.17 Look at the photo below. Read and listen to Mia talk about the people on her holiday. Complete 1–6 with the words in the box.

Spanish Luis Lucia Italian Ana

**MIA** This is [1] ______. She's my friend from Madrid. She's Spanish.
**NED** OK. And who's this?
**MIA** This is [2] ______. He's a teacher in Brazil.
**NED** Is he Brazilian?
**MIA** No, he isn't Brazilian. He's [3] ______.
**NED** Oh, really.
**MIA** And these are my friends [4] ______ and Matteo. They're married.
**NED** Are they American?
**MIA** No, they aren't American. They're [5] ______ – from Rome.

**b** Tell a partner about two of your friends. What nationality are they?

## 4 GRAMMAR *be*: *he* / *she* / *they* negative and questions

**a** Complete the tables with the words in the box.

they isn't is are aren't she

| + | – |
|---|---|
| She's Spanish. | She ______ Spanish. |
| They're Chinese. | They ______ Chinese. |

| ? |
|---|
| ______ ______ Spanish? |
| ______ ______ Chinese? |

**b** Now go to Grammar Focus 1B Part 2 on p. 116.

**c** 01.21 Complete the sentences. Listen and check.

1 **A** ______ he Italian?
**B** No, ______ ______.
2 **A** ______ they Spanish?
**B** Yes, ______ ______.
3 **A** ______ she Chinese?
**B** No, ______ ______.
4 **A** ______ they Mexican?
**B** No, ______ ______.
5 **A** ______ he British?
**B** Yes, ______ ______.

**d** Practise saying 1–5 in 4c with a partner.

**Language Plus** *this* / *these*

***This is*** *Ana*
*this* = one person

***These are*** *my friends Lucia and Matteo.*
*these* = two or more people

## 5 SPEAKING

Communication 1B Student a: Go to p. 104. Student B: Go to p. 106.

# 1C EVERYDAY ENGLISH
## Nice to meet you

Learn to meet and greet new people

P Intonation

W A personal profile

## 1 LISTENING

**a** Look at picture a. Is she in a new place?

**b** 01.22 Watch or listen to Part 1 and check your answer in 1a.

**c** 01.22 Watch or listen to Part 1 again. Complete the sentences with words in the box.

Hi Good morning

**RECEPTIONIST** ______, Electric Blue Technology.
**SOPHIA** ______, my name's Sophia Taylor. It's my first day.

## 2 USEFUL LANGUAGE Greeting people

**a** Complete 1–3 with the words in the box.

evening morning afternoon

7 am – 12 pm = [1]__________
12 pm – 5 pm = [2]__________
5 pm – 10 pm = [3]__________

**b** 01.23 **Pronunciation** Listen. How many syllables are in the words and expressions?

hi (1) good | mor | ning good | eve | ning
hel | lo good | af | ter | noon

**c** 01.23 Listen to the words and expressions in 2b again. Underline the stressed syllables.

hel<u>lo</u>

**d** Look at the times with a partner. Use the correct expression.

1 8 pm 3 11 am 5 6 am
2 3 pm 4 10 pm 6 1 pm

Good morning.

Good afternoon.

## 3 LISTENING AND USEFUL LANGUAGE
### Meeting new people 1

**a** 01.24 Watch or listen to Part 2. Sophia meets the manager of Electric Blue Technology. What's his name?

☐ Daniel ☐ Darren ☐ David

**b** 01.25 Listen to the sentences. Underline the words you hear. Are both options in 1–2 possible?

1 *I'm / My name's* Sophia Taylor.
2 *I'm / My name's* David.

**c** 01.26 **Pronunciation** Listen and notice the main stress.

**A** How <u>are</u> you?
**B** I'm <u>good</u>, thank you. And <u>you</u>?
**A** I'm <u>fine</u>, thanks.

**d** Practise the conversation in 3c with a partner.

**e** 01.27 Put the expressions in the table. Listen and check.

I'm fine, thanks. I'm OK, thank you.
Oh, not bad, thanks. I'm good, thank you.

| A ☺ | B 😐 |
|---|---|
| | |

**f** Practise the conversation in 3c again, but change roles and use expressions in 3e to reply.

## 4 LISTENING AND USEFUL LANGUAGE Meeting new people 2

**a** 01.28 Watch or listen to Part 3. Are Sophia and Megan friends?

**b** 01.28 Watch or listen to Part 3 again. Underline the correct answer.

1 **MEGAN** Nice to *meet / see* you too, Sophie.
2 **DAVID** So, this is your *home / office*.
3 **MEGAN** So, ... this is your *desk / chair*.

**c** 01.29 Put the conversation in the correct order. Listen and check.

☐ **MEGAN** Nice to meet you too, Sophie.
☐ **SOPHIA** Nice to meet you, Megan.
☐ **DAVID** This is Megan Jackson.

**d** Work in groups of three. Practise the conversation in 4c. Use your names.

This is Hassan.

Nice to meet you, Hassan.

## 5 PRONUNCIATION Intonation

**a** 01.30 Listen to phrases 1–5. Does the intonation change or stay the same →?

1 Hello.
2 How are you?
3 I'm good.
4 Nice to meet you.
5 Thank you.

**b** 01.30 Listen to the phrases in 5a again and repeat.

## 6 SPEAKING

**a** 01.31 Complete the conversation. Listen and check.

**LARISSA** Hi.
**AMIRA** Good evening.
**KARL** Hello.
**LARISSA** I'm Larissa and this [1]______ Amira.
**KARL** Nice to meet you. I'm Karl.
**AMIRA** Nice to [2]______ you too. How are you?
**KARL** I'm good. And [3]______?
**AMIRA** I'm fine.
**LARISSA** I'm [4]______ too.

**b** Work in groups of three. Practise the conversation in 6a. Use your names.

## 7 WRITING

**a** Read Sophia's profile. What information about her is new?

**ELECTRIC BLUE TECHNOLOGY**

**Our people in London**

Hi, my name's Sophia Taylor.
I'm from Toronto in Canada.
I'm in an office with
Megan Jackson.

**b** Now go to Writing Plus 1C on p. 158 for capital letters and full stops.

**c** Write a profile about you and your English class. Here are some ideas:

Hi/Hello, my ...
I'm from ... in ...
I'm in a class with ... in room ...

**d** Read other students' profiles. Is everyone from the same place?

**UNIT PROGRESS TEST**

**CHECK YOUR PROGRESS**

You can now do the Unit Progress Test.

# UNIT 1
# Review

## 1 GRAMMAR

**a** Underline the correct answer.

1 Hello. I*'m* / *are* Ana.
2 'Are you students?' 'Yes, *we're* / *we are*.'
3 You *am not* / *aren't* a teacher.
4 '*Am I* / *I am* right?' 'Yes, you are.'
5 Where *are you* / *you are*?
6 We*'re* / *am* at home.

**b** Add *is*, *isn't*, *are* or *aren't*.

1 'Is your name Sandy?' 'No, it ________.'
2 'Are Javier Hernández and Guillermo Ochoa from Mexico?' 'Yes, they ________.'
3 'Is Ricky Rubio Spanish?' 'Yes, he ________.'
4 '________ London and Manchester in the UK?' 'Yes, they are.'
5 'Are your friends football players?' 'No, they ________.'
6 '________ your teacher English?' 'No, she ________.'

**c** Ask and answer the questions in 1b.

**d** Correct the sentences.

> They's Spanish.
They're Spanish.

1 No, he aren't from China.
2 You are OK?
3 Yes, I'm.
4 She is Mexican?
5 I not am Italian.
6 They are from the UK?

## 2 VOCABULARY

**a** Write the names of the countries.

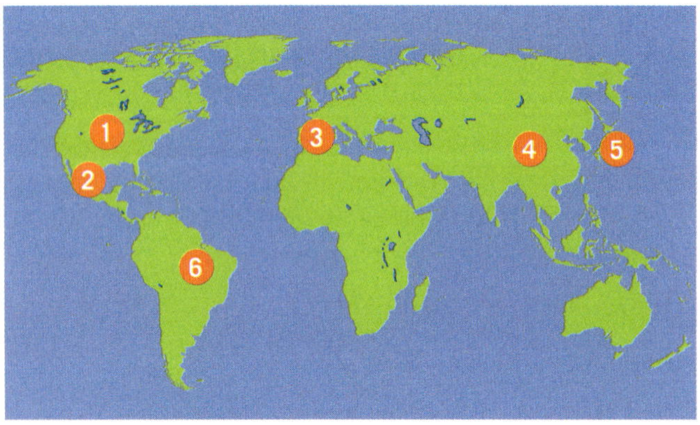


1 e n d i U t s S a t t e ________
2 e i x M c o ________
3 i p S a n ________
4 h i C a n ________
5 a n a J p ________
6 l a r B i z ________

**b** Complete the nationalities.

> Spa<u>nish</u>

1 Tur________

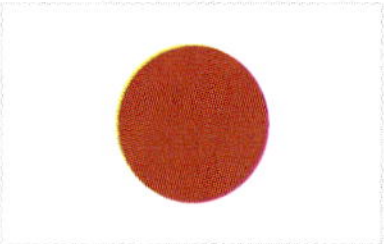

4 Jap________

2 Brazil________

5 Brit________

3 Mex________

6 Ital________

## 3 SOUND AND SPELLING

**a** Write the short forms in the table.

| Full forms | Short forms |
|---|---|
| I am | I'm |
| They are | They're |
| She is | ________ |
| We are | ________ |
| He is | ________ |
| I am not | ________ not |
| He is not | He ________ |

**b** 01.32 Listen and practise saying the short forms.

**c** 01.33 Listen to these phrases. Underline the stressed word or syllable.

1 Good <u>mor</u>ning.
2 How are you?
3 They're American.
4 We're teachers.
5 Nice to meet you.

**d** 01.33 Listen again to check. Practise saying the sentences.

## REVIEW YOUR PROGRESS

**How well did you do in this unit? Write 3, 2 or 1 for each objective.**
3 = very well 2 = well 1 = not so well

| I CAN ... | |
|---|---|
| say my name and country | ☐ |
| talk about people I know | ☐ |
| meet and greet new people. | ☐ |

## CAN DO OBJECTIVES

- Talk about your home town
- Talk about possessions and common objects
- Ask for and give personal information

UNIT 2

# ALL ABOUT ME

## GETTING STARTED

**a** Look at the picture and answer the questions.

1 Is it a … ?
- hot country
- big city
- new house

2 What country do you think it is?

3 Count (1, 2, 3 … ):
- the windows on the house
- the people in the picture

**b** What colours do you see on the house?

# 2A IT'S A BIG CITY

**Learn to talk about your home town**

**G** *be*: *it's* / *it isn't*; Possessive adjectives

**V** Common adjectives

## 1 LISTENING

**a** 02.01 Match the words in the box with pictures a–c. Listen and check.

city town village

Which are you from?

**b** 02.02 Listen and match pictures a–c with the names in the box.

Giovanna Nuria Robin

**c** 02.02 Listen again. Complete the sentences with the words in the box.

is it it's it isn't

**Conversation 1**

**A** Is [1]_______ a big city?

**B** No, no. [2]_______ a city.

**Conversation 2**

**A** [3]_______ a big city.

**B** Yes, it [4]_______.

**Conversation 3**

**A** [5]_______ it a city?

**B** No, it [6]_______.

## 2 GRAMMAR *be: it's / it isn't*

**a** Complete the table with *it* or *it's*.

| | | |
|---|---|---|
| + | Ravello is in Italy. | _______ in Italy. |
| – | Ravello isn't in Mexico. | _______ isn't in Mexico. |
| ? | Is Ravello in Italy? | Is _______ in Italy? |

**b** Complete the sentences with *he's*, *she's* or *it's*.

1 Giovanna's from Ravello in Italy. ____________ a town near Naples.
2 Robin's from Polperro in the UK. ____________ British.
3 Nuria's Spanish. ____________ from Valencia.
4 Akira's from Sōka in Japan. ____________ a city near Tokyo.
5 Selim's from Bursa in Turkey. ____________ a big city near Istanbul.

**c** 02.03 Listen and check.

**d** Now go to Grammar Focus 2A Part 1 on p. 118.

**Language Plus** *in / near*

*Naples is **in** Italy.*

*Ravello is **near** Naples.*

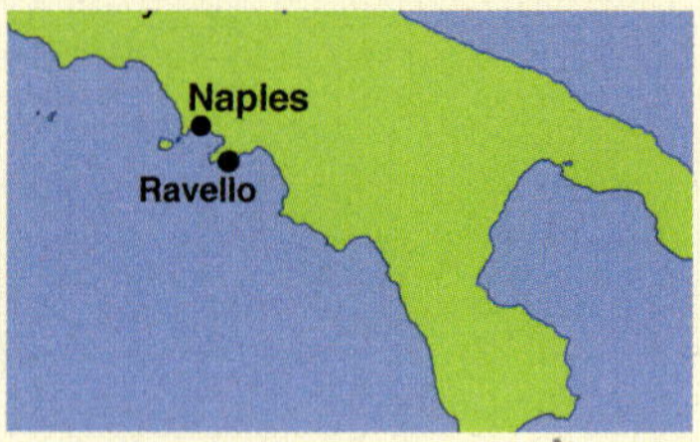


**e** Write sentences about you.

I'm from ... It's a (town / city) (in / near) ...

**f** Tell a partner your sentences.

## 3 READING AND VOCABULARY
### Common adjectives

**a** 02.06 Read and listen to *Our Homes*. Complete the table.

| | home | | home |
|---|---|---|---|
| Nuria | big flat | Miguel | |
| Giovanna | | Pietro and Susanna | |
| Robin | | Sonia | |

**b** **Sound and spelling** /h/ and /w/

1 02.07 Listen to the words. Which words have a /h/ sound? Which words have a /w/ sound?

home hi who what how hotel

2 Practise saying the words.

**c** 02.08 Complete the sentences with the words in the box. Listen and check.

big small old new

1 It's a ______ house.

2 It's a ______ flat.

3 It's a ______ city.

4 It's an ______ house.

**d** Now go to Vocabulary Focus 2A on p. 137.

# Our Homes

My flat is in a new part of Valencia. It's very big. My friend Miguel is from Sagunto. It's a beautiful town near Valencia. This is his home – it's a small house. **Nuria**

My flat in Ravello is big, old and beautiful. My friends Pietro and Susanna are from Naples. This is their home. It's a big flat in a nice part of town. **Giovanna**

My home is a small house in Polperro. It's an old village. My friend Sonia is from Plymouth. This is her home. It's a small flat, and it's new and beautiful. **Robin**

## 4 GRAMMAR
### Possessive adjectives

**a** Read *Our Homes* again. Complete the table.

| Pronoun | Possessive adjective |
|---|---|
| I | ______ |
| you | your |
| he | ______ |
| she | her |
| we | our |
| they | ______ |

**b** Complete the sentences.

1 Javier is from Barcelona. ______ home is in a nice part of the city.
2 Are you from Berlin? Where's ______ flat?
3 We're from Tokyo. ______ home is near a big hotel.
4 Sarah is from England. ______ town is near Hastings.
5 Pedro and Eva are from Mexico City. ______ flat is very big.

**c** Now go to Grammar Focus 2A Part 2 on p. 118.

**d** Complete the sentences about a friend.

My friend ______ is from ______. His / Her home is ______.

**e** Tell a partner about your friend's home.

## 5 SPEAKING

**Communication 2A**

Student A: Go to p. 104.
Student B: Go to p. 106.
Student C: Go to p. 108.

# 2B DO YOU HAVE A PHONE?

Learn to talk about possessions and common objects

G Plural nouns; *have*

V Common objects 1; Numbers 1

## 1 VOCABULARY Common objects 1

**a** 02.11 Match 1–10 in picture a with the words in the box. Listen and check.

a computer   a newspaper   a knife   a phone   a key
a watch   an umbrella   a ticket   a book   a bottle of water

**b** Two objects in 1a are not OK at an airport. What are they?

**Language Plus** *a / an*

We use *a* before most nouns. • *a key* • *a book*
We use *an* before *a, e, i, o, u*. • *an apple* • *an umbrella*

**c** Cover the words in the box in 1a. Ask a partner questions about the objects in the picture.

What's this?
It's a watch.

**d** Now go to Vocabulary Focus 2B Common objects 1 on p. 138.

## 2 LISTENING AND GRAMMAR Plural nouns

**a** 02.13 Listen to the conversation with an airport customs official. Tick (✓) the words you hear.

- ☐ books
- ☐ computers
- ☐ phones
- ☐ watches
- ☐ umbrellas
- ☐ bottles
- ☐ newspapers
- ☐ knives

**b** Complete the table.

| Singular (= 1) | Plural (= 2+) |
|---|---|
| a key | keys |
| a newspaper | ______ |
| a watch | ______ |
| a knife | ______ |

**c** Most nouns add *-s* in the plural. How are the plurals of *watch* and *knife* different?

**d Sound and spelling /s/, /z/ and /ɪz/**

1 02.14 Listen and practise these sounds. Which word has an extra syllable in the plural?
1 /s/ books 2 /z/ keys 3 /ɪz/ watches

2 02.15 Listen to these words. Which word has an extra syllable in the plural? Listen again and repeat.

knives bottles tickets apples villages phones

**e** Work in pairs.
Student A: Say a singular word.
Student B: Say the plural.

Then swap roles.

**f** Now go to Grammar Focus 2B on p. 118.

## 3 GRAMMAR *I have / you have*

**a** 02.16 Look at the X-ray picture and complete the conversation. Listen and check.

**A** What's in your bag?
**B** Mm, I have a [1]b______ and my [2]k______s and an [3]u______.
**A** Do you have a [4]p______?
**B** Yes. Oh, and a [5]b______ of w______. Sorry!

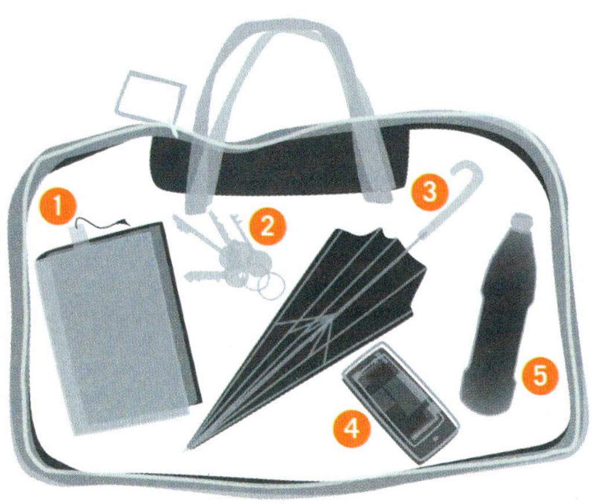


**b** 02.17 Listen to the forms of *have*.

| + | ? |
|---|---|
| I **have** a book. | **Do** you **have** a book? |

**c** 02.17 **Pronunciation** Listen again. Practise saying the sentences.

**d** Ask a partner about objects 1–5 in 3a. Ask about:
1 here (in class)
2 at home

Do you have an umbrella here?
No.
Do you have an umbrella at home?
Yes.

## 4 VOCABULARY Numbers 1

**a** 02.18 Listen and repeat the numbers.

**b** Match the words in the box with numbers 1–12 in 4a.

seven two nine four eight eleven
three six one ten twelve five

**c** Work in pairs.
Student A: Say a number.
Student B: Say the next number.

Then swap roles.

**d** **Communication 2B** Student A: Go to p. 104. Student B: Go to p. 106.

**e** Now go to Vocabulary Focus 2B Numbers 1 on p. 141.

## 5 SPEAKING

**a** Write three things you have in your bag.

*a bottle of water*

*an apple* *a computer*

**b** Guess what is in your partner's bag.

Do you have a phone?
Yes.
Do you have a knife?
No!

# 2C EVERYDAY ENGLISH

## What's your address?

**Learn to ask for and give personal information**

- P Intonation in questions
- W A form

## 1 LISTENING

**a** Think about a good home for you. Tick (✓) <u>four</u> boxes.

1 ☐ a house
  ☐ a flat
2 ☐ in a village
  ☐ in a city
3 ☐ old
  ☐ new
4 ☐ near a park
  ☐ near shops

**b** Tell a partner about your home in 1a.

A good home for me is …

**c** 02.21 Watch or listen to Part 1. Answer the questions.

1 Who asks questions, Sophia or the woman?
2 What kind of home does Sophia need, a flat or a house?

**d** 02.21 Watch or listen to Part 1 again. Tick (✓) the correct answer.

1 Sophia's surname:
  a ☐ Tailor  b ☐ Taylor
2 Her address in London:
  a ☐ Alpha Hotel  b ☐ Alfa Hotel
3 Her phone number:
  a ☐ 07832 674893  b ☐ 07832 647893

## 2 USEFUL LANGUAGE Asking for and giving personal information

**a** 02.22 <u>Underline</u> the correct answer. Listen and check.

1 **A** What's your surname?
  **B** *It's / I'm* Robinson.
2 **A** What's your address?
  **B** *It's / It's on* 7 King Street.
3 **A** What's your phone number?
  **B** *They're / It's* 0124 352738.
4 **A** What's your email address?
  **B** *He's / It's* chrisrobinson@powermail.com.

**b** 02.23 Listen to the answers to questions 3 and 4 in 2a again. Tick (✓) the correct answer.

1 a ☐ oh-one-two-four-three-five-two-seven-three-eight
  b ☐ oh-twelve-four-three-five-two-seven-three-eight
2 a ☐ chris-robinson-from-powermail-point-com
  b ☐ chris-robinson-at-powermail-dot-com

**c** 02.24 <u>Underline</u> the correct word. Listen and check your answer.

**RACHEL** Sophia Taylor. *What / How* do you spell that?
**SOPHIA** T-A-Y-L-O-R.

**d** 02.25 **Pronunciation** Listen to the questions. Notice the main stress in each question.

1 How do you <u>spell</u> that?
2 Can you <u>spell</u> that?
3 Sorry, what's the <u>spell</u>ing?

02.25 Listen again and repeat.

**e** Now go to Writing Plus 2C Part 1 on p. 158 for The alphabet.

**f** Ask a partner his/her surname. Then ask how to spell it.

**g** **Communication 2C** Student A: Go to p. 105. Student B: Go to p. 108.

## 3 LISTENING

a 02.27 Watch or listen to Part 2. What does Sophia think? Tick (✓) the correct sentence.

1 ☐ The flat's really nice.
2 ☐ The flat isn't very nice.

b 02.27 Watch or listen to Part 2 again. Tick (✓) the correct information about the flat.

1 ☐ small ☐ big
2 ☐ good for one person ☐ good for two people
3 ☐ near a supermarket ☐ near a park

## 4 PRONUNCIATION
### Intonation in questions

a 02.28 Listen to the questions. Does the intonation go up ↗ or down ↘ at the end?

1 What's your surname?
2 What's your phone number?

b 02.28 Listen again and repeat the questions.

c 02.29 Practise asking the questions with a partner. Then listen and check the intonation.

1 What's your address?
2 Where are you from?
3 What's the spelling?

## 5 SPEAKING

a Talk to different students. Ask about:

- names (first name and surname)
- phone number
- address
- email address

Write down the information. Ask about the spelling.

What's your last name?

It's Mishkin.

Can you spell that, please?

M-I-S-H-K-I-N.

## 6 WRITING

a Read about Sophia. What's the new information?

**Local Rentals: Customer Information**

| | |
|---|---|
| First name: | Sophia |
| Surname: | Taylor |
| Address: | Alpha Hotel, High Street |
| Phone number: | 07832 647893 |
| Email: | sophiat@electricblue.com |

b Now go to Writing Plus 2C Part 2 on p. 158 for Spelling.

c Complete the form with your information.

**Local Rentals: Customer Information**

| | |
|---|---|
| First name: | |
| Surname: | |
| Address: | |
| Phone number: | |
| Email: | |

## UNIT PROGRESS TEST

**CHECK YOUR PROGRESS**

You can now do the Unit Progress Test.

# UNIT 2
# Review

## 1 GRAMMAR

**a** Correct the underlined word.

> It's big houses. *They're*
1 This is Katia and this is she house.
2 'Excuse me! Is this you bag?' 'Yes, it is! Thank you.'
3 Hiro's from Sōka. She's a city in Japan.
4 It not a big flat.
5 They live in Madrid. This is they home.
6 'Hi, we're from New York. We city is big!'

**b** Complete the sentences with the plural form of the nouns in brackets.

1 They're my ______. (key)
2 Are they your ______? (knife)
3 I have two ______. (watch)
4 Are they your ______? (bottle of water)
5 Oxford and Cambridge are ______ in the UK. (city)
6 Where are the ______? (book)

**c** Complete the sentences with the words in the box.

are his is they they're it's it isn't

1 I'm from Ravello. ______ a town in Italy.
2 The men ______ at home.
3 'Are they big houses?' 'Yes, ______ are.'
4 ______ my books.
5 ______ it a city?
6 This is John and this is ______ flat.
7 'Is Madrid in Italy?' 'No, ______.'

## 2 VOCABULARY

**a** Match 1–6 with the opposite adjectives in the box.

boring difficult good happy old ~~small~~ wrong

> big *small*
1 easy ______
2 bad ______
3 right ______
4 sad ______
5 interesting ______
6 new ______

**b** Complete the crossword with the objects in pictures 1–8.

1 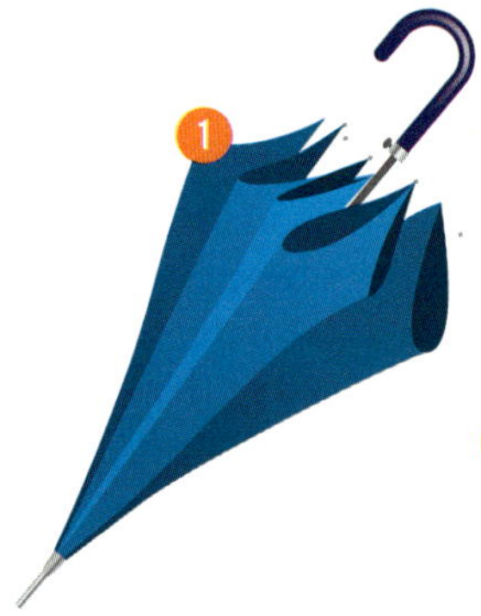
2 
3 
4 

5 

7 
8 

## 3 SOUND AND SPELLING

**a** 02.31 Look at the words in the box. Is the final sound /s/, /z/ or /ɪz/? Complete the table. Practise saying the words.

~~phones~~ watches keys addresses houses flats umbrellas tickets books computers

| /s/ | /z/ | /ɪz/ |
|---|---|---|
| | *phones* | |

**b** 02.32 Tick (✓) the words with a /h/ sound. Practise saying the words.

| | | | |
|---|---|---|---|
| ☐ hello | ☐ is | ☐ how | ☐ watch |
| ☐ her | ☐ home | ☐ who | ☐ happy |
| ☐ our | ☐ house | ☐ she | ☐ right |
| ☐ his | ☐ where | ☐ phone | |

## REVIEW YOUR PROGRESS

**How well did you do in this unit? Write 3, 2 or 1 for each objective.**
3 = very well 2 = well 1 = not so well

| I CAN ... | |
|---|---|
| talk about my home town | ☐ |
| talk about possessions and common objects | ☐ |
| ask for and give personal information. | ☐ |

## CAN DO OBJECTIVES

- Say what you eat and drink
- Talk about food and meals
- Order and pay in a café

UNIT 3

# FOOD AND DRINK

## GETTING STARTED

**a** Look at the picture and answer the questions.

1 What food can you see in the shopping trolley?
2 Which food in the shopping trolley do you like?
3 Which food in the shopping trolley don't you like?
4 What food do you buy?

**b** What other food do you know in English?

# 3A DO YOU LIKE FISH?

Learn to say what you eat and drink

**G** Present simple: *I / you / we / they*

**V** Food 1

## 1 VOCABULARY Food 1

**a** 03.01 Match pictures 1–7 with the words in the box. Then listen and check.

fruit rice meat bread vegetables eggs fish

1

2

3

4

5

6

7

**b** 03.01 **Pronunciation** Listen to the words in 1a again. Which word has more than one syllable? Underline the stressed syllable.

**c** Say two things you like ☺.

I like fruit and I like fish.

**d** **Sound and spelling** /iː/, /ɪ/ and /aɪ/

1 03.02 Listen and practise these sounds.
1 /iː/ m**ea**t 2 /ɪ/ f**i**sh 3 /aɪ/ **I**'m

2 03.03 Look at the words in the box. What sounds do the letters in **bold** have? Listen and add the words to the sound groups below.

b**i**g **ea**t n**i**ne s**i**ster **i**t's m**e** m**i**lk
Ch**i**na f**i**ve h**i**s t**ea**cher h**i**

| Sound 1 /iː/ | Sound 2 /ɪ/ | Sound 3 /aɪ/ |
|---|---|---|
| meat | fish | I'm |

3 Practise saying the words.

**e** Now go to Vocabulary Focus 3A on p. 139.

## 2 READING AND GRAMMAR Present simple: *I / you / we / they* positive and negative

**a** Which words in 1a can you see in pictures 1–3? Which word isn't in the pictures?

**b** 03.06 Read and listen to texts a–c. Match them with the families in pictures 1–3.

# FOOD FOR ONE WEEK

**a** They eat a lot of fruit and vegetables every day. And they eat meat with rice. They like eggs, but they don't eat bread or fish. They don't like fish. They drink a lot of water.

**b** They eat meat and eggs every day, but they don't eat fish. And they don't eat vegetables, but they eat fruit. They really like bread.

**c** They eat a lot of rice and vegetables. They like fruit and they eat bread. They don't eat fish or meat. They are vegetarians.

1 ☐

Tang family, China

**c** Complete the table.

| + | | | – | | |
|---|---|---|---|---|---|
| I<br>We<br>They | eat<br>like | meat.<br>fish. | I<br>We<br>They | ________ eat<br>________ like | meat.<br>fish. |

**d** <u>Underline</u> the correct words.

1 The Tangs *eat / don't eat* fish.
2 The Delgados *eat / don't eat* bread.
3 The Donatis *like / don't like* meat.
4 The Tangs *eat / don't eat* a lot of eggs.
5 The Donatis *like / don't like* vegetables.

**e** Which family's food would you like to have for a week? Why?

2 ☐

Donati family, Italy

3 ☐

Delgado family, Guatemala

## 3 LISTENING AND GRAMMAR Present simple: *I / you / we / they* questions

**a** 03.07 Listen to a conversation with Rajit. Tick (✓) the different food he eats.

☑ bread ☐ vegetables ☐ meat
☐ fish ☐ rice ☐ fruit

Rajit

**b** 03.07 Listen again. Complete the conversation.

**A** Rajit, what do you eat in a week?
**B** Oh, a lot of things. I eat rice every day, and bread. I eat a lot of fruit. I eat fish …
**A** [1]________ you eat meat?
**B** No, I don't like meat.
**A** Do you [2]________ vegetables?
**B** Oh yes, I like vegetables. I eat a lot of vegetables.
**A** Do you [3]________ them every day?
**B** Yes. They're very good for me.

**c** 03.08 Complete the questions in the table. Then listen and check.

| + | – | ? |
|---|---|---|
| I eat fish.<br>We like fruit. | I don't eat fish.<br>We don't like fruit. | _____ you _____ fish?<br>_____ you _____ fruit? |

**d** Now go to Grammar Focus 3A on p. 118.

**e** Practise the conversation in 3b with a partner.

## 4 SPEAKING

**a** Ask and answer questions with a partner. Complete the table with their answers.

Do you eat meat?
Yes, (I do).
Do you eat bread every day?
No, not every day.
Do you like fish?
No, I don't like fish.

| | yes / no? | every day? | like? |
|---|---|---|---|
| meat | | | |
| fish | | | |
| rice | | | |
| bread | | | |
| vegetables | | | |
| fruit | | | |
| eggs | | | |

**b** Write three words for drinks. Then ask your partner questions.

Do you drink cola?
Do you like milk?

# 3B I USUALLY HAVE DINNER EARLY

**Learn to talk about food and meals**

**G** Adverbs of frequency
**V** Food 2; Time

## 1 READING

**a** Tick (✓) the boxes about your breakfast.

**For my breakfast, I have ...**

| | YES | NO | | YES | NO |
|---|---|---|---|---|---|
| coffee | | | tea | | |
| bread | | | fruit | | |
| ice cream | | | fish | | |
| cold pizza | | | nothing | | |

**b** Talk about your answers in 1a with a partner.

> I have coffee – I don't have ice cream.

**c** Look at the pictures. What's the number one breakfast in Italy? Make a guess below.

☐ fruit

☐ cereal

☐ toast

☐ eggs

☐ coffee

☐ pastry

**d** Read the text and find the answer to 1c.

### THE NUMBER ONE BREAKFAST

In Italy, people like different food for breakfast. They sometimes eat cereal or fruit, but a pastry is the number one breakfast food. Italian people also like toast with jam for breakfast, or sometimes just biscuits. But Italians always have coffee with their food!

**e** What's the number one breakfast food in your country? What's the number one drink?

> I think ______ is the number one breakfast food in my country.

## 2 VOCABULARY Food 2; Time

**a** Match sentences 1–3 with pictures a–c.

1 I have lunch at *twelve* / *one* o'clock.
2 They have dinner at *six* / *seven* o'clock.
3 In my family, we have breakfast at *seven* / *eight* o'clock.

**a**

in the morning

**b**

in the afternoon

**c**

in the evening

**b** Now go to Vocabulary Focus 3B Food 2 on p. 140.

**c** 03.13 Listen to sentences 1–3 in 2a. Underline the correct words.

**d** 03.14 Match the clocks with the times. Listen and check.

☐ (a) quarter past four
☐ four o'clock
☐ (a) quarter to five
☐ half past four

**e** Point to a clock in 2d for a partner to say the time.

**f** Now go to Vocabulary Focus 3B Time on p. 141.

**g** **Sound and spelling** /ɑː/ and /ɔː/

1 03.16 Listen and practise these sounds.
1 /ɑː/ p**a**st h**a**lf 2 /ɔː/ f**our** qu**ar**ter

2 03.17 Look at the words in the box. What sounds do the letters in **bold** have? Listen and add the words to the sound groups below.

cl**a**ss **a**ll f**a**ther **a**fternoon w**a**ter d**au**ghter

| Sound 1 /ɑː/ | Sound 2 /ɔː/ |
|---|---|
| past | four |

3 Practise saying the words.

**h** **Communication 3B** Student A: Go to p. 105. Student B: Go to p. 107.

## 3 LISTENING

**a** 03.18 Listen to three people talk about dinner. Match 1–3 with a country in the box.

Turkey Spain the USA Brazil Mexico China

**b** 03.18 Listen again. Complete the table.

| Name | Dinner time | Food |
|---|---|---|
| Julie | | |
| Lucas | | |
| Monica | | |

**c** Do you like the same food as Julie, Lucas and Monica?

## 4 GRAMMAR Adverbs of frequency

**a** 03.19 Listen and complete the sentences with the words in the box.

always usually sometimes never

1 **JULIE** We ________ have rice with meat and vegetables.
2 **LUCAS** I ________ have fish for dinner.
3 **MONICA** People ________ have dinner early in Spain.
4 **MONICA** I ________ have bread and cheese.

**b** Complete 2 and 4 with words in the box in 4a.

1 always (100%)
2 ________ (80%)
3 sometimes (50%)
4 ________ (0%)

**c** Now go to Grammar Focus 3B on p. 120.

**d** Put the words in brackets in the correct place in the sentences.

1 I have breakfast at 9:00 at weekends. (sometimes)
2 I have a sandwich for lunch. (usually)
3 I have breakfast. (never)
4 In the evening, I have dinner at about 7:00. (always)

**e** Which sentences in 4d are true for you?

**Language Plus** *What time … ? / When … ?*

***What time** do you have dinner? = **When** do you have dinner?*

## 5 SPEAKING

**a** Answer questions 1–4. Write another question with your own idea.

1 In the morning, do you eat breakfast?
2 In the evening, do you eat a big dinner?
3 What time do you have lunch?
4 What do you eat for lunch?

**b** Ask and answer the questions in 5a with other students. Who has the same answers as you?

Jaime and I never eat breakfast.

# 3C EVERYDAY ENGLISH
## I'd like a cup of tea, please

**Learn to order and pay in a café**

P Sentence stress
W A text message

## 1 LISTENING

**a** What food on the menu do you like? Tell a partner.

**b** 03.21 **Pronunciation** Listen. This word has two syllables:

coff | ee

03.22 Which words have two syllables? Listen and check.

sandwich banana orange tomato

**c** 03.22 Listen to the words in 1b again. Underline the stressed syllable.

coffee

**d** Practise saying the words in 1b with a partner.

**e** Find 1–3 in pictures a–c.

1 a piece of chocolate cake 2 a key 3 ten pounds

**f** 03.23 Watch or listen. Put pictures a–c in the correct order.

**g** 03.23 Watch or listen again. Are the sentences true or false?

1 Sophia has a new flat.
2 Sophia has a cup of tea.
3 Sophia likes her flat.
4 The text message is from Sophia's cousin.

## 2 PRONUNCIATION Sentence stress

**a** 03.24 Listen to 1–3. Is the pronunciation of *of* the same?

1 of 2 a cup of tea 3 a glass of cola

**b** 03.25 Listen to these phrases. Which other word isn't stressed?

a cup of coffee a piece of banana cake

**c** Practise saying the phrases in 2b.

**d** Work in pairs. Practise more phrases with *a cup* / *a glass* / *a piece of* … . Use the menu in 1a or your ideas.

a ☐

b ☐

c ☐

## 3 USEFUL LANGUAGE Ordering and paying in a café

**a** 03.26 Listen and complete the sentences.

1 **MEGAN** I'd ______ a cup of coffee, please.
2 **SOPHIA** Can I ______ a cup of tea, a cup of coffee and a piece of chocolate cake, please?

03.26 Listen again and repeat.

**b** 03.27 Put the words in the correct order. Listen and check.

1 have / I / a cup of / can / coffee / please ?
2 please / an egg sandwich, / I'd like .
3 two / can / have / we / tomato sandwiches ?

**c** Practise saying the sentences in 3b with a partner.

**d** 03.28 Put the conversation in the correct order. Listen and check.

- ☐ A cheese sandwich, please.
- ☐ Of course. That's £6.00, please.
- ☐ Certainly. And to eat?
- ☐ Here you are.
- ☐ Can I have a glass of cola, please?
- ☐ Thank you.

**e** Practise the conversation in 3d with a partner. Change the drink, food and price.

Can I have a cup of tea, please?

## 4 SPEAKING

**a** Work with a partner. Student A: you work in a café. Student B: you're a customer. Use the menu on p. 28 and the conversation map below.

| A | B |
|---|---|
| Hello | |
| | Hello. I'd like … (*a drink*) |
| And something to eat? | |
| | Can I … ? |
| Of course. That's … | |
| | Here you are. |
| Thank you. | |

**b** Swap roles and repeat the conversation.

## 5 WRITING

**a** Read the text message. Who is it from? Who is it for?

Hi, James. I'm in a café with Sophia. She's my new friend at work. She's from Canada. She has a new flat here in London! Talk to you later. Megan.

Delivered

**b** Now go to Writing Plus 3C on p. 159 for Contractions.

**c** Write a text message to a friend. Here are some ideas:

Hi, …
I'm … (*at school / at work / in a café / in a restaurant*) with …
He's / She's … (*Spanish / a student / very nice*)
Talk (to you) / See you soon / later.

**d** Read a partner's text message. Who does he/she write about?

## UNIT PROGRESS TEST

**CHECK YOUR PROGRESS**

You can now do the Unit Progress Test.

# UNIT 3
## Review

## 1 GRAMMAR

**a** Write present simple sentences and questions with the words and phrases.

> (–) I / have / lunch at home.
*I don't have lunch at home.*

1 (?) you / like / eggs
2 (+) we / eat / bread every day.
3 (–) I / drink / fruit juice.
4 (–) we / eat / meat.
5 (+) you / like / fruit.
6 (?) they / eat / fish

**b** Underline the correct answer.

1 *Always I / I always* have a sandwich for lunch.
2 I *drink sometimes / sometimes drink* cola.
3 I *eat usually / usually eat* lunch at home.
4 I *never / never don't* drink milk.
5 *Never I have / I never have* dinner at 9:00.
6 I *don't sometimes / sometimes don't* have breakfast.

**c** Are the sentences in 1b true or false for you? Tell a partner.

**d** Correct the sentences.

> I not like rice.
*I don't like rice.*

1 No, we not do.
2 Always I have breakfast.
3 We not eat fish.
4 I drink usually water.
5 You like tea?
6 Yes, do I.

## 2 VOCABULARY

**a** Complete the groups with words in the box.

| coffee | dinner | fish | cakes | fruit juice | banana |
|---|---|---|---|---|---|

1 water, milk, ____________
2 tea, ____________
3 orange, apple, ____________
4 breakfast, lunch, ____________
5 meat, eggs, ____________
6 ice cream, biscuits, ____________

**b** Which is your favourite group in 2a?

**c** Look at 1–6 in the picture and complete the food words.

1 a__________s
2 o__________s
3 r__________
4 m__________
5 b__________
6 e__________s

## 3 SOUND AND SPELLING

**a** 03.29 Which sounds are the marked letters – /ɪ/, /iː/ or /aɪ/? Tick (✓) a or b. Practise saying the sentences.

> It's a biscuit.
a ☐ /iː/ /iː/ /iː/
b ☑ /ɪ/ /ɪ/ /ɪ/

1 Tea, please.
a ☐ /iː/ /iː/
b ☐ /ɪ/ /ɪ/

2 I'd like ice cream.
a ☐ /aɪ/ /aɪ/ /aɪ/ /iː/
b ☐ /iː/ /iː/ /iː/ /aɪ/

3 We drink milk.
a ☐ /aɪ/ /aɪ/ /iː/
b ☐ /iː/ /ɪ/ /ɪ/

4 Rice is nice.
a ☐ /aɪ/ /ɪ/ /aɪ/
b ☐ /iː/ /iː/ /iː/

**b** 03.30 Listen to the words. Tick (✓) the words with the /ɔː/ sound. Practise saying the words.

1 ☐ water
2 ☐ tomato
3 ☐ glass
4 ☐ morning
5 ☐ potato
6 ☐ orange
7 ☐ quarter
8 ☐ all

## REVIEW YOUR PROGRESS

**How well did you do in this unit? Write 3, 2 or 1 for each objective.**
3 = very well 2 = well 1 = not so well

| I CAN ... | |
|---|---|
| say what I eat and drink | ☐ |
| talk about food and meals | ☐ |
| order and pay in a café. | ☐ |

## CAN DO OBJECTIVES

- Talk about your life and ask about others'
- Talk about your family
- Ask and talk about photos

UNIT 4

# MY LIFE AND MY FAMILY

## GETTING STARTED

**a** Look at the picture and answer the questions.

1 Look at person a. Can you see … ?
- her mother
- her father
- her grandparents

2 Do you think this family all live together in one house?

3 Who in the picture … ?
- works
- studies

4 What do you think the people in the picture do next?

**b** Who lives in your home?

# 4A WHAT DO YOU STUDY?

Learn to ask and talk about your life

G Present simple: *Wh-* questions

V Common verbs

## 1 VOCABULARY Common verbs

**a** 04.01 Match sentences 1–5 with pictures a–e. Listen and check.

1. I **study** at university.
2. I **work** in an office.
3. I **speak** Japanese.
4. We **live** in London.
5. We **go** to the gym every day.

**b** Which sentences in 1a are true for you?

**c** Now go to Vocabulary Focus 4A on p. 142.

## 2 READING

**a** Read Matt's blog. Which sentence is true?

1. 'I live and I work in London.'
2. 'I live in Málaga and I work in London.'
3. 'I speak Spanish very well.'

**b** Read Matt's blog again. What does he say about these things?

1. flats in London
2. beaches in Málaga
3. number of days at work (in London)
4. number of days at work (in Málaga)
5. Spanish classes
6. Málaga

**c** What do you think of Matt's life?

**Language Plus** *study*

*study* … *at university / at school / at an English language school*
… *English / Spanish / Arabic*
… a subject (*art, maths*)

**d** Write sentences about you.

I live … I work / study … I study English …

**e** Tell a partner your sentences in 2d.

## Breakfast in MÁLAGA and Lunch in LONDON

# JUST A NORMAL DAY!

**I work in London.**

Flats are very expensive there. In Málaga, Spain, flats aren't very expensive and the beaches are beautiful. So I work in London, but I live in Málaga! I fly from Málaga to London on Monday. I work there for three days and I stay with my sister. Then I fly to Málaga again and I work at home two days a week. I don't speak Spanish very well, so I study Spanish at a language school and I go to classes on Saturday. I love Málaga – it's a beautiful city and it's great to live here!

## 3 LISTENING

a 04.03 Listen to Tom and Miriam. Who lives in Auckland, but works in Wellington?

b 04.03 Listen again. Underline the correct answers.

1 Miriam is *Brazilian / a New Zealander*.
2 Her home's in *Brazil / New Zealand*.
3 Her job *is / isn't* near her home.
4 She *is / isn't* married.
5 Miriam and Bernardo speak *English / Portuguese* together.

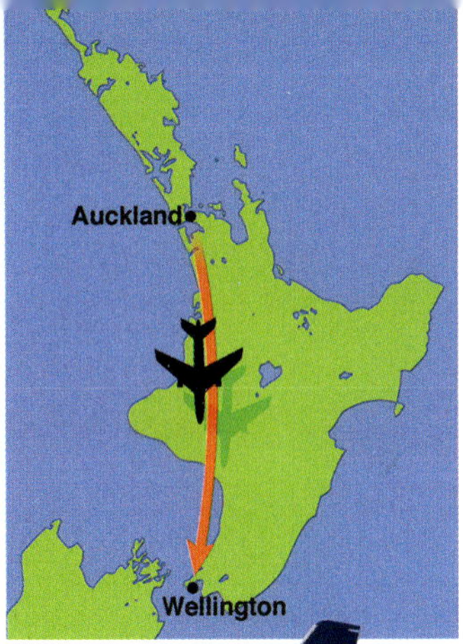

## 4 GRAMMAR
### Present simple: *Wh-* questions

a 04.04 Complete the questions in the table. Listen and check.

| ***Yes/No* questions** | |
|---|---|
| ______ you work at home? | Yes, I work two days at home.<br>No, I work in an office. |
| ***Wh-* questions** | |
| Where ______ you live?<br>When ______ you have dinner?<br>What ______ you study at university? | I live in Auckland.<br>I have dinner at 8:00.<br>I study Italian. |

b Now go to Grammar Focus 4A on p. 120.

c 04.07 Put the words in the correct order to make questions. Listen and check.

1 you work / do / in an office ?
2 do / where / you work ?
3 where / you live / do ?
4 university / study at / do you / what ?
5 do / speak Spanish / you ?

d 04.07 **Pronunciation** Listen to the questions in 4c again. Notice the stressed words and syllables.

1 *Do you work in an office?*

e 04.07 Tick (✓) the words we stress. Then listen to the questions in 4c again and repeat.

1 ☐ question word (e.g., *where*)
2 ☐ *do*
3 ☐ main verb (e.g., *work*)
4 ☐ preposition (e.g., *in*)

f Ask and answer the questions in 4c with a partner.

## 5 SPEAKING

**Communication 4A**

Student A: Go to p. 105.
Student B: Go to p. 108.

# 4B SHE HAS A SISTER AND A BROTHER

**Learn to talk about your family**

G Present simple: *he / she / it* positive

V Family and people; Numbers 2

## 1 READING AND LISTENING

**a** Match 1–6 with pictures a–f.

1 Football player Lionel Messi with his children.
2 Pop star Beyoncé with her husband, Jay-Z, and her sister Solange.
3 Film star Kate Hudson with her parents.
4 Film director Alejandro González Iñárritu with his wife, his son and his daughter.
5 Actor Colin Hanks and his father, Tom Hanks.
6 Singer Camila Cabello with her mother.

**b** 04.08 Listen and check.

**c** What other things do you know about the people in the pictures?

## 2 VOCABULARY Family and people

**a** Complete the table. Use words from 1a.

| (female) | (male) |
|---|---|
| mother | father |
| ______ | son |
| wife | ______ |
| ______ | brother |

**b** Which word in the sentences in 1a means … ?

1 mother and father
2 boys and girls

**c** Look at the family tree. Which people … ?

1 are married
2 have a brother
3 have a sister
4 have a child / children

**d** Work in pairs.

Student A: Choose a person from the family tree.
Student B: Ask questions to guess who Student A is.

Then swap roles.

Are you married?
Yes.
Do you have children?
Yes.

**e** Now go to Vocabulary Focus 4B Family and people on p. 143.

**f** Sound and spelling /ð/

1 04.11 Listen and practise this sound.
/ð/ mo**th**er

2 04.12 /ð/ is usually spelled *th*. Listen to the words and repeat.

this that father they brother then

3 Practise saying the words.

c

d

## 3 READING AND VOCABULARY Numbers 2

**a** Read *An International Family*. Are the sentences true (*T*) or false (*F*)?

1 Pablo and Alicia have two small children.
2 María is married and lives in Turkey.
3 Pablo and Alicia live in Mexico.

# An International Family

**Pablo and Alicia Moreno are married.** Pablo is from Spain and Alicia is from Buenos Aires, in Argentina, but they live in New York. Their family is very international!

Alicia has a sister and a brother. Her sister, Daniela, is 46. She lives in Buenos Aires and her mother lives there too. Her brother, Carlos, is 37. He lives in Brazil and he works in São Paulo.

Alicia and Pablo have two children. Their son, Alex, is 19. He's at university in Mexico and he lives there too. Their daughter, María, is 24. She lives in Istanbul with her Turkish husband, Mehmet.

**b** Where do they live? Write the names of the countries.

1 Daniela
2 Carlos
3 Alex
4 María
5 Mehmet

**c** Daniela is forty-six. How old is … ? (Write the numbers in words.)

1 Carlos 2 Alex 3 María

**Language Plus** *How old … ?*

***How old is** she?*
***She's** 25.*

***How old are** her children?*
***They're** three and five.*

***Note:*** We use *be*, not *have*, to talk about age.

**d** Now go to Vocabulary Focus 4B Numbers 2 on p. 141.

**e** Write the names of three famous people. How old are they? If you don't know, guess! Read out the names. What do other students think?

Lady Gaga

I think she's 38.

## 4 GRAMMAR Present simple: *he / she / it* positive

**a** Look at the verbs in the table and answer the questions.

1 How are the verbs in A different from the verbs in B?
2 How is *has* different?

| I / we / you / they | he / she / it |
|---|---|
| A | B |
| I **work** in an office. | He **works** in São Paulo. |
| We **have** two children. | She **has** a sister and a brother. |
| They **live** in New York. | She **lives** in Buenos Aires. |

**b** Complete the sentences with verbs from 4a.

1 He ______ in an office.
2 He ______ at home with his parents.
3 Her mother ______ a flat in New York.

**c** Now go to Grammar Focus 4B on p. 120.

**d** **Communication 4B** Student A: Go to p. 105. Student B: Go to p. 109.

## 5 SPEAKING

**a** Tell your partner about your family. Use the verbs in the box. Listen, but don't make notes.

have go study live work

My brother has two children – a boy and a girl.

**b** Say what you remember about your partner's family. Are you correct?

# EVERYDAY ENGLISH
## This is me with my father

**Learn to ask and talk about photos**

P Sound and spelling: /tʃ/ and /dʒ/

W Photo captions

a

b

## 1 LISTENING

**a** Ask and answer the questions.

1 Do you have photos of family and friends with you?
2 Where do you have them, on your phone or in your wallet?
3 How often do you look at them?

**b** Look at picture a and answer the questions.

1 Is Sophia happy or sad?
2 Why does she feel happy / sad?

**c** 04.15 Watch or listen to Part 1. Are your ideas in 1b correct?

**d** 04.16 Watch or listen to Part 2. Answer the questions.

1 How many people does Sophia talk about?
2 How many people does Megan talk about?

**e** 04.16 Complete the information about Sophia and Megan's families with the words in the box. Then watch or listen to Part 2 again and check your answers.

sister cousin teacher hotel computers supermarket

Sophia's mother's a [1] ______ and her father's the manager of a [2] ______. She has a [3] ______, Jackie. Jackie has two girls, Kylie and Amanda.

Megan has a brother, Mike. He works with [4] ______ and is married to Helen. She's the manager of a [5] ______. Megan also has a [6] ______, James.

**f** Talk about a favourite photo of your family. Who's in it?

## 2 USEFUL LANGUAGE Asking and talking about photos

**a** Look at expressions 1–7 from Part 2. Do we use them to … ?

a ask about photos
b talk about your photos
c talk about another person's photos

1 This is my mother.
2 Do you have photos of your family?
3 Nice picture!
4 Can I see them?
5 Who's this?
6 They're lovely.
7 This is my sister, Jackie.

**b** 04.17 Look at expressions 1–4. Are they in group a, b or c in 2a? Listen and check your answers in 2a and 2b.

1 This is a picture of my town.
2 It's really nice.
3 Do you have any pictures of your home?
4 These are my friends, Sayeed and Mona.

**c** 04.18 **Pronunciation** Listen to the sentence. Answer the questions. Listen again and repeat.

This is my mother.

1 Do the first two words join?
2 Is the pronunciation of *s* the same in *this* and *is*?

**d** 04.19 Complete the conversation with expressions in the box. Listen and check.

Great photo! Can I see them?
He's funny.
Do you have any photos of your friends?

**A** 1 ______________________
**B** Yes, I do.
**A** 2 ______________________
**B** Sure. This is a photo of my friend, Marco.
**A** 3 ______________________
**B** And this is me with my friend, Emilio.
**A** Yes, I know Emilio. 4 ______________
**B** You're right – he's really funny.

**e** Practise the conversation in 2d. Take turns to be A and B.

## 3 PRONUNCIATION Sound and spelling: /tʃ/ and /dʒ/

**a** 04.20 Listen and practise these sounds.

1 /tʃ/ tea**ch**er pic**t**ure 2 /dʒ/ mana**g**er **J**ames

**b** 04.21 Listen to the **marked** sounds in the words. Which one is different in each group?

1 **ch**ips **j**eans ques**t**ion
2 lar**ge** **j**ob **ch**oose
3 oran**ge** **ch**eap ma**tch**
4 pa**ge** **ch**eese **G**ermany

**c** Practise saying the words in 3b.

## 4 SPEAKING

Communication 4C Student A: Go to p. 105. Student B: Go to p. 108.

## 5 WRITING

**a** Read Sophia's information about her sister. What information is new?

This is my sister Jackie with her two beautiful daughters, Kylie and Amanda. They live in a new house in Toronto – it's very nice. Her husband Tom isn't there, because it's his photo! They're a great family.

**b** Now go to Writing Plus 4C on p. 159 for Word order.

**c** Write about your photo from 1f. Here are some ideas:

This is my … with … He's / She's / They're …
They live … It's nice / lovely / great!

**d** Read about your partner's photo. How many people does he/she write about?

### UNIT PROGRESS TEST

### CHECK YOUR PROGRESS

You can now do the Unit Progress Test.

# UNIT 4
## Review

## 1 GRAMMAR

**a** Look at the words and write present simple questions.

> where / you / live *Where do you live?*
1. what / your name
2. when / you / have lunch
3. what time / you / go to work
4. where / your friends / from
5. what / you / study
6. where / your school

**b** Ask and answer the questions in 1a.

**c** Correct the underlined words.

> My son like football. *likes*
1. Yoshi work in Berlin.
2. Our daughter eat rice every day.
3. My city haves two universities.
4. Naif go to school at 8:30.
5. My dad teachs Spanish.
6. My brother studys Spanish.

**d** Underline the correct answer.

1. When *are / 's / do* you work?
2. María *is live / live / lives* in Istanbul.
3. Where *are / is / do* you from?
4. What *are / is / do* you have for breakfast?
5. What *are / is / do* their names?
6. What time do you *gos / go / goes* to school?

## 2 VOCABULARY

**a** Cross out the answer that is NOT possible.

> I work *in a factory / in an office / ~~tennis~~*.
1. I meet *my friends for coffee / to the gym / people at work* every day.
2. I play *home / football / the guitar*.
3. I live in *Italian / a small house / a big city*.
4. I teach *at university / to the cinema / young children*.
5. I study *English / at university / to school*.
6. I speak *Spanish / Japan / Chinese*.

**b** Which information in 2a is true for you? Tell a partner.

**c** Complete the numbers.

> 29 *twenty-* nine
1. 31 ________ one
2. 24 ________ four
3. 75 ________ five
4. 82 ________ two
5. 96 ________ six
6. 53 ________ three
7. 48 ________ eight
8. 67 ________ seven
9. 100 a ________

**d** Match 1–6 with the words in the box.

baby boy girl men woman women

## 3 SOUND AND SPELLING

**a** 04.22 Underline ONE or TWO /ð/ sounds in each sentence. Practise saying the sentences.

1. These are my friends.
2. I study there.
3. This is my father.
4. They're at the cinema.
5. They teach at the university.
6. I like their daughter.

**b** 04.23 Look at the information in the table.

| /tʃ/ | /dʒ/ | /s/ |
|---|---|---|
| tea**ch** | mana**g**er | **s**tudy |
| pi**c**ture | **g**ym | offi**c**e |
| **ch**ild | **J**ulia | **c**inema |

**c** 04.24 Are the sounds in **bold** the same (S) or different (D)? Practise saying the sentences.

> We're on pa**g**e **s**eventy-two. *D*
> The offi**c**e is number **s**ixty-six. *S*
1. **G**ary is a mana**g**er.
2. **J**ohn speaks **G**erman.
3. It's a pic**t**ure of the **g**ym.
4. Is the univer**s**ity ni**c**e?
5. It's a ques**t**ion about **ch**ildren.
6. It's a **s**mall **c**inema.

## REVIEW YOUR PROGRESS

**How well did you do in this unit? Write 3, 2 or 1 for each objective.**
3 = very well 2 = well 1 = not so well

| I CAN ... | |
|---|---|
| talk about my life and ask about others | ☐ |
| talk about my family | ☐ |
| ask and talk about photos. | ☐ |

## CAN DO OBJECTIVES

- Describe a town
- Talk about hotels and hostels
- Ask about and say where places are

# UNIT 5

# PLACES

## GETTING STARTED

**a** Look at the picture and tick (✓) the things you think are in the museum.

- ☐ art
- ☐ photos
- ☐ a restaurant
- ☐ a phone
- ☐ tickets
- ☐ a shop

**b** Talk about the questions.

1 Who do you think visits this museum?
2 What other buildings do you think are near this museum?
3 Would you like to visit this museum?

# 5A THERE ARE A FEW SHOPS

**Learn to describe a town**

- **G** *there is / there are*: positive
- **V** Places in a town

## VERY HOT!

**Timbuktu, Mali**

Timbuktu is a small town in Mali in West Africa. It's in the desert, so it's very dry and there's sand in the streets. It's also very hot during the day – sometimes 49°C in the summer. There's a large market and it's a very important UNESCO World Heritage site. In the town, there's only one petrol station, but there are some shops and there are a few hotels and restaurants.

## VERY COLD!

**Harbin, China**

Harbin is a large city in China with a population of about 10 million people. It's nice in summer (25°C), but it's very cold in winter (–20°C). Lots of people call it the 'ice city'. From December to February every year, there is an ice and snow festival in Harbin. So, there are a lot of tourists in the winter. There are a lot of shops, good roads and hotels in the city.

## 1 READING

**a** Look at the pictures of Timbuktu and Harbin. Which place is … ?

- in a desert
- in the snow
- a good place for tourists

**b** Read about the two places and check your answers in 1a.

**c** Are the sentences about Timbuktu (T) or Harbin (H)?

1. 'We can only get petrol in one place here.'
2. 'It's always busy here in January.'
3. 'The shops are busy. There are a lot of people here.'
4. 'It's always hot here.'
5. 'Tourists come here in winter.'

**d** Do you think Timbuktu and Harbin are … ?

- nice places to live?
- nice places for a holiday?

Why / Why not?

**Language Plus** *a few, a lot of*

***a few** cars*

***a lot of** cars*

***a few** shops*

***a lot of** shops*

**Tip**

a lot of → **lots** of

## 2 GRAMMAR *there is / there are*: positive

**a** Complete the sentences. Check your answers in the texts in 1b.

Singular: [1]______ is a market / a petrol station.
Plural: There [2]______ good roads / hotels.

**b** 05.01 **Pronunciation** Listen and write the sentences. Tell the sentences to your partner.

**c** Now go to Grammar Focus 5A on p. 122.

**d** Cover the texts. Make sentences about the two places:

- hotels
- restaurants
- a market
- shops
- good roads
- tourists

**e** Write two true sentences about your street. Use *there is* or *there are*. Check your partner's sentences.

## 3 VOCABULARY Places in a town

**a** 05.03 Match the words in the box with the places in pictures a–f. Listen and check.

café shop restaurant
school bank hotel

**b** Which places in 3a are these?

1 'My daughter goes there every day.'
2 'We go there for dinner every Saturday night.'
3 'I often drink coffee there with my friends.'
4 'You're in room 305. Here's your key.'
5 'They have fruit and vegetables and also newspapers and magazines.'
6 'I'd like £500, please.'

**c** Now go to Vocabulary Focus 5A on p. 144.

**d** **Sound and spelling /uː/ and /ʌ/**

1 05.05 Listen and practise these sounds.
1 /uː/ sch**oo**l 2 /ʌ/ l**u**nch

2 05.06 Look at the words in the box. What sounds do the letters in **bold** have? Listen and add the words to the sound groups below.

f**oo**d n**ew** tw**o** wh**o** m**o**ther
**u**mbrella b**eau**tiful s**o**metimes

| Sound 1 /uː/ | Sound 2 /ʌ/ |
|---|---|
| school | lunch |

3 Practise saying the words.

## 4 LISTENING

**a** 05.07 Listen to a conversation about places in a town. Look at the map and match 1–5 with the words in the box.

bookshop café bank restaurant supermarket

**b** 05.07 Listen again. Are the sentences true (*T*) or false (*F*)?

1 There are lots of shops on New Street.
2 Nice people work in the bookshop.
3 The café is Italian.
4 The coffee and cakes in the café aren't good.
5 It's a Chinese restaurant.
6 The restaurant is cheap.

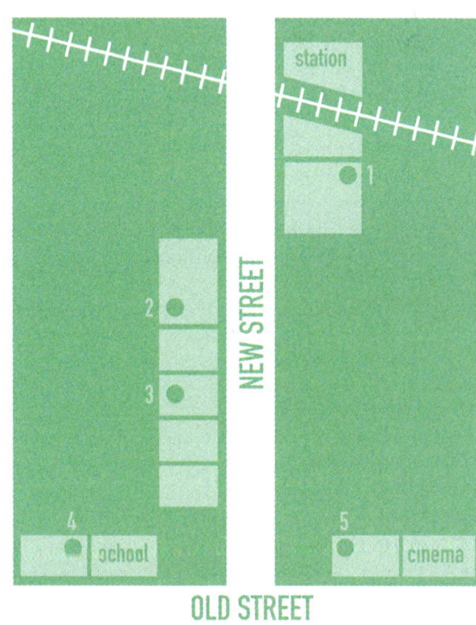


**c** What is the same about the town on the map and your town?

## 5 SPEAKING

**a** Think of a street in the town where you are now. Make notes. Use words from this lesson.

*There's a … There are … It's in … It's near …*

**b** Describe your street, but don't say its name. Do other students know the name of the street?

# 5B IS THERE A HOSTEL IN YOUR TOWN?

Learn to talk about hotels and hostels

G *there is / there are*: negative and questions

V Hotels

## 1 VOCABULARY Hotels

**a** 05.08 Match the words in the box with pictures 1–5. Listen and check.

| bath | room | bed | TV | shower |
|---|---|---|---|---|

**b** Sound and spelling /ʃ/

1 05.09 Listen and practise this sound.
/ʃ/ **sh**ower

2 05.10 Listen to the words in the box. <u>Underline</u> the /ʃ/ sound in each word.

| shop | fish | sure | station |
|---|---|---|---|

3 Practise saying the words.

**c** Now go to Vocabulary Focus 5B on p. 138.

**d** 05.12 Pronunciation Listen to the words. Notice the stressed syllables. Practise saying them.

<u>hos</u>tel  ho<u>tel</u>

**e** Which things in pictures 1–5 in 1a aren't in a hostel room?

## 2 READING

**a** Look at pictures 1–3 of Turkey. Choose adjectives to talk about them. Compare your ideas with your partner.

- beautiful
- great
- nice
- boring
- exciting
- interesting
- old
- big

**b** Read Sandra's review of a hostel in Turkey. Does Sandra like the hostel?

**c** Read the review again. Tick (✓) what's in the hostel.

| | | | |
|---|---|---|---|
| second floor | ☐ small rooms | ☐ big rooms | ☐ café |
| first floor | ☐ restaurant | ☐ TV room | ☐ small rooms |
| ground floor | ☐ café | ☐ kitchen | ☐ TV room |

**d** Would you like to stay at the hostel? Why / Why not?

### HOSTEL REVIEWS

**The Cave Hostel** ★★★★★

This is a great hostel in Göreme, in Turkey. It's in Cappadocia, a very old part of the country. You can do a lot of things here. My favourite thing is going in a hot air balloon. You can see really beautiful places from the air.

The hostel has different rooms with different prices. On the first floor, there are small rooms for two people with baths. On the second floor, there are big rooms with six beds in them. They're very cheap, but there isn't a shower or a bath in the big rooms. There aren't any blankets or pillows – you pay for those. There isn't a restaurant or café in the hostel, but there's a kitchen on the ground floor. There aren't any TVs in the rooms, but there's free wi-fi. It's a very simple place to stay and it's clean. And the people are very friendly. Faruk, the manager, sings karaoke really well!

***Sandra***

## 3 GRAMMAR *there is / there are*: negative

**a** 05.13 Complete the sentences with *isn't* or *aren't*. Listen and check.

1 There ______ any blankets.
2 There ______ a restaurant.

**b** Find more examples of *there isn't* and *there aren't* in Sandra's review.

**c** Think about the town or city you're in now. Tick (✓) the sentences that are true. Correct the false sentences.

1 ☐ There's a big museum in this town / city.
2 ☐ There are a lot of shops here.
3 ☐ There aren't any hostels.
4 ☐ There are two stations.
5 ☐ There aren't any parks.

**d** Read your sentences and listen to your partner's sentences. Are they the same?

There aren't any museums in this town.

Yes, there is a museum in this town – on Cromwell Road.

## 4 LISTENING

**a** 05.14 Listen to a hostel receptionist and George, a guest. Is George happy with the hostel?

**b** 05.14 Listen again. Tick (✓) the things in the hostel.

☐ free rooms ☐ café ☐ wi-fi
☐ car park ☐ kitchen ☐ showers

**c** Why do people like hostels? Why do people like hotels?

## 5 GRAMMAR *there is / there are*: questions

**a** 05.15 Complete the questions. Listen and check.

1 Singular: ______ ______ a car park here?
Yes, there's a car park here.
2 Plural: ______ ______ any cafés near here?
Yes, there are cafés near here.

**b** Now go to Grammar Focus 5B on p. 122.

**c** Write questions using *Is there … ?* and *Are there … ?* about your partner's town, city or street. Here are some ideas:

- cafés
- supermarket
- swimming pool
- hospital
- cinema
- restaurants

**d** Ask your partner about their town, city or street.

Are there any cafés in your town?

Yes, there are two cafés.

Is there a supermarket on your street?

No, but there are two shops.

## 6 SPEAKING

**Communication 5B**
Student A: Go to p. 109.
Student B: Go to p. 107.

3

2

# 5C EVERYDAY ENGLISH

## Is there a supermarket near here?

**Learn to ask and say where places are**

- P Emphasising what you say 1
- W An email about a place

## 1 LISTENING

**a** Ask and answer the questions.

1 What food shops or markets are there near your home?
2 Do you go to these shops or markets? How often?
3 Is the food good / expensive?

**b** 05.18 Watch or listen to Part 1. Answer the questions.

1 Does Megan like Sophia's flat?
2 What does Sophia need?
3 Does Sophia know where to buy food near her flat?

## 2 PRONUNCIATION Emphasising what you say 1

**a** 05.19 Listen to the sentence.

**MEGAN** It's a really nice flat, Sophia.

05.20 Listen to the sentence again. Is *really* more or less stressed the second time?

**b** Tick (✓) the correct rule.

We say *really* with a strong stress to:
1 ☐ speak loudly
2 ☐ make the meaning stronger

**c** 05.21 Listen to the sentences. Underline one word with strong stress in each sentence.

1 My country is very hot in the summer.
2 James's new car is really fast.
3 This film is so boring.

**d** 05.21 Listen again and repeat.

## 3 LISTENING

**a** 05.22 Watch or listen to Part 2. Answer the questions.

1 Do Sophia and Megan find a shop?
2 Who do they meet in the street?

**b** 05.22 Watch or listen to Part 2 again. Are the sentences true (*T*) or false (*F*)?

1 Sophia thinks a café is a shop.
2 James sees Megan and Sophia first.
3 James lives in the next street.
4 There's a supermarket in the next street.
5 There's a shop near James's flat.

## 4 USEFUL LANGUAGE Asking and saying where places are

**a** 05.23 Complete the questions with words in the box. Listen and check.

near where there

1 ______'s your flat?
2 Is ______ a supermarket near here?
3 Are there any shops ______ here?

**b** 05.24 Match the two possible answers in a–c with questions 1–3 in 4a. Listen and check.

a Yes, there are. There's one in this street. / No, sorry, there aren't.
b Yes, there's one near my flat. / No, sorry, there isn't.
c It's in the next street. / It's in this street.

**c** 05.25 Put the conversation in the correct order. Listen and check.

**A** ☐ Great, thank you. And is there a good restaurant in this part of town?
**A** 1 Excuse me, can you help me?
**A** ☐ OK, thanks for your help.
**A** ☐ Are there any good cafés near here?

**B** ☐ Yes, there's one in the next street – Café Milano.
**B** ☐ No, I'm sorry, there aren't any restaurants near here. But there's one near the station.
**B** ☐ Yes, of course.
**B** ☐ No problem.

**d** Practise the conversation in 4c with a partner.

## 5 SPEAKING

Communication 5C Student A: Look at the information below. Student B: Go to p. 106.

**a** **Conversation 1.** You're on a street you don't know. Ask Student B about:

- a hotel
- cafés

**b** **Conversation 2.** Now you're on a street you know. Use the information to answer Student B's questions.

- a bank: in the next street
- shops: not near here – near the hospital

## 6 WRITING

**a** Read part of an email from Sophia to her parents. She writes about her new flat. Does she only write about the good things?

> My new flat is great. It's big and it's in a nice part of town. The flat is near my office and there's a beautiful park in the next street. There isn't a supermarket near me, but there's a shop in the next street.
> ...

**b** Go to Writing Plus 5C on p. 160 for *and* and *but*.

**c** Write about your part of town. Use *there's / there isn't / there are / there aren't*. Use *and* and *but*.

**d** Read about your partner's part of town. Is it the same?

## UNIT PROGRESS TEST

### CHECK YOUR PROGRESS

You can now do the Unit Progress Test.

# UNIT 5
## Review

## 1 GRAMMAR

**a** Correct the sentences.

> There an Italian restaurant. *There's an Italian restaurant.*
1 There is a hotel on this street?
2 Yes, there's.
3 There are a shower.
4 There aren't a free rooms.
5 Is there swimming pool at the hotel?
6 No, there not is.

**b** Complete the sentences.

1 Is ___________ a bank near here?
2 Are there ___________ bottles of water in the room?
3 ___________ there a supermarket on this street?
4 Is there ___________ TV in the room?
5 ___________ there any cafés near here?
6 Is there ___________ teacher in the room?

**c** Ask and answer the questions in 1b.

## 2 VOCABULARY

**a** What are these places? Use the words to complete the crossword.

1 
2 
3 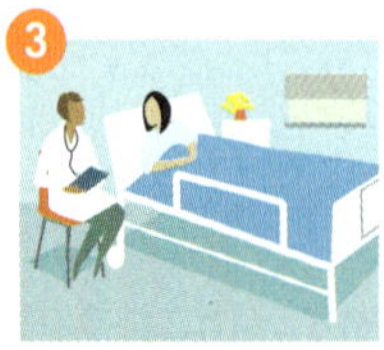
4 
5 
6 
7 
8 

**b** Write the words.

1 deb ___________

2 werhos ___________

3 ipowll ___________

4 thab ___________

5 orom ___________

6 wotel ___________

7 iw-if ___________

8 kanblet ___________

## 3 SOUND AND SPELLING

**a** 05.26 Complete the table with the words in the box. Practise saying the words.

~~**u**p~~ ~~y**ou**~~ **u**mbrella l**o**vely b**eau**tiful n**ew**
br**o**ther sch**oo**l m**o**ther m**u**seum p**oo**l

| /uː/ | /ʌ/ |
|---|---|
| *you* | *up* |

**b** 05.27 Look at the information in the table.

| /ɒ/ | /aʊ/ | /əʊ/ |
|---|---|---|
| sh**o**p | sh**ow**er | pill**ow** |
| h**o**spital | fl**ow**er | kn**ow** |
| h**o**t | t**ow**el | h**o**tel |

**c** 05.28 Are the sounds in **bold** the same (S) or different (D)? Practise saying the words.

> t**ow**n – sh**o**p *D*
1 h**o**t – h**o**tel
2 sh**ow**er – h**ow**
3 **O**K – kn**ow**
4 g**o** – pill**ow**
5 h**o**t – t**ow**el
6 fl**ow**er – h**o**spital

## REVIEW YOUR PROGRESS

**How well did you do in this unit? Write 3, 2 or 1 for each objective.**
3 = very well 2 = well 1 = not so well

| I CAN ... | |
|---|---|
| describe a town | ☐ |
| talk about hotels and hostels | ☐ |
| ask and say where places are. | ☐ |

## CAN DO OBJECTIVES

- Talk about people's jobs
- Talk about daily routines and habits
- Make and accept offers

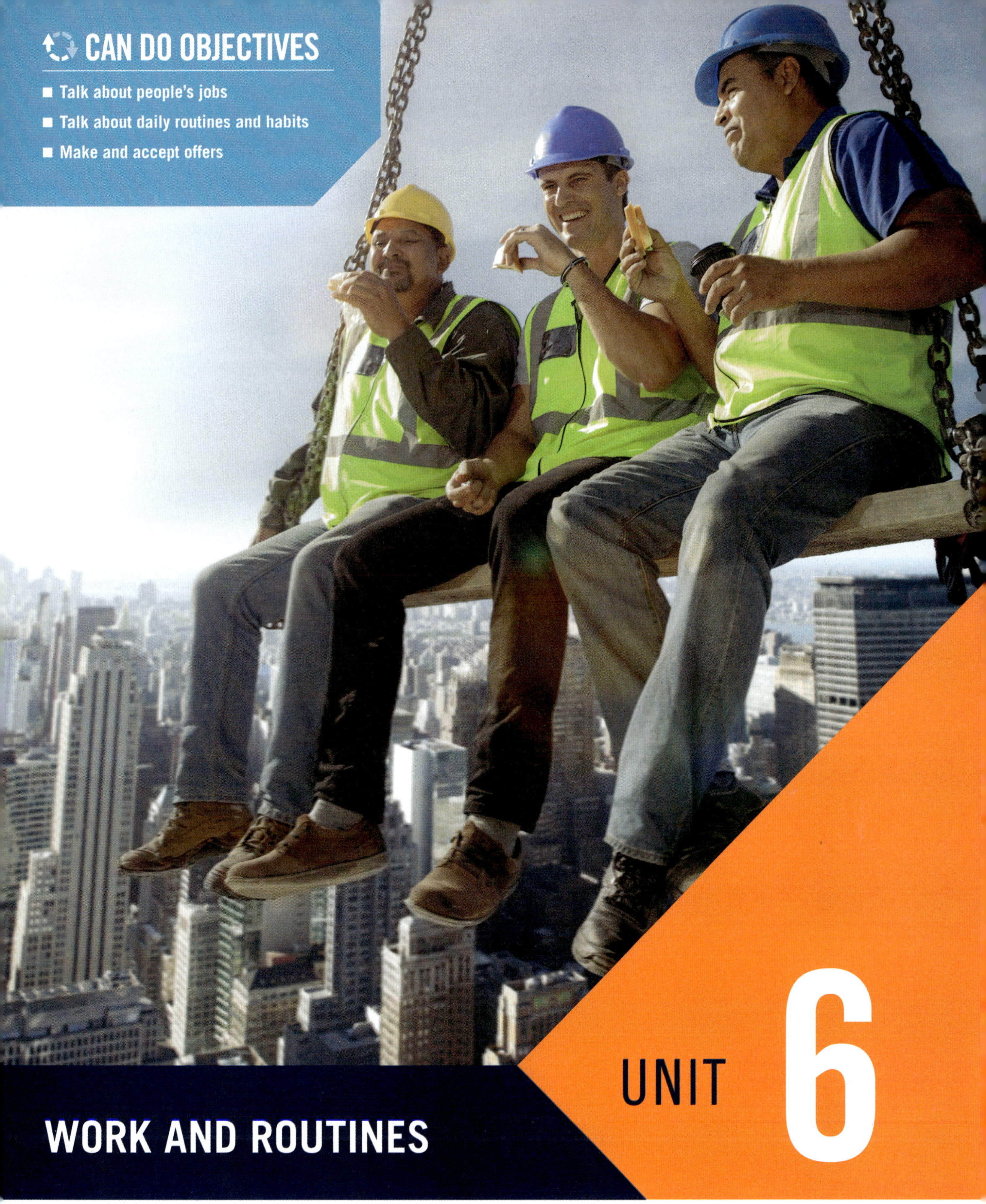

# UNIT 6

# WORK AND ROUTINES

## GETTING STARTED

**a** Look at the picture and answer the questions.

1 What do the people do?
2 Where do the people work?
3 Would you like to do this job?

**b** Think of two questions to ask the people in the picture.

# 6A I DON'T WORK AT NIGHT

**Learn to talk about people's jobs**

G Present simple: *he / she / it* negative

V Jobs

JOBS INTERNATIONAL

HOME NEWS ABOUT

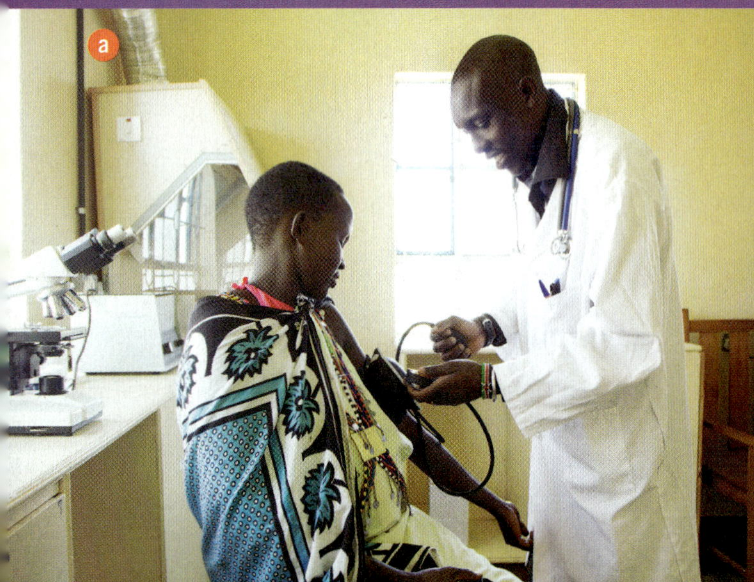

## HELP AROUND THE WORLD ...

**Welcome to Jobs International. Our people go around the world and help others. Meet two of them.**

I'm a doctor from Brazil and I work in a small hospital in Ghana. I love the work here because it's very interesting. I do different things every day. And the people are so friendly. Life isn't always easy here, but it's great to help people.

I'm a teacher at a school in Samoa, but I'm from Australia. I teach English here and after school, I play sports with the children. They love rugby and volleyball. The children are really happy – a lot of fun. This is a really good job.

## 1 READING

**a** Look at pictures a and b. What places are in the pictures? What jobs do people do there?

**b** Read about Luiza and Fred on the *Jobs International* website. Are your ideas in 1a correct?

**c** Read the website again. Are the sentences true or false?

1 *Jobs International* people don't work in their home countries.
2 Luiza works in a big hospital.
3 Her work is sometimes boring.
4 She likes the people in Ghana.
5 Fred goes home after classes.
6 His students like playing sport.

**d** Write questions for Luiza and Fred.

*What … do? → What do you do?*

1 Where … work?
2 … like the people?
3 … like the job?

**e** You are Luiza or Fred. Ask and answer the questions in 1d.

What do you do?

I'm a teacher.

**Language Plus** *work / job*

| | |
|---|---|
| *I **work** in a hospital.* | *work* = verb |
| *I like my **work**.* | *work* = noun |
| *It's a good **job**.* | *job* = noun (*doctor, teacher*) |

## 2 LISTENING AND VOCABULARY Jobs

**a** Match the words in the box with pictures a–h.

| football player | student | receptionist | waiter | taxi driver | factory worker | office worker | shop assistant |
|---|---|---|---|---|---|---|---|

**b** 06.01 **Pronunciation** Listen to the two-word jobs in 2a. Which word is stressed?

1 the first word
2 the second word

Practise saying the words.

**c** 06.02 Listen to four people talk about their jobs. What do they do?

1 ____________ 3 ____________
2 ____________ 4 ____________

**d** 06.02 Listen again. Complete the sentences with the words in the box.

| study | play (x2) | sit | meet (x2) |
|---|---|---|---|

1 **DIANA** I ________ all day, but I ________ some interesting people and go to a lot of different places. I don't work at night.
2 **FELIPE** I ________ in a team, and the weekend is the most important time of the week in my job. I don't ________ games in the week – well, sometimes on Wednesdays.
3 **FATIMA** I ________ business at university. It's really interesting.
4 **SHONA** I work in a shop and ________ a lot of different people.

**e** Which job do you like in 2c? Which job don't you like? Say why.

**f** Now go to Vocabulary Focus 6A on p. 145.

## 3 GRAMMAR Present simple: *he / she / it* negative

**a** 06.04 Complete the sentences with *does* or *doesn't*. Listen and check.

**DIANA** I don't work at night.
1 She ____________ work at night.
**FELIPE** I don't play games in the week.
2 He ____________ play games in the week.

**b** Now go to Grammar Focus 6A on p. 124.

**c** Complete the sentences with the correct form of the verbs in brackets.

1 Alex is a taxi driver. He ____________ in the morning. (not work)
2 Sam is a bank worker. He ____________ his job. (not like)
3 Lucy is a shop assistant. She ____________ much each day. (not sit)
4 Matteo is a waiter. He ____________ on Monday. (not work)

**d** **Sound and spelling /ɜː/**

1 06.06 Listen to the words. Do the **marked** letters sound the same?
w**or**k   univ**er**sity

2 06.07 Listen to the words in the box. Which words have the sound /ɜː/?

| f**ir**st | v**er**b | n**ear** | g**ir**l | rec**ep**tionist | w**or**ld |
|---|---|---|---|---|---|

3 Which letter often comes after the vowel to spell the sound /ɜː/?
4 Practise saying the words with /ɜː/.

## 4 SPEAKING

**Communication 6A** Student A: Go to p. 109. Student B: Go to p. 107.

# 6B I WAKE UP AT 4:00

Learn to talk about daily routine and habits

G Present simple: *he / she / it* questions

V Daily routine

## A Good Night's Sleep

People say it's good to sleep for eight hours every night … but is it true? Some people sleep for only five or six hours, and they feel fine in the morning. And some people sleep twice every night …

**Anneli Hanka, 24, Finland**

I always **wake up** at about 4:00 in the morning. I don't want to sleep, so I **get up** and I do yoga. Then I **go to bed** again. Then I get up at 8:00 in the morning and I go to work. I feel fine – I never feel tired.

**Beatriz Romero, 32, USA**

I finish work at 6:00 in the evening, and I arrive home at 6:30. I read the news or text a friend. Then I go to bed for three hours. My husband works in a restaurant and he gets home at about 12:00 at night. So I get up, we have dinner and then we watch TV until about 3:00. Then I sleep until 7:00.

## 1 READING AND VOCABULARY Daily routine

**a** Talk about when you do these things. Use the phrases in the box.

in the morning   in the afternoon   in the evening   at night

1 have dinner
2 go to English class
3 work
4 have coffee
5 read the news
6 sleep

**b** Read the text above. Match what Beatriz and Anneli say with pictures a and b.

**c** Match the underlined words from the text with pictures 1–3.

**d** Complete the verb phrases with the words in the box. Then read the text again to check your answers.

have   watch   go   arrive / get   finish

1 ______ to work
2 ______ home
3 ______ dinner
4 ______ TV
5 ______ work

**e** Now go to Vocabulary Focus 6B on p. 146.

**f** Ask and answer the questions with a partner.

1 Do you sleep … ?
- for eight hours
- twice every night
- for five or six hours

2 When do you usually … ?
- wake up
- get up
- go to bed

3 When do you usually … ?
- go to work or school
- get home in the evening
- finish work or school

**Language Plus** *for, from … to … , until*

8 hours
11:00 pm — 7:00 am

*I sleep **for** eight hours.*
*I sleep **from** 11:00 **to** 7:00.*
*I sleep **until** 7:00.*

**g** **Sound and spelling** Consonant clusters

1 06.10 These words start with two consonant sounds together. Listen and practise saying them.
**sl**eep **br**eakfast **tw**elve

2 06.11 Listen to the words in the box. Underline the two consonant sounds that are together.

play   small   bread   fruit   flat   study   speak

3 Practise saying the words.

## 2 LISTENING

a 06.12 Listen to an interview with Paul. What are his answers to the questions?

1 Do you go to bed early?
2 When do you wake up?
3 What do you do then?
4 What about your wife? Does she wake up then?

b Talk about the questions with a partner.

1 What do you think about Paul's daily routine?
2 What do you think about his photos? Think of adjectives to talk about them.

## 3 GRAMMAR Present simple: *he / she / it* questions

a Complete the questions in the table with *do* or *does*.

| you | he/she/it |
|---|---|
| Do you go to bed early? | ______ she wake up? |
| When ______ you wake up? | When ______ he get up? |

b Now go to Grammar Focus 6B on p. 124.

c 06.15 **Pronunciation** Listen to the questions with *when* in 3a and notice the stressed words. Tick (✓) the words we stress.

1 ☐ question word (*when*)
2 ☐ *do*
3 ☐ *up*

d Write questions about Beatriz and Anneli on page 50.

1 What time / Beatriz / finish work?
2 Where / her husband / work?
3 What time / he / get home?
4 When / Anneli / wake up?
5 What / she / do then?
6 How / she / feel in the morning?

e Ask and answer the questions in 3d with a partner.

f Ask about your partner's routine.

- the morning
- meals
- work / school / university
- the evening
- sleep

When do you get up?

I get up at 7:30.

g Work with a new partner. Ask questions about their first partner's routine.

When does Emma get up?

Emma gets up at 7:30.

## 4 SPEAKING

**Communication 6B** Student A: Go to p. 109. Student B: Go to p. 107.

# 6C EVERYDAY ENGLISH
## I'll come with you

**Learn to make and accept offers**

P Emphasising what you say 2

W An email about your day

## 1 LISTENING

**a** It's your first week in a new flat. Tick (✓) four things you need.

1 ☐ a bowl
2 ☐ a glass
3 ☐ a cup
4 ☐ a spoon
5 ☐ a knife
6 ☐ a plate

**b** Tell a partner your ideas in 1a. Do you need the same things?

**c** 06.16 Watch or listen to Part 1. Answer the questions.

1 Who do Megan and Sophia meet?
2 Where do they all go?

**d** 06.16 Watch or listen to Part 1 again. <u>Underline</u> the correct word.

1 The flowers are for *Megan / Sophia*.
2 Megan and James want *tea / coffee*.
3 Sophia needs another *cup / spoon*.
4 Sophia wants to go shopping *today / tomorrow*.

## 2 USEFUL LANGUAGE Making and accepting offers 1

**a** 06.17 Complete the conversations with the words in the box. Listen and check.

thanks please like (x2)

1 **SOPHIA** Would you ______ a cup of coffee?
**JAMES** Yes, ______.
2 **SOPHIA** ... I have biscuits! Would you ______ one, Megan?
**MEGAN** No, it's OK, ______.

**b** 06.17 Pronunciation Listen to the mini-conversations in 2a again. Do you hear a /l/ or a /d/ sound in *would*? Listen again and repeat.

**c** 06.18 Put A's questions in the correct order in the conversation. Listen and check.

**A** like a / would you / cup of tea ?
**B** Yes, please.
**A** piece of cake / you like a / and would ?
**B** No, it's OK, thanks.

**d** Practise the conversation in 2c with a partner. Ask about different food and drinks.

## 3 LISTENING AND USEFUL LANGUAGE
### Making and accepting offers 2

**a** 06.19 Watch or listen to Part 2. Answer the questions.

1 What does James want to do?
2 Do Sophia and Megan want him to help?

**b** 06.20 Complete the sentences with words in the box. Listen and check.

can help I'll

1 I ______ go with you.
2 I'll ______ you buy things.
3 ______ come with you.

**c** 06.21 Do these replies answer yes or no? Listen and check.

That's great, thanks. Don't worry, it's OK.
Thanks, but I'm fine. Thank you, that's very kind.

**d** 06.22 Complete the conversation with the words in the box. Listen and check.

great can help right supermarket

**A** I need to go to the [1]______.
**B** I [2]______ come with you.
**A** That's [3]______! And I need to make dinner.
**B** I'll [4]______ you.
**A** All [5]______, thank you very much.

**e** Practise the conversation in 3d with a partner.

**f** Use different words and expressions to make a new conversation.

I need to go to the shops.

I'll go with you.

## 4 PRONUNCIATION
### Emphasising what you say 2

**a** 06.23 Listen to the sentences and notice the strong stress. Then listen again and repeat.

1 I can go with you. 2 I'll come with you.

**b** 06.24 Listen to the mini-conversations. Underline the strong stress.

**Conversation 1**
**A** I can't do this exercise.
**B** Joe can help you.
**Conversation 2**
**C** I need to get to the station this afternoon.
**D** I'll drive you.

**c** Practise the mini-conversations in 4b with a partner.

## 5 SPEAKING

**a** You're in a café with your partner. Use the ideas below to make a conversation.

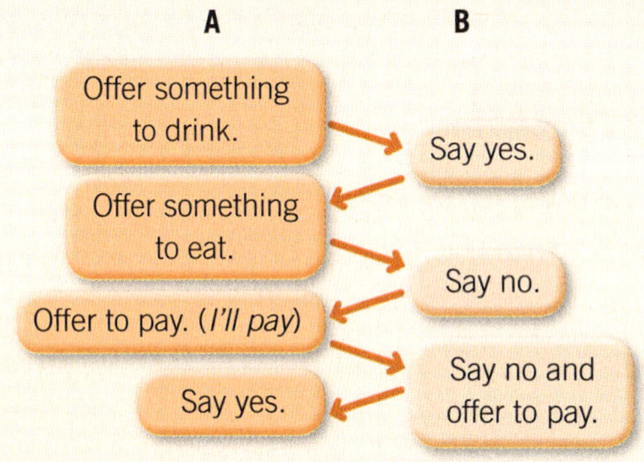


## 6 WRITING

**a** Read part of an email from Sophia to her sister. She writes about a day in her life in London. Where do Sophia and Megan have coffee? Why?

> I walk to work every day because my flat is near the office. I start work at 8:30 and I finish at 5:30. I work with Megan. We go out to a café for coffee every day because the coffee machine in the office isn't very good. We also have lunch there. They have nice sandwiches and chocolate cake – my favourite! Megan always says, 'I'll pay.' She's very nice.

**b** Now go to Writing Plus 6C on p. 160 for *because* and *also*.

**c** Write about a day in your life. Use *because* and *also*.

**d** Read about your partner's day. Do you do the same?

**UNIT PROGRESS TEST**

**CHECK YOUR PROGRESS**

You can now do the Unit Progress Test.

# UNIT 6
## Review

## 1 GRAMMAR

**a** Tick (✓) the sentences that are correct. Correct the mistakes.

> My sister doesn't lives at home.
*My sister doesn't live at home.*
> ☑ I don't study Chinese.
1 ☐ She don't like cake.
2 ☐ Marcus doesn't meets many people.
3 ☐ This town doesn't have a university.
4 ☐ I work not on Fridays.
5 ☐ We don't talk much at work.
6 ☐ Isabella speaks not Italian.

**b** Complete the sentences with *do*, *don't*, *does* or *doesn't*.

1 ________ your sister work in a bank?
No, she 2 ________.
3 ________ you meet people at work?
Yes, I 4 ________.
5 ________ you and your friends play football?
No, we 6 ________.

**c** Write present simple questions with the words and phrases.

> what time / you / get up
*What time do you get up?*
1 what / you / eat in the morning
2 where / your brother / work
3 you / speak / English
4 your teacher / speak / Spanish
5 what time / the lesson / start
6 when / it / finish

**d** Ask and answer the questions in 1c.

## 2 VOCABULARY

**a** Complete the job words.

1 w________s

2 t____i d____r

3 d________r

4 r________t

5 t________r

6 c________f

**b** Complete the table with the words and phrases in the box.

arrive get start to bed lunch shower ~~to school~~

| | |
|---|---|
| go | *to school* / to work<br>1 ________ |
| wake<br>2 ________ | up |
| 3 ________<br>finish | work |
| have | breakfast / 4 ________ / dinner<br>a coffee / a 5 ________ |
| 6 ________<br>get | home |

**c** What do you do every day? Tell a partner.

## 3 SOUND AND SPELLING

**a** 06.25 Look at the information in the table.

| /ʌ/ | /ɔː/ |
|---|---|
| **u**p, l**u**nch, c**u**p, r**u**gby<br>c**o**me, l**o**vely, w**o**rry | sp**or**t, b**or**ing<br>f**our**<br>sm**a**ll, **a**lways |

**b** 06.26 Are the **marked** sounds the same (S) or different (D)? Practise saying the words.

1 **a**lways – b**or**ing
2 sm**a**ll – l**u**nch
3 l**o**vely – r**u**gby
4 f**our** – c**u**ps
5 sp**or**t – w**o**rry
6 c**o**me – **u**p

**c** 06.27 Match the words that start with the same consonant group. Practise saying the words.

bread class ~~flowers~~ player sport start twenty

> **fl**at – *flowers*
1 **tw**elve – ________
2 **st**udy – ________
3 **pl**ate – ________
4 **cl**ock – ________
5 **br**eakfast – ________
6 **sp**oon – ________

## REVIEW YOUR PROGRESS

**How well did you do in this unit? Write 3, 2 or 1 for each objective.**
3 = very well 2 = well 1 = not so well

| I CAN ... | |
|---|---|
| talk about people's jobs | ☐ |
| talk about daily routines and habits | ☐ |
| make and accept offers. | ☐ |

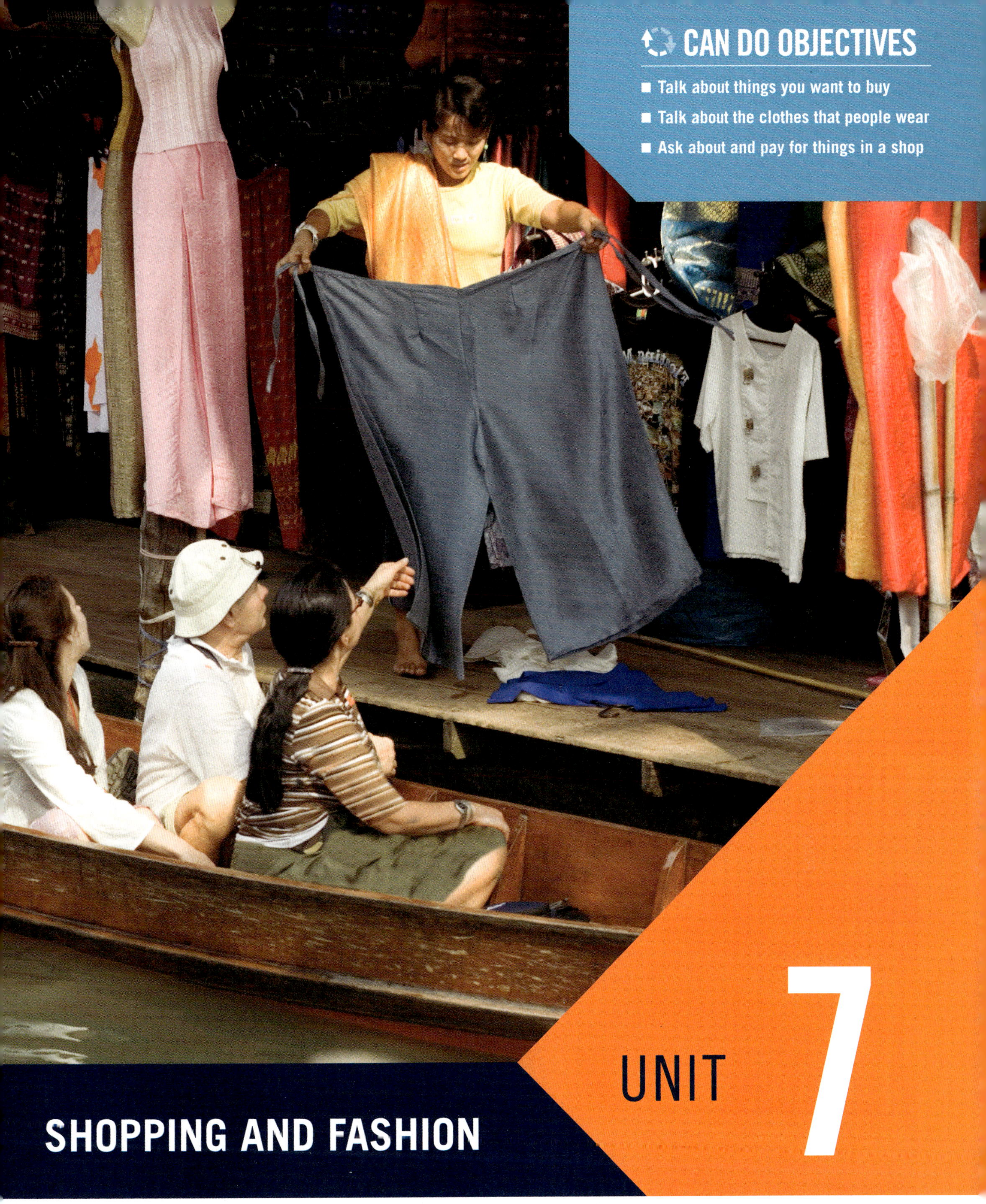

## CAN DO OBJECTIVES

- Talk about things you want to buy
- Talk about the clothes that people wear
- Ask about and pay for things in a shop

# UNIT 7

# SHOPPING AND FASHION

## GETTING STARTED

**a** Look at the picture and answer the questions.

1 Are the people in the boat ... ?

- ☐ on holiday
- ☐ shopping for food
- ☐ shopping for clothes
- ☐ friends
- ☐ family

2 What question does the woman in the boat ask?

3 What clothes can you see in the picture?

**b** Talk about the questions.

1 What do you like to buy when you go shopping?

2 What clothes do you have?

3 What colour clothes do you like?

# 7A I LIKE THIS LAMP

Learn to talk about things you want to buy

G *this, that, these, those*

V Common objects 2; Prices

## 1 READING AND VOCABULARY Common objects 2

**a** Read about three places to shop. Which place is in the pictures?

**b** Which place is good for these people?

1 'I want a new bed for my flat.'
2 'I love old books and magazines.'
3 'I always finish work at 7:00 pm.'
4 'I think old lamps are beautiful.'

**c** Look at the pictures and read about The Sunday Flea Market again. Match the objects a–f with the words in the box.

suitcase lamp clock guitar picture chair

**d** Talk with other students about which object you would like to buy in the pictures. Say why. Which object do most people want?

**e** Now go to Vocabulary Focus 7A on p. 147.

**f** **Sound and spelling /b/, /p/, /g/ and /k/**

1 Complete the words in the table. They are all common objects.

| Sound 1 /b/ | Sound 2 /p/ | Sound 3 /g/ | Sound 4 /k/ |
|---|---|---|---|
| __ag | __lant | __lass | __up |
| foot__all | __late | __uitar | suit__ase |
| | __icture | | __lo__ __ |

2 07.02 Listen and check.
3 Which sound is spelled in different ways in the table?
4 Practise saying the words.

**g** Work in pairs.

Student A: You have a stall at the flea market. Write five things you sell. Don't show Student B.
Student B: What does Student A sell?

Do you sell guitars?

No, sorry.

Do you have glasses?

Yes, I do. Here you are.

# SHOPPING
## PLACES TO GO

### MEGA HOME STORE

**Open 8 am–8 pm**

A great place to buy things for your home. They sell beds, pillows, tables, chairs and lamps. Everything is new, but it isn't expensive. There's also a good café with drinks, pizza and sandwiches.

### THE SUNDAY FLEA MARKET

**Open 6 am–4 pm**

Here you can buy something for your home or you can just look around. They sell a lot of old things. You can buy clocks, guitars, suitcases, lamps, pictures, chairs … anything! Just look at these pictures from our readers!

### BOOKS & CO.

**Open 9 am–6 pm**

A very interesting bookshop. They sell old and new books and they also have magazines, pictures, old photographs and music. If you like old books and pictures, this is the place for you.

## 2 LISTENING AND GRAMMAR *this, that, these, those*

**a** 07.03 Kate and Edward are at Mega Home Store. Listen to their conversation and answer the questions.

1 Who likes the plant and the chairs?
2 Who likes the phone, Kate or Edward?
3 How much is the speaker?
4 Does Kate think it's a good price?

**b** 07.04 Listen to Kate and Edward. Complete the sentences with *this*, *that*, *these* or *those*.

1 'I like ________ plant. What do you think?'
2 'Or ________ chairs. They're really nice.'
3 'Oh, look. ________ plates are beautiful.'
4 'Look at ________ speaker! That's so cool.'

**c** Complete the table with the words in 2b.

| Singular | this | |
|---|---|---|
| Plural | | |

Which words mean … ?
1 here, near me
2 there, not near me

**d** **Sound and spelling** *this*, *that*, *these* and *those*

1 07.05 Listen to *this*, *that*, *these* and *those*. Which words … ?
- end in a /s/ sound
- end in a /z/ sound

2 Practise saying the words.

**e** Now go to Grammar Focus 7A on p. 126.

**f** You and your partner are in the shop below. Talk about the objects in the box with *this*, *that*, *these* or *those*.

glasses plates speaker plant chairs phone lamp

## 3 VOCABULARY Prices

**a** 07.07 Listen to the prices. Tick (✓) the phrase you hear.

1 £3.80
 a ☐ three pound eighty
 b ☐ three pounds eighty
 c ☐ three pounds and eighty
2 €25
 a ☐ twenty-five euro
 b ☐ twenty-five euros
 c ☐ twenty-five of euros

**b** 07.08 Practise saying the prices below. Listen and check.

1 £5.99
2 $16.50
3 €4.50
4 $100

**c** 07.09 Listen. Then complete the conversation.

**A** Excuse me. [1]______ ______ is that **clock**?
**B** [2]______ €13.50.
**A** Hmm. And [3]______ ______ are these **cups**?
**B** [4]______ €5 each.

**d** Practise the conversation in 3c with a partner. Change the words in **bold** and the prices.

**e** How much are these things in your country?
- a cup of coffee in a café
- a phone
- a pizza
- a bottle of water

## 4 SPEAKING

**Communication 7A**

Student A: Go to p. 113.
Student B: Go to p. 111.

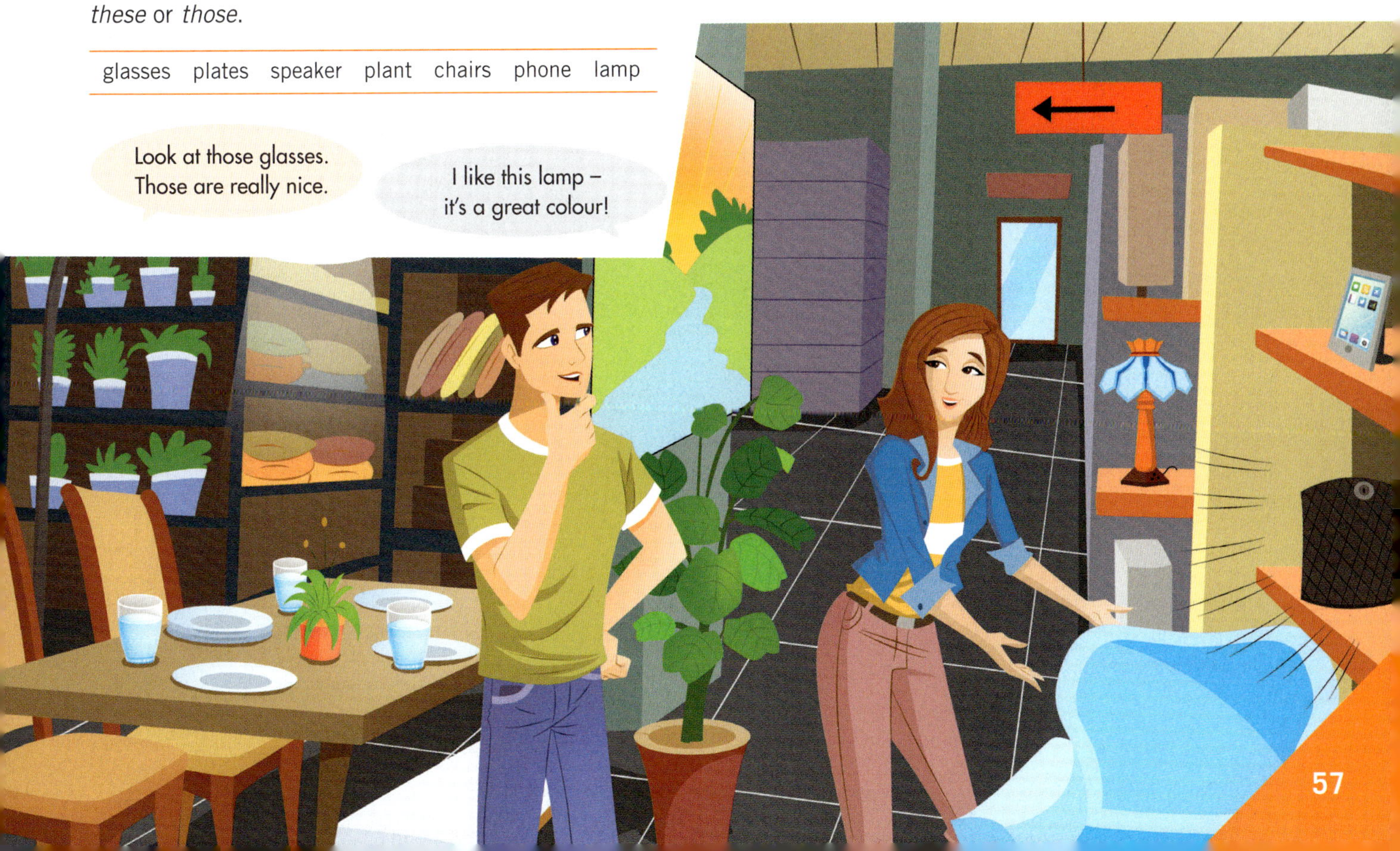

# 7B IT'S GREG'S T-SHIRT

**Learn to talk about clothes that people wear**

G Possessive *'s*; Revision of adverbs

V Clothes; Colours

## They make colourful clothes, but do they wear them?

Fashion designers often make very different and interesting clothes for people, but they don't usually wear colourful clothes. They often wear the same clothes and the same colours.

**TOM FORD** makes beautiful clothes for men and for women, but he often wears a white shirt and a black or dark grey jacket.

## 1 VOCABULARY Clothes

**a** Look at the pictures of the models and the fashion designers. Which clothes do you like?

**b** 07.10 Match the words in the box with a–h in the pictures. Listen and check.

jacket coat shirt skirt trousers T-shirt dress blouse

**c** Which clothes do you often wear together?

**d** **Sound and spelling** /ʃ/ and /dʒ/

1 07.11 Listen and practise these sounds.
1 /ʃ/ **sh**irt 2 /dʒ/ **j**acket

2 07.12 Look at the words in the box. What sounds do the letters in **bold** have? Listen and add the words to the sound groups below.

**G**erman interna**t**ional fa**sh**ion lar**g**e langua**g**e villa**g**e **s**ugar

| Sound 1 /ʃ/ | Sound 2 /dʒ/ |
| --- | --- |
| shirt | jacket |

3 Practise saying the words.

**e** **Communication 7B** Student A: Go to p. 110. Student B: Go to p. 114.

## 2 READING

**a** Read about the fashion designers. What is the same about them?

**b** Read the text again. Are the sentences true (*T*) or false (*F*)? Correct the false sentences.

1 Fashion designers sometimes wear boring clothes.
2 Tom Ford never wears a black jacket.
3 Carolina Herrera often wears a white skirt.
4 Michael Kors often wears a jacket.

**c** Is it a good idea for fashion designers to wear their clothes? Why / Why not?

## 3 VOCABULARY Colours

**a** Look at the picture of Tom Ford. Complete the sentence about him with colours in the box.

black ● grey ● white ○

Tom Ford often wears a ________ shirt and a ________ or dark ________ jacket.

**CAROLINA HERRERA** makes clothes with a lot of different colours, but she usually wears a black skirt and a white blouse.

**MICHAEL KORS** designs colourful clothes, but he often wears a black T-shirt, black trousers and a black jacket.

**Language Plus** *dark / light*

| | |
|---|---|
| ***dark*** *blue* | ***light*** *blue* |
| ***dark*** *green* | ***light*** *green* |

**b** Now go to Vocabulary Focus 7B on p. 148.

**c** Work with a partner.

Student A: Choose a picture in 1a. Don't tell your partner! Talk about the colours and the clothes.
Student B: Guess the picture your partner talks about.

Then swap roles.

## 4 LISTENING

**a** 07.15 Listen to Kate and Giuseppe Costa. Tick (✓) the clothes you hear.

☐ T-shirt ☐ skirt ☐ shoes
☐ jeans ☐ trousers ☐ shirt

**b** 07.15 Listen again and complete the information.

| Who? | What clothes? | Why? |
|---|---|---|
| Greg | ______ | *doesn't wear / doesn't like* |
| Sara | ______ | *doesn't wear / doesn't like* |
| Giuseppe | ______ | *doesn't wear / doesn't like* |

## 5 GRAMMAR Possessive *'s*; Revision of adverbs

**a** 07.16 Complete the sentences with a name from 4b. Listen and check.

1 **GIUSEPPE** Is this my old T-shirt?
**KATE** No, it's ______**'s** T-shirt. (= It's **his** T-shirt.)
2 **GIUSEPPE** Are these your jeans?
**KATE** No, they're ______**'s** jeans. (= They're **her** jeans.)

**b** Now go to Grammar Focus 7B on p. 126.

**c** Look at the picture of Greg, Sara, Giuseppe and Kate. Ask and answer questions about the Costa family.

Who's Giuseppe?
He's Kate's husband.

**d** 07.18 Kate talks about the people in her office. Put the word in brackets in the correct place in the sentences. Listen and check.

"Everyone wears different clothes at work. [1]My boss wears a blouse and trousers (always). [2]She wears a skirt (never) – she doesn't like them. [3]Johnnie wears jeans and a white shirt (usually), [4]but he wears black trousers (sometimes). [5]And Fran wears a dress (often), [6]but on Fridays she wears jeans (usually)."

**e** Think of people you work or study with. What do they usually wear? Tell a partner.

## 6 SPEAKING

**a** Put the words and phrases in the correct order to make questions. Write another question with your own idea.

1 wear / at work (or school) / do you / what ?
2 wear / do you / what colour clothes ?
3 your brother's (or sister's, father's, mother's) clothes / do you / wear ?
4 at home / do you / wear shoes ?

**b** Ask and answer the questions in 6a. Add extra information to your answers.

What do you wear at work?
I usually wear a blue or black dress and dark shoes. I like dark colours.

# 7C EVERYDAY ENGLISH

## Can I help you?

**Learn to ask about and pay for things in a shop**

P Connected speech

W An email request for information

## 1 LISTENING

**a** Number the things you can buy from 1 to 4.
1 = I like going shopping for this / these very much.
4 = I really don't like going shopping for this / these.

☐ food ☐ clothes ☐ things for the home ☐ IT things

**b** Talk with a partner about your ideas in 1a. Do you like shopping for the same things?

**c** 07.19 Watch or listen to Part 1. Answer the questions.

1 Who sees some nice cups?
2 Who buys something?

**d** 07.19 Watch or listen to Part 1 again. Complete the information about the cups with a number.

1 Price: £ ____
2 Number in the shop: ____
3 Sophia needs: ____
4 Megan wants: ____

## 2 USEFUL LANGUAGE Going shopping 1

**a** 07.20 Who says each expression – the customer (C) or the shop assistant (S)? Listen and check.

1 How much are these cups?
2 I'd like two of these cups, please.
3 They're three pounds each.
4 Certainly.
5 Can I look around?
6 Can I help you?
7 Of course.

**b** 07.21 Put the conversation in the correct order. Listen and check.

☐ It's fifteen pounds.
☐ Certainly.
☐ It's ten pounds for the small one.
1 Can I help you?
☐ And how much is the small bowl?
☐ OK, then I'd like the large bowl, please.
☐ Yes, thank you. How much is this large bowl?

**c** Practise the conversation in 2b with a partner.

**d** Practise the conversation in 2b again, but ask about glasses. Change the prices.

## 3 PRONUNCIATION Connected speech

**a** 07.22 Listen and notice the extra sounds in these sentences.

1 We /j/ only have three.
2 I'd like two /w/ of these cups.

Practise saying the sentences.

**b** Complete the rules with the sounds in the box.

/w/ /j/

We add a ______ sound between words ending with /iː/ and words starting with a vowel.
We add a ______ sound between words ending with /uː/ and words starting with a vowel.

**c** 07.23 Listen to these sentences. Which extra /j/ or /w/ sound can you hear? Listen again and repeat.

1 Would you like two or three?
2 These are for me and you.
3 Would you like three or four?
4 Are they for you or me?

**d** Practise the sentences in 3c with a partner.

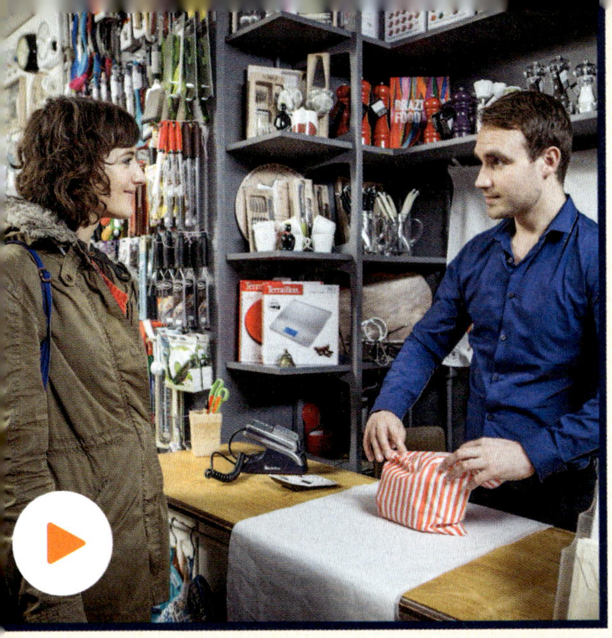

## 4 LISTENING AND USEFUL LANGUAGE
### Going shopping 2

**a** 07.24 Watch or listen to Part 2. Are the sentences true (*T*) or false (*F*)?

1 Megan pays five pounds.
2 She uses a card to pay.
3 Sophia doesn't buy anything.

**b** 07.25 Complete the sentences with words in the box. Listen and check.

your that's here's you no

**S** OK, ______ ten pounds, please.
**C** Here ______ are.
**S** Enter ______ PIN, please.
**C** OK, ______ problem.
**S** ______ your receipt.

**c** 07.26 Complete a conversation between a shop assistant and customer. Use phrases in 4b. Listen and check.

**C** How much … ? (*shoes*)
**S** Twenty pounds.
**C** Here …
**S** Enter …
**C** OK …
**S** And … receipt

**d** Practise the conversation in 4c with a partner. Change the things you buy and the price.

## 5 SPEAKING

Communication 7C
Student A: Go to p. 111.
Student B: Go to p. 112.

## 6 WRITING

**a** Sophia saw an online advertisement.

**FOR SALE**

Chairs, lamps, small tables, a big bed –
*all in good condition.*
**Not expensive!**

Email me for more information **jack@icemail.com**

Read her email. What information does she want to know?

Dear Jack,
You have an online ad for things you want to sell. I need a chair, a bed and a lamp. How old are these things? How much are they? Can I pay online by credit card?
Thank you!
Sophia

**b** Now go to Writing Plus 7C on p. 161 for Commas, exclamation marks and question marks.

**c** You see these online advertisements.

**FOR SALE**

Sports T-shirts and balls – a lot of different sports – signed by professional players: football, basketball, rugby and more.
**Great prices!**

Email me for more information **ilovesports@travelmail.com**

**FOR SALE**

Books for learning English – dictionaries, grammar books, coursebooks.
**All in good condition.**

Email me for more information **melissa@mymail.com**

Write an email to ask about one of the advertisements. Here are some ideas:

You have a / an / some …
I need …
How old … ?
How much … ?
Can I pay … ?

**d** Read a partner's email. What objects does your partner ask about? Do you ask about the same things?

## UNIT PROGRESS TEST

**CHECK YOUR PROGRESS**

You can now do the Unit Progress Test.

# UNIT 7
# Review

## 1 GRAMMAR

**a** Complete the sentences with the phrases in the box.

these this those that's

1 ______ is my dad's car.

2 I love ______ flowers.

3 ______ an expensive car.

4 ______ flowers in the windows are nice!

**b** Underline the correct answers to complete the conversation.

**ZOE** Hi, Lee. Do you know Kate? [1]*This / That / These* are [2]*Kate's / Kates / Kates'* daughters, Amy and Anna.
**LEE** Hello! Nice to meet you, girls. Who's who?
**ZOE** This [3]*is / are* Amy.
**ANNA** And I'm Anna.
**LEE** I like your bag, Anna.
**ANNA** Oh, thanks. It's [4]*Amys / Amys' / Amy's*. Amy and I have a swimming lesson today.
**ZOE** Yes, the [5]*girl's / girls / girls'* lesson starts at nine.
**ANNA** And then we go to our favourite restaurant!

**c** Practise the conversation in 1b in groups of three.

## 2 VOCABULARY

**a** Complete the names of these common objects.

1 a p______________e

2 a g______________r

3 a c______________r

4 a g______________s

5 a l______________p

6 a p______________t

**b** Complete the descriptions using the colours and clothes.

white light blue light brown red green dark blue

shirt coat skirt jeans shoes

1 a ______ dress
2 ______ trousers and black ______
3 a grey ______ and a ______ jacket
4 a light green ______ and a ______ hat
5 a ______ blouse and a red ______
6 dark blue ______ and a ______ T-shirt

**c** How many hats/coats/jackets/shoes do you have? What colour are they? Tell a partner.

## 3 SOUND AND SPELLING

**a** 07.27 Answer the questions. Practise saying the words.

1 Which words have the /k/ sound? Underline them.

suitcase clock place chair cup jacket coat dark

2 Which words have the /b/ sound? Underline them.

blue black brown blouse bed bowl

3 Which words have the /p/ sound? Underline them.

pink lamp photograph picture pillow plate plant

4 Which words have the /g/ sound? Underline them.

magazine bag light grey green thing

**b** 07.28 Complete the table with the words in the box. Practise saying the words.

dress ~~shoes~~ sugar Spain international jeans large fashion T-shirt jacket Germany this skirt

| /ʃ/ | /s/ | /dʒ/ |
|---|---|---|
| shoes | | |

## REVIEW YOUR PROGRESS

**How well did you do in this unit? Write 3, 2 or 1 for each objective.**
3 = very well 2 = well 1 = not so well

| I CAN ... | |
|---|---|
| talk about things I want to buy | ☐ |
| talk about the clothes that people wear | ☐ |
| ask about and pay for things in a shop. | ☐ |

## CAN DO OBJECTIVES

- Talk about past events
- Describe events in the past
- Make and respond to suggestions

# UNIT 8

# PAST EVENTS

## GETTING STARTED

**a** Look at the picture of a New Year's Eve celebration and talk about the questions.

1 Do you want to go there? Why / Why not?

2 What do you think is happening at this New Year's Eve celebration? Here are some ideas:

- ☐ music
- ☐ dancing
- ☐ shopping
- ☐ fireworks
- ☐ eating food
- ☐ meeting friends

**b** Talk about the questions.

1 Where were you last New Year's Eve?

2 Who were you with?

3 What things did you do?

4 Did you have fun?

# 8A I WAS ON TOUR WITH MY BAND

**Learn to talk about past events**

G Past simple: *be*

V Past time expressions

## 1 READING

**a** Look at the events in pictures a–d. Choose one you like and one you don't like. Tell a partner. Say why.

a party

a sports game

a concert

a meeting

**b** Read about Cara, Antonio and Ava. Which events in 1a do they talk about?

**c** Read the texts again. Which cities does each person talk about?

**d** Talk about Cara, Antonio and Ava's lives with a partner. Who would you like to meet? Why?

My name's Cara. I'm a photographer. I was in New York three days ago for work and then I was in Dublin yesterday at a meeting about newspaper photography. Life's busy right now!

**'Yesterday I was in Dublin.'**

**'I was at a game in Bristol. It was the Final!'**

### The people in our team ...

My name's Antonio Marotto. I'm the doctor for our team. It's a great job – I really like helping our players. I often go away with the team. We were in Newcastle two weeks ago for a game and we were in Bristol last week. It's fun to travel with the team.

### Ava on the road ...

Hi everyone, it's Ava. Last week I was on tour with my band in Europe – three cities in five days. We were in Munich on Wednesday and then we were in Vienna on Thursday. But Saturday was the best night. We were in Milan and about 1,000 people were at our concert.

**'In this photo we were in Milan.'**

## 2 GRAMMAR Past simple: *be* positive

**a** Complete the table. Find examples of the past simple of *be* in the texts about Cara, Antonio and Ava.

| + | |
|---|---|
| I [1]________ | we [3]________ |
| you were | you were |
| he/she/it [2]________ | they were |

**b** 08.01 **Pronunciation** Listen to sentences 1–4. Are *was* and *were* stressed? Practise saying the sentences.

1 We were in Munich.
2 I was in Madrid.
3 We were in Newcastle.
4 I was in New York.

**c** Now go to Grammar Focus 8A Part 1 on p. 128.

**d** Write sentences about where you were:

- this morning
- last night
- yesterday afternoon

**e** Compare your sentences in 2d with a partner. Were you in the same places?

Chan and I were at the supermarket yesterday afternoon.

## 3 VOCABULARY Past time expressions

**a** Today is Friday of week 3. Put the number of sentences 1–4 in the correct place on the timeline.

week 1 | week 2 | week 3
Monday Tuesday Wednesday Thursday Friday

1 We were in Munich on Wednesday.
2 We were in Madrid two weeks ago.
3 … we were in Bristol last week.
4 I was in Dublin yesterday.

**b** Look at the underlined words in 3a. Replace them with words in the box.

months this morning Saturday year

**c** Now go to Vocabulary Focus 8A on p. 149.

**d** Work in pairs.
Student A: Say a past time expression.
Student B: Say where a person you know was.
Then swap roles.

last weekend

My parents were in London last weekend.

two years ago

My friend Marco was in Thailand two years ago.

## 4 LISTENING AND GRAMMAR Past simple: *be* negative and questions

**a** 08.06 Review the texts about Cara, Antonio and Ava again. Then listen to them talking to friends. Write the correct name for each conversation.

**Conversation 1** ____________
**Conversation 2** ____________
**Conversation 3** ____________

**b** 08.06 Match events 1–3 with adjectives a–c. Listen again and check.

1 the meeting
2 the game
3 the concert

a exciting
b interesting
c fun

**c** 08.07 Listen to Conversation 1 again. Complete the conversation with the words in the box.

was (x2) were (x2) wasn't

**WILL** ________ you at work yesterday?
**CARA** Yes, I ________, but I ________ here in the office.
**WILL** Where ________ you?
**CARA** I was at a meeting in Dublin.
**WILL** Oh, ________ it interesting?
**CARA** Yes, it was really interesting.

**d** Now go to Grammar Focus 8A Part 2 on p. 128.

**e** 08.11 Complete the conversation with *was*, *were*, *wasn't* or *weren't*. Listen and check.

**A** You ________ at work yesterday.
**B** No, it ________ a holiday for me.
**A** Nice. ________ you at home all day?
**B** No, I ________. I ________ in town in the morning and then I ________ at a party last night.
**A** ________ the party good?
**B** Yes, it ________ a lot of fun.

**f** Practise the conversation in 4e with a partner. Change some of the information.

I was at a football match in the morning and then at the cinema last night.

Was the film good?

## 5 SPEAKING

**Communication 8A** Student A: Go to p. 113. Student B: Go to p. 111. Student C: Go to p. 115.

# 8B HE SAW A BEAR

**Learn to describe events in the past**

G Past simple: positive

V Free time activities

## 1 READING

**a** Look at pictures 1–3 below. Match the pictures to the animal names. Where do they usually live? What do you know about them?

______ deer ______ bear ______ hippo

**b** Read the stories below. Write the story titles next to the sentences.

1 Hippos were on a rugby field. ____________

2 Three deer were in a woman's flat. ____________

3 A bear was in a man's garden. ____________

**c** Read the stories again. Complete the information.

| | Where? | When? | Animal activity? |
|---|---|---|---|
| Andrew from Utah | at home | | |
| Ben from South Africa | | evening | |
| A woman from Indiana | | | jump |

**d** Talk about the questions.

1 Which story do you like?

2 Which animals sometimes come into houses in your country?

cat

dog

bird

snake

3 What do you do if a wild animal comes into your house?

# WILD STORIES!

1

### CURIOUS CREATURE

Andrew Singer from Utah was at home in his house on a farm. One evening he was in the kitchen and he heard something strange in the garden, so he looked out of the window. He saw a bear in the garden. The bear walked around the garden and looked in the windows of the house. It tried to open the kitchen door and Andrew was really scared. It wasn't possible for the bear to get in, so it went away. Andrew thinks the bear was hungry, but it's not a good idea to give bears food.

2

### SURPRISE VISITORS

A woman from Indiana had a ground floor flat with a garden. In the evening, she went into her living room and watched TV. She heard something in her bedroom, so she went to look. She saw three deer near her bed. They came into the living room and jumped on her sofa, then they went into the bathroom. The woman called the police and they came to catch the deer. She had an exciting night with her three new friends!

3

### READY TO PLAY

Ben Kruger from South Africa loves playing rugby. He has a business in Limpopo, a city in the north of South Africa. One night after work, he went to a rugby field nearby. It was dark and he saw something on the field. It was large, but it wasn't a person – it was a hippopotamus (hippo)! Then he saw another hippo and then another – there were a lot of them. The hippos ate some grass and then went away. Ben thinks the hippos were from a river near the rugby field.

## 2 GRAMMAR Past simple: positive

**a** 08.12 Read the stories again and find the past simple forms of the verbs in the table. Listen and check.

| A | | B | |
|---|---|---|---|
| **Verb** | **Past form** | **Verb** | **Past form** |
| look | *looked* | have | *had* |
| watch | | hear | |
| call | | eat | |
| jump | | see | |
| walk | | go | |
| try | | come | |

**b** Answer the questions about the table in 2a.

1 What do we add to the verbs in A to make the past form?
2 Do the verbs in B all change in the same way or in different ways?

**c** **Sound and spelling** /t/ and /d/

1 08.13 Listen and practise these sounds.
1 /t/ talk**ed** 2 /d/ liv**ed**

2 08.14 Listen to the past forms in the box. Which *-ed* endings sound … ?
- more like /t/
- more like /d/

looked watched called tried
walked played finished

3 Practise saying the words.

**d** Cover the table in 2a. Test a partner.
Student A: Say a verb.
Student B: Say the past form.
Then swap roles.

**e** Now go to Grammar Focus 8B on p. 128.

**f** Complete the sentences so they are true for you.

1 Yesterday I called ____________. (a person)
2 Last month I saw ____________. (a TV programme)
3 Last weekend I went to ____________. (a place)
4 Last night I ate ____________. (food)

Tell your partner about your sentences.

## 3 LISTENING AND VOCABULARY Free time activities

**a** 08.17 Listen to three conversations about the three stories. In each conversation, some information is incorrect. What is the wrong information?

1 ____________
2 ____________
3 ____________

**b** 08.18 Listen to the sentences from the conversations. Use the correct verb in the box.

read (x2) talked went had watched heard

1 I just ________ to a café.
2 I ________ a large coffee.
3 And I ________ the newspaper.
4 I ________ this funny story.
5 I ________ this story on a podcast.
6 I ________ to my friend Katie last night.
7 She ________ the video online.

**c** Match verbs 1 to 6 with a word or phrase in the box to make more past simple phrases.

a book to my parents home dinner a film
for a walk breakfast a song on the radio to my friend

1 went ______, ______
2 had ______, ______
3 read ______
4 heard ______
5 talked ______, ______
6 watched ______

**d** 08.19 Listen to Emily talk about the things she did yesterday. Put pictures a–e in the correct order.

a

b

c

d

e

**e** 08.19 Complete what Emily says with phrases from 3c. Then listen again and check.

Yesterday I [1]____________ at about 9:00, and then I went to a café and had coffee with my friend Karen. After that, I went to work and was there all day. I [2]____________ with my brother and then I [3]____________ and called my parents. I [4]____________ Rosie in Brazil on Skype. After that, I [5]____________ online and then I went to bed and [6]____________ before going to sleep.

**f** Now go to Vocabulary Focus 8B on p. 150.

**g** Complete the sentences about free time activities.

1 When I was a child, I ______.
2 After work / school, I often ______.
3 On weekends, I like to ______.

**h** Tell other students your sentences in 3g. What free time activities were/are popular … ?

a when everyone was a child
b after work / school
c at the weekend

## 4 SPEAKING

**Communication 8B** Student A: Go to p. 113. Student B: Go to p. 111.

# 8C EVERYDAY ENGLISH

## Let's go somewhere this weekend

**Learn to make and respond to suggestions**

- P Main stress and intonation
- W Thank you note

## 1 LISTENING

**a** Ask and answer the questions.

1 On the first day at work / university / school after the weekend, how do you feel?
2 What do you talk to your friends about on this day?

**b** Sophia arrives at work. Choose the answer you think is correct.

1 Sophia asks David about:
   a London and work
   b his home town and family
2 Sophia and Megan talk about:
   a shopping
   b a party

**c** 08.22 Watch or listen to Part 1. Are your answers in 1b correct?

**d** 08.22 Watch or listen to Part 1 again. Tick (✓) the correct sentence.

1 a ☐ Sophia helped Megan on Saturday.
  b ☐ Sophia doesn't like shopping.
  c ☐ Sophia and Megan both enjoyed shopping.

2 a ☐ Sophia wants to go shopping again.
  b ☐ Megan wants to go shopping this afternoon.
  c ☐ Sophia wants to go to a café and then go shopping.

**e** 08.23 Watch or listen to Part 2. Who went to a party? Who watched TV?

**f** 08.23 Watch or listen to Part 2 again and answer the questions.

1 What was the problem with the party?
2 What's difficult for Sophia?
3 What's Megan's idea for next weekend?
4 Does Sophia feel happy or sad at the end of the conversation? Why?

**g** Talk about the questions.

1 Is it difficult to meet new people in your town / city? Why / Why not?
2 What are good ways to meet new people?

## 2 USEFUL LANGUAGE Making and responding to suggestions

**a** 08.24 Listen to the conversations. Underline the word you hear. Are both options possible?

1 **MEGAN** We *can / could* go shopping again some time.
**SOPHIA** Yes, OK. *Good / Great* idea.

2 **MEGAN** So, *shall we / let's* go there for the day next Saturday?
**SOPHIA** OK, that's a *nice / lovely* idea.

**b** 08.25 Complete the conversation with the words in the box. Listen and check.

we idea go sorry

**A** Let's ______ for dinner on Saturday.
**B** Saturday? I'm ______, I can't. I'm away on Saturday.
**A** Shall ______ go on Sunday?
**B** Yes, that's a great ______.

**c** Practise the conversation in 2b with a partner.

**d** Complete the conversation with words or expressions in 2a and 2b. There is sometimes more than one answer.

**A** ______ go to the cinema tonight.
**B** ______, I'm not free. I have a dinner with my family.
**A** ______ go tomorrow night.
**B** OK, ______.

**e** Practise the conversation in 2d with a partner. Take turns to be A and B.

## 3 PRONUNCIATION Main stress and intonation

**a** 08.26 Listen to the expressions. Notice the main stress.

1 Yes, that's a great idea. 2 Yes, that's a lovely idea.

**b** 08.26 Listen to the expressions in 3a again. Does the intonation rise ↗ or fall ↘ after the main stress?

**c** Work with a partner.
Student A: say sentences 1 and 2.
Student B: answer with phrases in 3a.

1 Let's have a cup of coffee. 2 Shall we go for a walk?

Then swap roles.

## 4 SPEAKING

**a** Work in pairs. Read the ideas below and think about what you want to say.

| A | B |
|---|---|
| Suggest going to a restaurant on Friday. → | You're not free on Friday. You have a work dinner. |
| ← Suggest Saturday. → | Say yes. Suggest an Italian restaurant. |
| ← You went to an Italian restaurant last weekend. Suggest a Mexican restaurant. → | Say yes. Suggest a time. |
| ← Agree with Student B. Say goodbye. → | Thank Student A and say goodbye. |

**b** Have a phone conversation with your partner. Then swap roles.

Shall we go to a restaurant on Friday?

I'm sorry, I'm not free. I have a work dinner.

## 5 WRITING

**a** Read Sophia's text to Megan. Why did Sophia write it?

> Hi Megan!
> Thank you for your help on Saturday.
> It was fun to go shopping with you and you helped me find some good shops. I hope we can go shopping again some time soon. See you soon!

**b** Now go to Writing Plus 8C on p. 161 for Writing short emails, notes and texts.

**c** Write a note to a friend to thank them for something. Here are some ideas:

Here are some flowers / chocolates to say thank you for …
It was … I hope …

**d** Read another student's note. What do they say thank you for?

**UNIT PROGRESS TEST**

**CHECK YOUR PROGRESS**

You can now do the Unit Progress Test.

# UNIT 8
## Review

### 1 GRAMMAR

**a** Write past simple sentences and questions with *be* and the words and phrases.

> (?) where / you yesterday
*Where were you yesterday?*
1 (+) I / in a meeting.
2 (?) / you OK
3 (–) James / at work this morning.
4 (?) where / he
5 (+) Yasmin and Kylie / in New York two weeks ago.
6 (–) we / in Paris six years ago

**b** Complete the text with the past simple form of the verb in brackets.

Last week my family and I [1]__________ (be) in Dublin. We [2]__________ (arrive) on Wednesday morning. First, we [3]__________ (visit) my dad's family. My dad and his brothers [4]__________ (talk) for a long time. Then we [5]__________ (go) to a big museum in the city centre. We [6]__________ (see) lots of interesting things there. In the evening, we [7]__________ (watch) a film at the cinema. We [8]__________ (stay) at the Dylan Hotel. The rooms [9]__________ (not / be) very big, but I [10]__________ (like) the bathroom and the food [11]__________ (be) great! Every morning I [12]__________ (have) toast, eggs, fruit and coffee for breakfast.

### 2 VOCABULARY

**a** Tick (✓) the correct answer.

**Today is WEDNESDAY 21 OCTOBER.**
**It's 7:30 pm.**

1 Wednesday 7 October
a ☐ two weeks ago
b ☐ yesterday
2 2:30 pm on Wednesday 21 October
a ☐ last night
b ☐ this afternoon
3 21 August
a ☐ two months ago
b ☐ last month
4 Tuesday 20 October
a ☐ yesterday
b ☐ a few days ago
5 Saturday 17 October
a ☐ this morning
b ☐ last Saturday
6 Sunday 18 October
a ☐ six months ago
b ☐ last Sunday

**b** Ask and answer questions with *Where were you … ?* and a past time expression.

**c** Complete the table with the words and phrases in the box.

a video game  a football match (x2)
a magazine  a pizza  a podcast  a shower

| | |
|---|---|
| have | a drink, a coffee, [1]__________, [2]__________ |
| listen to | music, [3]__________ |
| watch | [4]__________, a film |
| read | a book, [5]__________, the newspaper |
| play | the guitar, [6]__________, football |
| go to | the cinema, a party, [7]__________, a café |

**d** Correct the sentences.

1 I was in Munich before two weeks ago.
2 We were in Milan last the weekend.
3 I had coffee with Lily at Friday.
4 We went a party yesterday.
5 I listened music last night.
6 We played the football this morning.

### 3 SOUND AND SPELLING

**a** 08.27 Look at the words in the box. Is the final sound /t/ or /d/? Complete the table. Practise saying the words.

~~called~~  talked  lived  watched
listened  played  finished

| /t/ | /d/ |
|---|---|
| | *called* |

**b** 08.28 Look at the information in the table.

| /eɪ/ | /aɪ/ |
|---|---|
| play, stay, day<br>game, paper, radio<br>great, grey | white, knife, wife<br>night, right |

**c** 08.29 Are the **marked** sounds the same (S) or different (D)? Practise saying the words.

1 white – night
2 great – game
3 right – day
4 stay – grey
5 paper – knife
6 radio – play

## REVIEW YOUR PROGRESS

**How well did you do in this unit? Write 3, 2 or 1 for each objective.**
3 = very well  2 = well  1 = not so well

| I CAN … | |
|---|---|
| talk about past events | ☐ |
| describe events in the past | ☐ |
| make and respond to suggestions. | ☐ |

## CAN DO OBJECTIVES

- Talk about travel and holiday experiences
- Talk about past holidays
- Make and respond to requests

# UNIT 9

# HOLIDAYS

## GETTING STARTED

**a** Look at the picture and answer the questions.

1 What country do you think this is?
2 What transport can you see?
3 What time of year is it?
4 What is the weather like in this place?

**b** Talk about the questions.

1 Where did you go on your last holiday?
2 What weather do you like while on holiday? Why?

**c** Ask your partner one question about their last holiday.

# 9A I DIDN'T STAY IN A HOTEL

Learn to talk about travel and holiday experience

G Past simple: negative

V Transport

## GARDEN CAMPING

Home | Find A Garden | Reviews | Contact Us

### How Does It Work?

Do you want a cheap holiday in a beautiful place? Why not camp in someone's garden? It's cheap and you can make new friends. We have more than 1,000 gardens in 70 countries and you can camp in all of them!

STEVE'S PLACE, MELBOURNE, AUSTRALIA

Modern house with a big garden on a lake. 20 minutes from Melbourne airport.

**COST** $15 a night

**HOW TO GET THERE**
Go to Jolimont Station by bus, train or tram. Then get a taxi or drive a car to the house (10 minutes).

YOUSSEF'S PLACE, MARRAKESH, MOROCCO

42 big tents with beds and showers inside. 40 minutes from the city of Marrakesh.

**COST** $30 a night

**HOW TO GET THERE**
Fly to Marrakesh and then take a taxi or drive a car.

## 1 READING

**a** Where do you usually stay on holiday? Here are some ideas:

- at a hotel
- at a hostel
- at a campsite
- with friends or family

**b** Read *How Does It Work?* on the *Garden Camping* website. What do you think of the idea?

It's a great idea!

Hmm, interesting.

No, thanks!

**c** Read about three gardens on the *Garden Camping* website. Which answers (a–d) are incorrect? Correct the wrong answers.

1 Steve's place:
   - a old house
   - b big garden
   - c in Melbourne
   - d near the train station

2 Youssef's place:
   - a small tents
   - b showers
   - c not in Marrakesh
   - d not very cheap

3 Guadalupe's place:
   - a big garden
   - b pool
   - c near some restaurants
   - d expensive

## 2 VOCABULARY Transport

**a** 09.01 Find words on the *Garden Camping* website to match pictures 1–7. Listen and check.

**b** Find words on the *Garden Camping* website to complete the tables.

| go ______ | bus train<br>plane tram |
|---|---|

| ______/______ | a bus<br>a taxi |
|---|---|

**c** Find verbs in the texts that mean:

a go by car
b go by plane

**d** Now go to Vocabulary Focus 9A on p. 151.

**e** How do you … ?

1 go to work or school
2 go to a big town or city nearby
3 go home late at night
4 go to a party
5 go on holiday

I usually get a bus to work.

House with a big garden and swimming pool. Free bikes. Near restaurants, a river and a zoo.

**COST:** $4 a night

**HOW TO GET THERE:** Go to Villavicencio by plane or get a bus. Then take a taxi or another bus to our house.

**GUADALUPE'S PLACE, CUMARAL, COLOMBIA**

**Language Plus** *go*

***go** to the cinema*

***go** to work* NOT ~~*to the work*~~

***go** home* NOT ~~*to home*~~

***go** on holiday*

**f** **Sound and spelling** the letter *a*

1 09.04 The letter *a* can have different sounds. Listen and practise the words.
1 /æ/ t**a**xi 2 /ɑː/ c**a**r 3 /eɪ/ pl**a**ne 4 /ɒ/ w**a**tch

2 09.05 Listen to these words. Are the letters in **bold** Sound 1, 2, 3 or 4?

wh**a**t fl**a**t tr**a**in f**a**ther

3 09.06 Listen to these words. Which one in each group has a different *a* sound?

| | | | |
|---|---|---|---|
| 1 | b**a**nk | w**a**nt | m**a**n |
| 2 | h**a**ve | c**a**ke | Sp**a**in |
| 3 | p**a**rty | b**a**g | g**a**rden |
| 4 | pl**a**nt | gl**a**ss | w**a**nt |

4 Practise saying the words.

## 3 GRAMMAR AND LISTENING
### Past simple: negative

**a** Read the post from Julian's travel blog. Which place from the *Garden Camping* website does he write about?

Julian

**WEEK 3**

### Through the Country by Bus

We didn't go to big cities. We went by bus, and we stayed in small places in the country. In one place, we stayed with a family. We didn't stay in their house – we camped in their garden. We bought food in the town and we cooked meals in the house. And we went swimming every morning in their pool. It was very cheap and the family were very friendly. We stayed for four days!

15 7

**b** Read the blog post again. Tick (✓) the correct sentences.

1 a ☐ They went to small places.
  b ☐ They didn't go to small places.
2 a ☐ They had a car.
  b ☐ They didn't have a car.
3 a ☐ They stayed in the house.
  b ☐ They didn't stay in the house.
4 a ☐ They used the kitchen.
  b ☐ They didn't use the kitchen.

**c** Look at the b sentences in 3b. Complete the rule.

Past simple negative (–):
*I / you / he / she / it / we / they* + ______ + verb

**d** Now go to Grammar Focus 9A on p. 130.

**e** 09.08 **Pronunciation** Listen to the sentences. Is *didn't* stressed or unstressed?

1 We didn't stay in their house.
2 We didn't have a car.

**f** 09.09 Listen to Julian. He says more things about his trip. What does he say about … ?

- emails
- money
- bikes
- photos

**g** What do you like about Julian's holiday? What don't you like?

**h** Think about your last holiday. Which sentences are true? If they aren't true, make them negative. Then write a true positive sentence.

1 I stayed in a hotel.
2 I visited museums.
3 I bought a lot of clothes.
4 I had my computer with me.
5 I went to bed early.
6 I cooked my own food.
7 I watched TV.
8 I read a lot of books.

1 *I didn't stay in a hotel. I stayed in a hostel.*

**i** Tell a partner your sentences in 3h.

I didn't visit museums. I went to the zoo.

## 4 SPEAKING

**Communication 9A** Student A: Go to p. 114. Student B: Go to p. 110.

# 9B HOW DID YOU GET THERE?

**Learn to talk about past holidays**

- **G** Past simple: questions
- **V** The seasons; The weather

## 1 VOCABULARY The seasons

**a** 09.10 Match the words in the box with pictures a–d. Listen and check.

| winter | summer | spring | autumn |
|---|---|---|---|

a

b

c

d

**b** Ask and answer the questions.

1 Do you have four seasons in your country?
2 Which seasons do you like? Which seasons don't you like?

## 2 READING

**a** Read about the Ortega family's holiday. What was different about this New Year's Eve and New Year's Day for them?

**b** Complete Miguel's notes with the words in the box.

| party | shopping | watched | cold |
|---|---|---|---|

Notes — Done

Thursday: [1] ____________ with family in Union Square.

New Year's Eve: [2] ____________ in Times Square – great fireworks!

Friday: [3] ____________ and snowy weather; everyone stayed inside and [4] ____________ a film.

The Ortega family from Tenerife went to New York City for New Year's Eve. Read Miguel Ortega's blog post.

MY BLOG

**MIGUEL ORTEGA**

## New Year's Fun in the BIG APPLE

Times Square ball drop

### Thursday 31 December

We went shopping in Union Square – it has a lot of big shops, restaurants and cafés. The weather is cold and windy in December, but we enjoyed it! We went to a big New Year's Eve party in Times Square in the evening and watched the ball drop. My sister and I loved the fireworks!

### Friday 1 January

It's winter here, and it's very different to have our New Year in the cold. I like the hot, sunny weather in Tenerife on New Year's Day, but in New York it was very cold and snowy. It didn't feel like New Year's Day. Everyone stayed inside and watched a film!

## 3 VOCABULARY The weather

**a** ▶ 09.11 What does Miguel say about the weather in New York City and Tenerife? Complete the sentences with *hot* or *cold*. Listen and check.

1 The weather is ______ and windy in December.

2 I like the ______, sunny weather in Tenerife on New Year's Day.

**Language Plus** *like*

*I **like** sunny weather.* = I think sunny weather is good.
*What's the weather **like**?* = How's the weather?

**b** Now go to Vocabulary Focus 9B on p. 152.

**c** **Sound and spelling** the letter *o*

1 ▶ 09.14 The letter *o* can have different sounds. Listen and repeat the words.

1 /əʊ/ sn**o**w   2 /aʊ/ cl**o**udy   3 /ɒ/ h**o**t

2 ▶ 09.15 Listen to these words. Are the letters in **bold** Sound 1, 2 or 3?

h**o**liday   t**o**wn   c**o**ld

3 ▶ 09.16 Listen to these words. Which one in each group has a different *o* sound? Listen again and repeat.

| | | | |
|---|---|---|---|
| 1 | g**o**t | j**o**b | g**o** |
| 2 | kn**ow** | n**o**t | sl**ow** |
| 3 | ph**o**ne | n**ow** | d**ow**n |

**d** **Communication 9B** Student A: Go to p. 111. Student B: Go to p. 113.

## 4 LISTENING AND GRAMMAR Past simple: questions

**a** ▶ 09.17 Listen to Kiril and Angie talk about summer holidays. Tick (✓) the correct sentence.

1 ☐ They're on holiday now.
2 ☐ They talk about past and future holidays.
3 ☐ They only talk about past holidays.

**b** ▶ 09.17 Listen again. Match 1–3 with a–c.

1 Kiril last year — a an island in Greece
2 Angie last year — b the south of France
3 Angie two years ago — c Moscow

**c** ▶ 09.18 Listen to the end of the conversation. Choose one word from the box to complete the two questions.

do   did

**Kiril** How ______ you get there?
**Angie** By train. And, you know, the weather was really warm.
**Kiril** ______ you enjoy it there?
**Angie** Yes, I did. I had a great time. Try to go this year!

**d** Now go to Grammar Focus 9B on p. 130.

**e** ▶ 09.21 Complete the two conversations about last weekend. Listen and check your answers.

**Conversation 1**
**A** go / cinema last weekend?
**B** Yes, I did.
**A** What / see?
**B** The new James Bond film.

**Conversation 2**
**C** go / restaurant last night?
**D** Yes, I did.
**C** Where / go?
**D** A new Thai restaurant.

**f** Tell a partner about last weekend. Use the conversations in 4e and your own ideas.

Did you see your friends last weekend?
Yes, I did.
Who did you see?
I saw Daniele.

**g** Work in new pairs. Tell your new partner about your first partner.

Jacob saw his friend Daniele last weekend.

## 5 SPEAKING

**a** Think about a past holiday. Make notes about the:

- place
- weather
- food
- things you did

**b** Write questions to ask about your partner's holiday.

1 When … the holiday? *When was the holiday?*
2 Where … go?
3 What … the weather like?
4 What … eat?
5 What … do?
6 (your idea for a question)

**c** Ask and answer the questions in 5b about your holiday.

When was the holiday?
It was last spring.
Where did you go?
We went to Lombok, in Indonesia.
What was the weather like?
It was hot and sunny.

# 9C EVERYDAY ENGLISH
## Can you do something for me?

**Learn to make and respond to requests**

P Syllables

W An online post

## 1 LISTENING

**a** Talk about a place near your town or city with a partner. Ask and answer the questions.

1 Where's a nice place to visit for a day? Why?
2 What can you see and do there?
3 Do you go there often?

**b** 09.22 Look at pictures a and b and talk about the questions. Watch or listen to Part 1 and check your answers.

1 Do you think Sophia and Megan like Henley?
2 What do they see in the shop?

**c** 09.22 Watch or listen to Part 1 again. Are the sentences true (*T*) or false (*F*)?

1 They decide to go to the museum before lunch.
2 Megan decides to go in the shop.
3 The clock is difficult to carry.

**d** What do you buy when you visit another place?

## 2 PRONUNCIATION Syllables and spelling

**a** 09.23 Listen to the **marked** word in the sentence. Do you hear all the letters?

It's very **different** from Toronto.

09.23 Listen again and repeat the **marked** word.

**b** 09.24 Listen to these words. Underline the letters you don't hear.

restaurant interesting favourite
every family vegetable camera

**c** Practise saying the words in 2b.

## 3 LISTENING

**a** 09.25 Look at picture c and answer the questions. Watch or listen to Part 2 and check your answers.

1 Who does Megan call? 2 What does she want?

**b** 09.25 Watch or listen to Part 2 again. Underline the correct answer.

1 Sophia and Megan *take the train* / *drive* home.
2 Megan says the problem is the *clock* / *weather*.
3 James *can* / *can't* meet Megan and Sophia at the station.

**c** Who do you usually ask for help – a friend or someone in your family? Why?

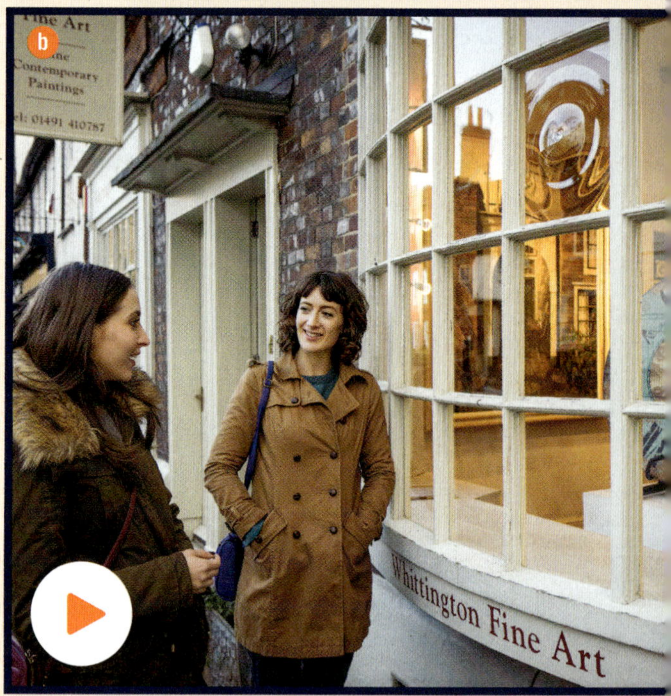

## 4 USEFUL LANGUAGE Making and responding to requests

**a** 09.26 Listen to the questions. Underline the word you hear. Then answer the question below.

1 *Can* / *Could* you take it for a minute?
2 *Can* / *Could* you do something for me?
3 *Can* / *Could* you pick us up from the station later, please?
4 *Can* / *Could* you meet us at the station, please?

Is it OK to use *can* and *could* in all the sentences?

**b** 09.27 Put the possible replies to the questions in 4a into the table. Listen and check your answers.

Of course. No, I can't. Yes, certainly.
I'm sorry, I can't. Sure, no problem.

| Yes | No |
|---|---|
| | |

**c** 09.28 Complete mini-conversations 1 and 2 with the phrases in the box. Listen and check.

Oh, OK, I'll do it then.
Thanks, that's really kind of you.

1 **A** Could you help me with the shopping?
**B** Sure, no problem.
**A** ______.

2 **C** Can you get the children from school?
**D** I'm sorry, I can't. I have a lot of work to finish.
**C** ______.

**d** Work in pairs. Take turns to make requests and reply. Use the ideas below and *can* / *could*.

1 help me with my work
2 give me your book
3 meet me after class
4 phone me this evening

Could you meet me after class?

I'm sorry, I can't. I'm busy.

## 5 SPEAKING

**a** Work in pairs. You talk on the phone. Look at the ideas below and think about what you want to say.

| A | B |
|---|---|
| Say hello and who you are. | |
| | Say hello and ask how Student A is. |
| Answer. Ask for help with something. | |
| | Say yes. |
| Ask Student B to come shopping with you today. | |
| | Say no – you're busy today. |
| Ask about tomorrow. | |
| | Say yes. |
| Say thanks and goodbye. | |
| | Say goodbye. |

**b** Have a phone conversation with your partner. Then swap roles.

## 6 WRITING

**a** Read what Sophia wrote online about her weekend. What information about the clock is new?

Last weekend I went to Henley with my new friend, Megan. First, we went for a walk by the river. It was beautiful. Next, we went to a small museum and had lunch. Then, we went shopping and I saw a lovely clock. It was quite expensive (£150!), but I bought it and we took it back to London. It was really heavy! Henley is a nice town – it's very different from Toronto.

12 3

**b** Now go to Writing Plus 9C on p. 162 for Making the order clear.

**c** Write an online post about a trip to another place. Here are some ideas:

Last weekend, / month, / summer, I went to … with …
First, we … It was … Next, we … Then, we …
… is a nice / beautiful / lovely city / town / place.

**d** Read another student's online post. Do you like the activities he / she did?

### UNIT PROGRESS TEST

### CHECK YOUR PROGRESS

You can now do the Unit Progress Test.

# UNIT 9
## Review

## 1 GRAMMAR

**a** Underline the correct answer.

1 We didn't *stay / stayed* in a hotel last year.
2 I didn't *take / took* any photos this morning.
3 She *doesn't / didn't* buy a book yesterday.
4 They didn't *have / had* fish for dinner last night.
5 We *don't watched / didn't watch* a film last week.
6 He *didn't got / didn't get* a taxi to the airport.

**b** Look at the answers and complete the questions.

> 'Did it rain yesterday?' 'Yes, it did. It rained in the morning.'
1 '__________ football last week?' 'No, I didn't – but I played tennis!'
2 'What time __________ yesterday?' 'I got up at six o'clock.'
3 '__________ any photos on New Year's Eve?' 'Yes, I did. I took some photos at the party.'
4 'Where __________ yesterday?' 'I went to the park.'
5 '__________ your phone yesterday?' 'Yes, of course! I use my phone every day!'
6 'What __________ for breakfast today?' 'I had cereal and coffee.'

**c** Work in pairs. Ask and answer the questions in 1b.

**d** Correct the past simple sentences.

> Where they did stay? *Where did they stay?*
1 Do you arrived last night?
2 Yes, I do arrived.
3 No, I not.
4 What did you bought?
5 I didn't watched TV.
6 What you cooked?
7 We don't visit Pedro yesterday.
8 Saw you the garden?

## 2 VOCABULARY

**a** Write the words.

1 ritan __________
2 atix __________
3 rungedundro __________
4 mart __________
5 elnap __________
6 pish __________

**b** Underline the correct answers.

**A** Was it [1] *cold / wet / warm*?
**B** Yes! It was –10°C! There was a lot of [2] *snow / snowy*.
**A** Wow! It never [3] *snows / snowy* in my country.

**C** Do I need an umbrella?
**D** I don't know. It's [4] *rainy / rain* – but it's very [5] *wind / windy* too!

**E** Was it [6] *wet / hot* ?
**F** Yes, very! It was about 35°C! But it was [7] *cloud / cloudy* all the time. We didn't see the sun.

## 3 SOUND AND SPELLING

**a** 09.29 Which of the letters in **bold** in each group has a different sound? Underline the word. Practise saying the words.

1 tr**ai**n c**a**r pl**a**ne r**ai**n
2 c**a**mp wh**a**t h**o**t n**o**t
3 g**o** b**oa**t sn**ow** w**i**nd
4 fl**a**t c**a**mp t**a**ke tr**a**m
5 cl**ou**d h**o**me c**o**ld n**o**
6 b**u**s s**u**n dr**o**ve l**o**vely

**b** 09.30 Complete the table with words in the box.

~~cinema~~ beautiful ~~different~~ expensive interesting camera lovely difficult restaurant business favourite museum

| We always say all the letters | We don't always say all the letters |
|---|---|
| *cinema* | *different* |

## REVIEW YOUR PROGRESS

**How well did you do in this unit? Write 3, 2 or 1 for each objective.**
3 = very well 2 = well 1 = not so well

| I CAN ... | |
|---|---|
| talk about travel and holiday experiences | ☐ |
| talk about past holidays | ☐ |
| make and respond to requests. | ☐ |

## CAN DO OBJECTIVES

- Talk about your home
- Ask where people are and what they're doing
- Ask for travel information

UNIT 10

# HERE AND NOW

## GETTING STARTED

**a** Look at the picture and answer the questions.

1 What is the boy doing?
2 Who is the woman? Where is she?
3 What do you think they're saying?
4 How often do you think they do this?
5 How do they feel? Why?

**b** Talk about the questions.

1 Do you speak to family and friends online? How often? Who do you speak to?
2 What programs or apps do you use to talk to people online?
3 What are the good things and bad things about using the Internet to speak to people?

# 10A WE'RE WATCHING THE MATCH

**Learn to talk about your home**

**G** Present continuous: positive

**V** The home

## 1 VOCABULARY The home

**a** 10.01 Match the words in the box with pictures a–f. Listen and check.

bedroom garden living room
dining room kitchen bathroom

**b** Now go to Vocabulary Focus 10A on p. 153.

**c Sound and spelling /tʃ/ and /θ/**

1 10.03 Listen and practise these sounds.
1 /tʃ/ kit**ch**en 2 /θ/ ba**th**room

2 10.04 What sound do you hear in the words in the box, Sound 1 or Sound 2? Listen and add the words to the sound groups below.

cheese month birthday thanks chips
both March question three watch

| Sound 1 /tʃ/ | Sound 2 /θ/ |
|---|---|
| kit**ch**en | ba**th**room |

3 Which letters usually spell /tʃ/ and which spell /θ/?

4 Practise saying the words.

**d** Ask and answer the questions with a partner.

1 How many bedrooms are there in your home?
2 Where do you eat your dinner?
3 Is there a TV in your home? Where?
4 Do you have a garden? If yes, is it big or small?
5 Which room is your favourite?

## 2 LISTENING AND SPEAKING

**a** 10.05 Listen to Grace talk about her flat. Put pictures a–c on page 81 in the order Grace talks about them.

**b** 10.05 Listen again. Are the sentences True (*T*) or false (*F*)?

1 Grace's flat isn't big.
2 The light in her flat is good.
3 There isn't a TV in the living room.
4 There's a dining room in her flat.
5 She uses her computer in her living room.

**c** Do you like Grace's flat? Why / Why not?

**Language Plus** *in / on*

| ***in*** + room | ***on*** + floor, wall |
|---|---|
| *There's a desk **in** my bedroom.* | *The books are **on** the floor.* |
| *Put the cake **in** the kitchen.* | *There are pictures **on** the wall.* |

**d** Think about your home and the rooms it has. Tell a partner about your home.

In my home there are four bedrooms and a big bathroom.

**e** Choose a room in your home and write the names of some objects in that room. Then tell your partner about them.

In my bedroom there's a bed, a chair and a small desk.

## 3 READING

**a** Read the texts. Are they for people who are near or far away?

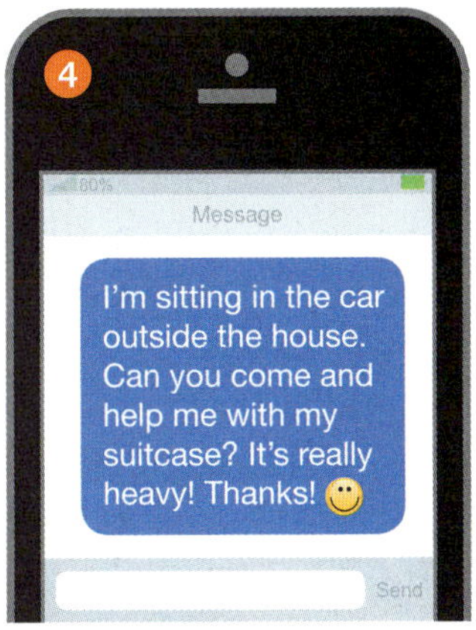

**b** Read the texts again. Where are the writers?

**c** Do you sometimes send a text to someone when you're in the same place? Why / Why not?

## 4 GRAMMAR
### Present continuous: positive

**a** Look at the sentence from text 1. Does it mean *now* or *usually*?

We're watching the match.

**b** Complete the rule with *-ing* and *be*.

> Present continuous positive (+):
> *I/you/he/she/it/we/they* + ______ + verb + ______

**c** 10.06 **Pronunciation** Listen to the sentence in 4a. Underline the stressed words.

**d** Underline four more examples of the present continuous in texts 2–5 in 3a.

**e** Now go to Grammar Focus 10A on p. 130.

**f** It's 2 pm on Sunday. What are you doing? Write a text to a friend.

*Hi!*
*I'm having lunch at a new restaurant in the centre of town with my sister. It's really good! We're eating lots of food.*

**g** Read your text to the class. Listen to the other students. Is anyone doing the same thing?

## 5 SPEAKING

**Communication 10A** Student A: Go to p. 115. Student B: Go to p. 112.

# 10B ARE YOU WORKING?

Learn to ask where people are and what they're doing

**G** Present continuous: negative and questions

**V** Place phrases with prepositions

## How much do you use your phone?

**Some people always have their phone on and they use it all the time — in a café, in the car, even in bed! Is this a good idea? Tell us what you think! And do you use your phone all the time?**

RAOUL
My phone's always on, day and night, and I use it all the time – I talk on it, play games on it, send messages. When I wake up, I sit in bed, check my messages and read the news on my phone. It's a great way to start the day!

YASMIN
I never talk on the phone when I'm with people in a restaurant. I have it on 'silent' and put it in my bag – I don't want to talk while I'm eating. But I often take photos of the food with it. It's always by my bed at night, so I can wake up in the morning. I don't like talking on the phone much – I usually send text messages.

BRYAN
I always have my phone with me – when I'm at home and when I'm at work and I use it on the way to work to talk and check my emails. But I don't have it by the bed at night – I put it on 'silent' and leave it in the kitchen. I want to sleep!

SAM
I use my phone all the time, but not at the cinema and not on a plane. I have it on at night by the bed. You never know – maybe someone needs to call you.

JENNY
My phone is usually off and I don't use it much. I use it to call people at the airport or on a bus – sometimes I need to say I'm late. But I don't like sending text messages.

a

b

## 1 READING

**a** Match the phrases in the box with pictures a–e.

at the cinema   in bed   in the car
in a restaurant   on a mountain

**b** Look at pictures a–e again. Answer the questions.

1 What object is in all the pictures?
2 Which are … ?
- a good idea
- normal
- a bad idea

**c** Read the message board comments and answer the questions.

1 You call the five people. They're in a restaurant. Who answers?
2 You call the five people at 3 am. Who answers?

**d** Which person do you think … ?

a has good ideas
b has a problem

**e** Write a comment about you and your phone for the message board.

**f** Read your comment to your partner. Are you the same?

## 2 VOCABULARY Place phrases with prepositions

**a** Find phrases in the message board with *in*, *on* or *at* and the nouns in the box. Add them to the table.

~~café~~   airport   car   work   bed   plane
cinema   bus   restaurant   home

| in | on | at |
|---|---|---|
| *in a café* ______ ______ | ______ | ______ ______ |
| ______ ______ | ______ | ______ ______ |

**b** You're in a place in 2a and your partner calls you. Tell your partner what you're doing. Your partner guesses the place.

*I'm going to work.*

*Are you in the car?*

**c** Now go to Vocabulary Focus 10B on p. 147.

**d** **Sound and spelling /ə/**

1 10.09 Listen to the sound /ə/ in these words. Is it stressed or unstressed?
teach**er**   stud**e**nt   cin**e**m**a**   stat**io**n

2 10.10 Listen to these words. <u>Underline</u> the /ə/ sound in each word.

dinner   England   garden   television
waiter   breakfast   listen   driver

3 Practise saying the words.

## 3 LISTENING AND GRAMMAR Present continuous: negative and questions

**a** 10.11 Listen and match conversations 1–5 with pictures a–e.

**b** Do you think … ?

1 Dan likes Lou
2 Lou likes Dan

How do you know?

**c** 10.12 Complete the table. Listen and check.

| + | – |
|---|---|
| I'm working. | I'm ______ ______. |
| I'm having dinner. | I'm ______ ______ dinner. |

**d** 10.13 Complete Dan's questions. Listen and check.

1 **DAN** What ______ ______ doing?
**LOU** I'm at the bus stop. I'm going home.
2 **DAN** ______ ______ working?
**LOU** No, I'm not working.
3 **LOU** I'm watching a film.
**DAN** Oh, what ______ ______ watching?

**e** 10.14 **Pronunciation** Listen to the questions in 3d again. Which word has the main stress in each question?

**f** Now go to Grammar Focus 10B on p. 132.

**g** **Communication 10B** Student A: Go to p. 114. Student B: Go to p. 112.

## 4 SPEAKING

**a** You and a partner are in different places. You want to meet. Before you speak on the phone, make notes. Think about these questions:

- Where are you? (Choose a place from Vocabulary Focus 10B on page 147.)
- What are you doing? (Think of two or more activities.)
- When do you want to meet? (Think of a day, a time and a place.)

**b** Phone your partner and have a conversation.

- Ask where your partner is and what he/she is doing.
- Plan when and where to meet your partner.

Hi, Tom. What are you doing?

I'm writing a report.

Are you free this evening? Do you want to go to Café Cabana?

# 10C EVERYDAY ENGLISH
## What time's the next train to London?

**Learn to ask for travel information**

P Sound and spelling: /ɪə/ and /eə/

W A message asking for information

## 1 LISTENING

**a** Look at picture a and talk about the questions.

1 How does Sophia feel?
2 What does Megan offer to do?

**b** 10.18 Watch or listen to Part 1. Check your ideas in 1a.

**c** 10.18 Watch or listen to Part 1 again. Answer the questions.

1 What does Megan say about James?
2 Do they know what time the train leaves?

## 2 PRONUNCIATION Sound and spelling: /ɪə/ and /eə/

**a** 10.19 Listen to these words. Which word has a different sound?

**he**re **yeah** **rea**lly

**b** 10.20 Listen and complete the table with the words in the box.

chair care hear real hair
near there clear pair meal

| Sound 1 /ɪə/ | Sound 2 /eə/ |
|---|---|
| *here* | *yeah* |

**c** 10.20 Listen again and repeat.

## 3 LISTENING

**a** Look at picture b. What questions do Megan and Sophia ask the station official?

**b** 10.21 Watch or listen to Part 2. Check your ideas in 3a.

**c** 10.21 Watch or listen to Part 2 again. Complete the information.

1 Time of next train: ______
2 Time now: ______
3 Platform: ______

**d** In your country, what is an easy way to travel – train, bus, car?

## 4 USEFUL LANGUAGE Asking for travel information

**a** Who says these expressions – a passenger (P) or the station official (SO)?

1 The next train is at 4:35.
2 Which platform is it?
3 Excuse me.
4 The train leaves in three minutes.
5 No, you change at Reading.
6 Yes? How can I help you?
7 What time's the next train to London?
8 Is it a direct train?
9 It's Platform 3.

**b** 10.22 Listen and check your answers in 4a. Then listen again and repeat.

**c** 10.23 Complete the sentences with *at* or *in*. Listen and check.

1 The next train leaves ______ half an hour.
2 The next train leaves ______ five o'clock.

**d** 10.24 Put the conversation in the correct order. Then listen and check.

**A**
☐ So, at 5:15. And is it a direct bus?
☐ Great! Thanks for your help.
☐ What time's the next bus to Cambridge?
1 Excuse me.
☐ OK, and which bus stop is it?

**B**
☐ The next bus leaves in 20 minutes.
☐ It's Stop 7, near the ticket office.
☐ No problem.
☐ Yes? How can I help you?
☐ No, you change at Birmingham.

**e** Practise the conversation in 4d with a partner. Take turns to be the station official and the passenger. Change the times, kind of transport and the platforms / bus stops.

## 5 SPEAKING

Communication 10C
Student A: Go to p. 110.
Student B: Go to p. 112.

## 6 WRITING

**a** Megan helped her friend Amelia plan a holiday in Paris. Amelia sends Megan a message. Read it and answer the questions.

1 Where's Amelia now?
2 Which two questions does she ask?

Hi, Megan. I'm travelling to Paris right now on the train. Sorry, I can't remember two things. First, where can I find a taxi at the station? And how much is it from the station to the hotel? I don't have a lot of euros with me! Thanks!

**b** Now go to Writing Plus 10C on p. 162 for Word order in questions.

**c** Write a message to a friend. Ask two questions in your message. Here are some ideas:

Hi …
I'm going / doing / having …
Sorry, I can't remember …
Where / How / When … ?
Thanks …

**d** Read another student's message. Try to answer the questions.

## UNIT PROGRESS TEST

### CHECK YOUR PROGRESS

You can now do the Unit Progress Test.

# UNIT 10
## Review

### 1 GRAMMAR

**a** Correct the present continuous sentences.

> Carmen be wearing a yellow T-shirt.
*Carmen's wearing a yellow T-shirt.*

1 You wearing my shoes!
2 They're geting a taxi.
3 I'm writeing to Kelly.
4 The lesson starting.
5 She's haveing lunch.
6 We waiting.

**b** Write present continuous questions with the words and phrases.

1 where / you / sit ?
2 you / wear / black shoes ?
3 it / rain ?
4 you / use / a computer ?
5 why / you / study / English ?
6 what / your friends / do ?

**c** Ask and answer the questions in 1b.

**d** Complete the phone conversation with the verbs in brackets.

**GABY** Hi, it's me.
**JUAN** Oh, hi. What [1]______ (you / do)?
**GABY** I [2]______ (talk) to you, of course. I'm on the train.
**JUAN** Oh, very funny. Well, I [3]______ (cook) dinner. So, [4]______ (you / listen to) music?
**GABY** Mm, no. I [5]______ (read) a book.
**JUAN** Oh, great. What's the weather like there?
**GABY** Not good. It [6]______ (rain) outside.
**JUAN** Well, it [7]______ (not / rain) here – it [8]______ (snow)! But Gwen and Carla are in the garden.
**GABY** The garden? Why? What [9]______ (they / do)?
**JUAN** They [10]______ (make) a snowman!

### 2 VOCABULARY

**a** Write the rooms.

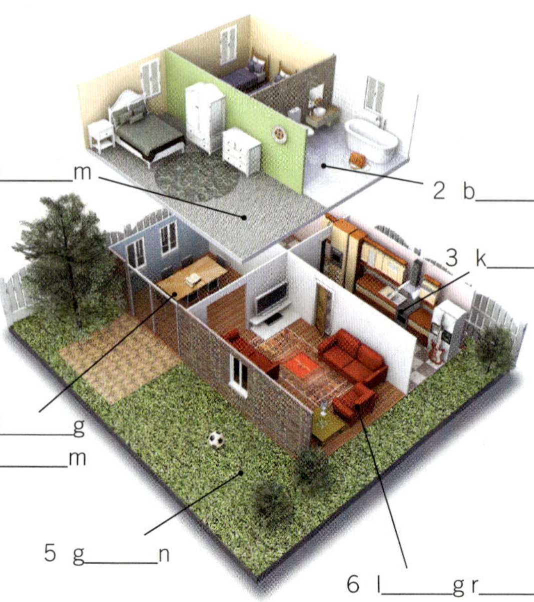

1 b______m
2 b______m
3 k______n
4 d______g r______m
5 g______n
6 l______g r______m

**b** Complete the questions with *in*, *on* or *at*.

1 Do you listen to music ______ the car?
2 Do you sleep ______ trains / buses / planes?
3 Do you read ______ bed?
4 Do you eat ______ the cinema?
5 Were you ______ home yesterday for lunch?
6 Did you play football ______ school?
7 What's ______ the floor in this room?
8 Are there any pictures ______ the walls?

**c** Ask and answer the questions in 2b.

### 3 SOUND AND SPELLING

**a** Notice the two sounds and the letters in **bold**.

1 /tʃ/ **ch**oose
2 /θ/ **th**ree
3 /ð/ **th**ey're

**b** 10.25 Complete the table with the words in the box. Practise saying the words.

bathroom birthday change ~~choose~~ kitchen mother question thanks the ~~three~~ ~~they're~~ weather

| /tʃ/ | /θ/ | /ð/ |
|---|---|---|
| *choose* | *three* | *they're* |

**c** 10.26 Are the two sounds in **bold** in each sentence the same (S) or different (D)? Practise saying the sentences.

1 **We're** h**ere**.
2 **Wear** a p**air** of shoes.
3 Th**eir** house is n**ear**.
4 It's r**eal** h**air**.
5 **Yeah**, it's th**ere**.
6 Wh**ere**'s the ch**air**?

### REVIEW YOUR PROGRESS

**How well did you do in this unit? Write 3, 2 or 1 for each objective.**
3 = very well 2 = well 1 = not so well

| I CAN ... | |
|---|---|
| talk about my home | ☐ |
| ask where people are and what they're doing | ☐ |
| ask for travel information. | ☐ |

## CAN DO OBJECTIVES

- Talk about people's lives
- Talk about things you know how to do
- Talk about opinions

# UNIT 11

# ACHIEVERS

## GETTING STARTED

**a** Look at the picture and answer the questions.

1 What did this man do before he went into his tent? What are his plans tomorrow?

2 Tick (✓) the things the man can do in his tent tonight. Why can't he do some things?

- ☐ listen to music
- ☐ read a magazine
- ☐ play the guitar
- ☐ cook dinner
- ☐ do yoga
- ☐ sleep well

3 What do you think he is writing in his book?

4 What questions do you want to ask him? Write down three.

**b** Would you like to be where this man is? Why / Why not?

# 11A SHE WENT AROUND THE EARTH

**Learn to talk about people's lives**

G Object pronouns

V Life events

## 1 READING

**a** Think of two famous people from your country (present or past). Ask and answer the questions with a partner.

1 Why are / were they famous?
2 What do you know about them?
3 Do you think people from other countries know about them? Why / Why not?

**b** Read *They Were the First!* Who … ?

1 died over 15 years ago
2 had new ideas for computers
3 studied and worked at the same time
4 came from a poor family
5 lived in a few different places
6 had one child

**c** Read *They Were the First!* again. Choose one thing about each person you think is interesting and say why.

# THEY WERE THE FIRST!

### #1 THE FIRST WOMAN IN SPACE

**Valentina Tereshkova (born 1937)**

### Who is she?

A Russian cosmonaut.

### What did she do?

In 1963, she flew in *Vostok 6*. She went around the Earth 48 times and she was in space for almost three days.

### Her life

She was born in 1937 in a small village in Russia. Her father was a tractor driver and her mother worked in a factory. She finished school at 16 and started work in a factory. In her free time, she studied and she also went parachute jumping.

In 1963 she got married and the next year she had a daughter, Elena. After that, Valentina never flew into space again.

## 2 VOCABULARY Life events

**a** 11.01 Look at these events in a person's life. Match events 1–6 with pictures a–f. Listen and check.

1 die
2 grow up
3 finish university
4 get married
5 go to school
6 be born

**b** Write the events in three lists.

1 everyone does this
2 most people do this
3 only some people do this

**c** Compare your lists with other students. Are they the same?

**d** Read *They Were the First!* again. Write past simple sentences about the years below.

Valentina Tereshkova
• 1937 • 1953 • 1963 • 1964

William Higinbotham
• 1910 • 1928 • 1932 • 1949

*1937 – Valentina was born.*

**Language Plus** Years

To say a year, we usually say the numbers in pairs:

1937 → 19 37 *nineteen thirty-seven* 2021 → 20 21 *twenty twenty-one*

We usually use *two thousand and* with single-digit years after 2000, but not with double-digit numbers:

2001 = *two thousand and one* 2015 = *twenty fifteen*

**Note**: 1900 = *nineteen hundred* 2000 = *two thousand*
1905 = *nineteen oh five*

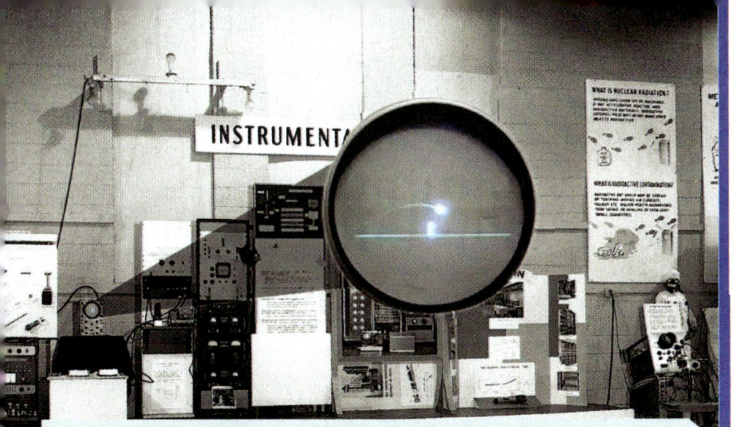


## #2 THE GRANDFATHER OF VIDEO GAMES

**William Higinbotham (1910–1994)**

### Who was he?

An American scientist

### What did he do?

In 1958, he made a video game called 'Tennis for Two'. It was the first video game in the world and people waited in line all day to play it.

### His life

He was born in 1910 and he grew up in Caledonia, New York. When he was 18 he went to college and four years later he studied at Cornell University.

When he was 39 he got married and moved to Bellport, New York, where he worked at a science lab. William wanted to make a fun game for people to play at his science lab, so he made 'Tennis for Two', and he showed it during Visitor Day. It was a big success – but he didn't make any money from it!

**e Sound and spelling /ɜː/**

1 11.02 Listen to the words.

university worked thirty

Are the **marked** letters … ?

a all the same sound
b two different sounds
c three different sounds

2 11.03 Underline the letters in these words that have the sound /ɜː/. Listen and check.

Thursday first world shirt early weren't girl

3 Practise saying the words.

**f** Now go to Vocabulary Focus 11A on p. 154.

## 3 LISTENING AND GRAMMAR

### Object pronouns

**a** 11.06 Listen to two friends talking about Valentina Tereshkova. Tick (✓) the questions you can answer after listening to their conversation.

1 ☐ Where did she go to school?
2 ☐ Why did she get the job?
3 ☐ How did she meet her husband?
4 ☐ Where does she live now?
5 ☐ What does she want to do in the future?

**b** 11.06 Listen again and answer the questions you ticked in 3a.

**c** 11.07 Complete the sentences from the conversation with the words in the box. Listen and check.

he him she her

1 ______'s a Russian cosmonaut. Do you know about ______?
2 She married a cosmonaut. She met ______ in 1963. ______ was in the same space programme.

**d** Underline the correct words to complete the rules.

1 We use **he** and **she** *before* / *after* a verb.
2 We use **him** and **her** *before* / *after* a verb or preposition.

**e** Now go to Grammar Focus 11A on p. 132.

## 4 SPEAKING

**a** Write four or five events in your life and the years.

2005–2019 – I lived in Florence.
2019 – I started university.

**b** Work in pairs. Read your partner's sentences and ask some questions.

Where did you …?
When did you …?
Why did you …?

**c** Tell the class two things about your partner's life.

# 11B SHE CAN PULL A PLANE

Learn to talk about things you know how to do

G *can* for ability

V Abilities

## 1 READING

**a** Look at 1–3 below. What's difficult for you to do? Why / Why not?

1 be cold for a long time
2 swim underwater
3 pull or carry big objects

**b** Read *Amazing Humans*. Are the amazing humans real or not?

**c** Read *Amazing Humans* again. Answer the questions.

1 How long can Wim Hof stay in a cold bath?
2 How long can the Bajau Laut people stay underwater?
3 How does Seema Bhadoria pull things?

**d** Which real person/people in *Amazing Humans* can do something useful?

## 2 GRAMMAR *can*: positive and negative

**a** Complete the table. Check your answers in the text.

| **Positive** | | | |
|---|---|---|---|
| I **can**<br>You **can**<br>He/She ______ | swim underwater. | We **can**<br>They ______ | swim underwater. |
| **Negative** | | | |
| I **can't**<br>You **can't**<br>He/She ______ | make ice. | We **can't**<br>They ______ | make ice. |

**b** Underline examples of *can*/*can't* in *Amazing Humans*. What is after *can*/*can't*, a noun or a verb?

**c** Now go to Grammar Focus 11B Part 1 on p. 134.

# AMAZING HUMANS

**Do you sometimes do things that are different and interesting? Do you make videos of these things? Maybe you're not Superman or Wonder Woman, but you can do something amazing. Here are some stories about people who can do amazing things!**

### THE ICEMAN

Wim Hof is from the Netherlands and he's often called 'The Iceman'. He can't make ice, but he can sit in a bath of ice for one hour, 52 minutes and two seconds. He doesn't feel cold. In 2009, he ran more than 40 kilometres in –20°C wearing only shorts!

### THE FISHMEN

The Bajau Laut people in Southeast Asia can swim underwater for a long time. Sometimes they can go underwater for more than five minutes. They can also see very well in the water – it helps them to see the fish!

### THE STRONG WOMAN

Seema Bhadoria is an amazing young woman from India – she can pull really big objects with only her teeth. When she was only 18 years old she pulled a plane with her teeth! She can also pull a ship or a big truck.

## 3 VOCABULARY Abilities

**a** Match the verbs in the box with pictures a–d.

cook sing swim paint

a

b

c

d

**b** Now go to Vocabulary Focus 11B on p. 155.

**Language Plus** (*very / quite*) *well*

*I can swim* ***very well***. = I'm very good.
*I can swim* ***well***. = I'm good.
*I can swim* ***quite well***. = I'm OK.
*I can****'t*** *swim* ***at all***. = It's impossible for me.

**c** Talk about people you know and what they can or can't do.

My brother can't dance very well.

## 4 LISTENING

**a** Read the job description. Does the school want someone who can do one thing or a lot of things?

JOB ALERT CLOSE ⊗

**We need people to work at our summer school in Chapel Hill.**

We want people who can do a lot of different things – sing, dance, play the guitar, draw, ride a horse, but we also want good teachers!

If you're interested, please send us an email or give us a call …

**b** 11.12 Listen to Celia, the head teacher at the school, talk to Andy. Is he a good person for the job?

**c** 11.12 Listen again. What can Andy do? Complete sentences 1–4 with the words and phrases in the box.

teach ride a horse play the guitar sing dance

1 He can ______ and ______ quite well.
2 He can ______ very well.
3 He can't ______ very well.
4 He can't ______ at all.

## 5 GRAMMAR *can*: questions

**a** 11.13 Complete the conversations. Listen and check your answers.

1 **CELIA** And ______ ______ sing?
**ANDY** Yes, ______ ______.
2 **CELIA** ______ ______ dance well?
**ANDY** No, ______ ______.

**b** Now go to Grammar Focus 11B Part 2 on p. 134.

**c** 11.15 **Pronunciation** Listen to the sentences. Tick (✓) when *can* / *can't* is stressed.

1 ☐ I can sing quite well.
2 ☐ I can't dance very well.
3 ☐ Can you sing?
4 ☐ Yes, I can.

**d** Practise saying the sentences. Underline the correct words to complete the rules.

***Can*** *is / isn't* stressed in positive sentences and questions.
***Can*** *is / isn't* stressed in negative sentences and short answers.

**e** 11.16 Complete the conversation with the correct form of *can*. Listen and check.

**A** ______ Andy play the guitar?
**B** Yes, he ______.
**A** And ______ he ride a horse?
**B** Yes, he ______ ride a horse very well.
**A** ______ he teach?
**B** No, he ______ teach at all.

**f** Practise the conversation in 5e with a partner.

## 6 SPEAKING

**a** Work in pairs. Write one question with *can* for each topic.

- sports — *Can you play tennis?*
- food — *Can you make a cake?*
- language
- music / art

**b** Work with a new partner. Ask and answer your questions in 6a.

Can you play tennis?

No, I can't play tennis at all.

**c** Work with your first partner again. Tell them about your second partner.

Lola can speak German quite well, but she can't speak Italian.

# 11C EVERYDAY ENGLISH

## What do you think?

**Learn to talk about opinions**

P Consonant clusters

W An email to a friend

## 1 LISTENING

**a** Ask and answer the questions.

1 What's your favourite room in your house?
2 What things have you got there?

**b** Look at pictures a–c. Which is the best description of the story, 1 or 2?

1 Sophia, Megan and James arrive home. They tell James about the fun things they did in Henley. Sophia knows where she wants to put the clock.
2 Sophia, Megan and James arrive home. Megan and James talk about places to visit in London. They like different places. Sophia can't choose a good place for the clock.

**c** 11.17 Watch or listen. Check your answer in 1b.

**d** 11.17 Watch or listen again and answer the questions.

1 What does James think of the clock?
2 What did Sophia think of Henley?
3 Why doesn't Megan like London Zoo?
4 Why doesn't James like the Tower of London?
5 Why does James think a clock in the bedroom is a bad idea?
6 Where does Sophia choose to put the clock?

**e** Are there any interesting places to visit in / near your town or city?

a

b

## 2 USEFUL LANGUAGE Talking about opinions

**a** Look at the expressions. Do we use them to … ?

a ask an opinion
b give an opinion
c have the same opinion
d have a different opinion

1 Did you like Henley?
2 I don't think so.
3 Maybe you're right.
4 I don't think the bedroom is a good idea.
5 I think London Zoo is very nice.
6 What about the Tower of London?
7 I think you're right.
8 What do you think?

11.18 Listen and check your answers.

**b** 11.18 Pronunciation Listen to sentences 1–8 in 2a again. Underline the main stress. Listen again and repeat.

**c** 11.19 Look at expressions 1–4. Are they in group a, b, c or d in 2a? Listen and check.

1 Yes, I agree.
2 Do you like this clock?
3 What do you think of London?
4 I'm not so sure.

**d** 11.20 Put the words in the correct order to make expressions. Listen and check.

1 very interesting / museum is / I think the .
2 you think / what do / new restaurant / of the ?
3 you're / I think / right .
4 so / think / I don't .
5 the colour blue / I don't think / is a good idea .

**e** Complete the conversation with your ideas.

**A** What do you think of English?
**YOU** ______________________
**A** Yes, maybe you're right. What about the grammar?
**YOU** ______________________
**A** Really? I don't think so. I think your language is very difficult.
**YOU** ______________________
**A** Well, all languages are a bit difficult.
**YOU** ______________________

**f** Practise the conversation in 2e with a partner. Take turns to be A.

## 3 PRONUNCIATION Consonant clusters

**a** 11.21 Listen to the words. Notice how the **marked** letters are pronounced. Listen again and repeat.

1 /t/ rig**ht**
2 /ŋk/ thi**nk**
3 /st/ touri**st**

**b** 11.22 Listen and match the **marked** letters in 1–6 with a–f.

| | | |
|---|---|---|
| 1 a**sk** | 3 fi**nd** | 5 restaura**nt** |
| 2 da**nce** | 4 difficu**lt** | 6 si**x** |
| a /nt/ | c /sk/ | e /nd/ |
| b /lt/ | d /ks/ | f /ns/ |

**c** Practise saying the words.

## 4 SPEAKING

Communication 11C
Student A: Go to p. 113.
Student B: Go to p. 114.

## 5 WRITING

**a** Read Sophia's email to a friend in Canada. What does she like about her life in London?

> Hi Lisa,
>
> Thanks for your email – it was nice to hear from you.
>
> Things in London are going well. It's a big city and there are lots of things I can do. I'm making some new friends here. I work in an office with a girl called Megan. She's from London and she's very friendly. She helped me a lot when I arrived. I also know her cousin James. He's very kind. I often see them at the weekend.
>
> My flat is quite big. It's comfortable and I like it a lot. It's near my office, so I can walk to work every day. I like that!
>
> I miss my family at home and I miss my friends, too! Write again soon.
>
> Love,
>
> Sophia

**b** Now go to Writing Plus 11C on p. 163 for Pronouns.

**c** Write an email to a friend. Tell them about your life now. Here are some ideas:

- Say hi and thank the person for his/her email. (*Hi … Thanks …* )
- Write about your life – your job or studies. (*I'm working / studying …* )
- Write about family and/or friends. (*My parents are well … I see my friend Luisa every …* )
- Say goodbye and ask the person to write to you. (*Goodbye for now … Love / Best wishes …* )

**d** Read another student's email. What's interesting about their life?

## UNIT PROGRESS TEST

### CHECK YOUR PROGRESS

You can now do the Unit Progress Test.

# UNIT 11
## Review

## 1 GRAMMAR

**a** Complete the sentences with the correct pronoun.

1 I like Rob, but I don't think he likes ______.
2 Those shoes are beautiful. Can I buy ______, please?
3 Sarah's a good friend. I met ______ at university.
4 My husband and I live in the city, but my parents live in a small village. They sometimes visit ______ at the weekend.
5 They had a baby boy and they called ______ Antonio.
6 Happy birthday! I got ______ a present!
7 Your car is dirty. You need to clean ______.

**b** Look at the table. Then complete the conversation with the words and phrases in the box.

| | dance | play tennis | ride a horse |
|---|---|---|---|
| Beto | ✗ | ✓✓ | ✓ |
| Melanie | ✓ | ✗ | ✓✓ |

can (x4) can't can she can you
he can't I can she can

**A** [1]______ Beto dance?
**B** No, [2]______ . But he [3]______ play tennis very well and he [4]______ ride a horse.
**A** What about Melanie? [5]______ ride a horse?
**B** Yes, [6]______. She can ride a horse very well and she [7]______ dance, but she [8]______ play tennis.
**A** What about you? [9]______ play tennis?
**B** Yes, [10]______ .

**c** Ask a partner about the activities in 1b. Use *Can you … ?*

## 2 VOCABULARY

**a** Complete the text with the correct form of the verb phrases in the box.

have a baby boy finish school be born
go to university die grow up get married

My parents met in London and I [1] ______ in England, but my family came here to New Zealand when I was three. I [2] ______ here and I don't remember anything about England. I [3] ______ when I was sixteen. I got a job at a hotel, but it wasn't very interesting.
Then I [4] ______ in Australia. I studied engineering and I met Daniela – she's now my wife!
Daniela and I [5] ______ five years ago. We both got good jobs in Australia, but then my father [6] ______, so we came back here to New Zealand to be near my mum.
We [7] ______ last year. Life is good!

**b** Complete the verb phrases with the words in the box.

dinner basketball a motorbike songs to work walls

| | |
|---|---|
| play | cards, [1]______, volleyball |
| sing | [2]______ |
| paint | a picture, [3]______ |
| ride | a horse, [4]______, a bike |
| drive | a car, [5]______ |
| cook | [6]______ |

**c** Which of the things in 2b do you do every day? Which do you sometimes do? Which do you never do?

## 3 SOUND AND SPELLING

**a** 11.23 Tick (✓) the words with an /ɜː/ sound. Practise saying the words.

- ☐ thirteen
- ☐ born
- ☐ university
- ☐ rode
- ☐ sand
- ☐ weren't
- ☐ cooked
- ☐ swam
- ☐ thirty
- ☐ worked
- ☐ married

**b** 11.24 Are the sounds in **bold** the same (S) or different (D)? Practise saying the words.

1 si**x** – than**ks**
2 dan**ce** – an**sw**er
3 **r**ight – **wh**ite
4 touri**st** – dan**ced**
5 **ask** – **sch**ool
6 s**ing** – s**ang**

## REVIEW YOUR PROGRESS

**How well did you do in this unit? Write 3, 2 or 1 for each objective.**
3 = very well 2 = well 1 = not so well

| I CAN … | |
|---|---|
| talk about people's lives | ☐ |
| talk about things I know how to do | ☐ |
| talk about opinions. | ☐ |

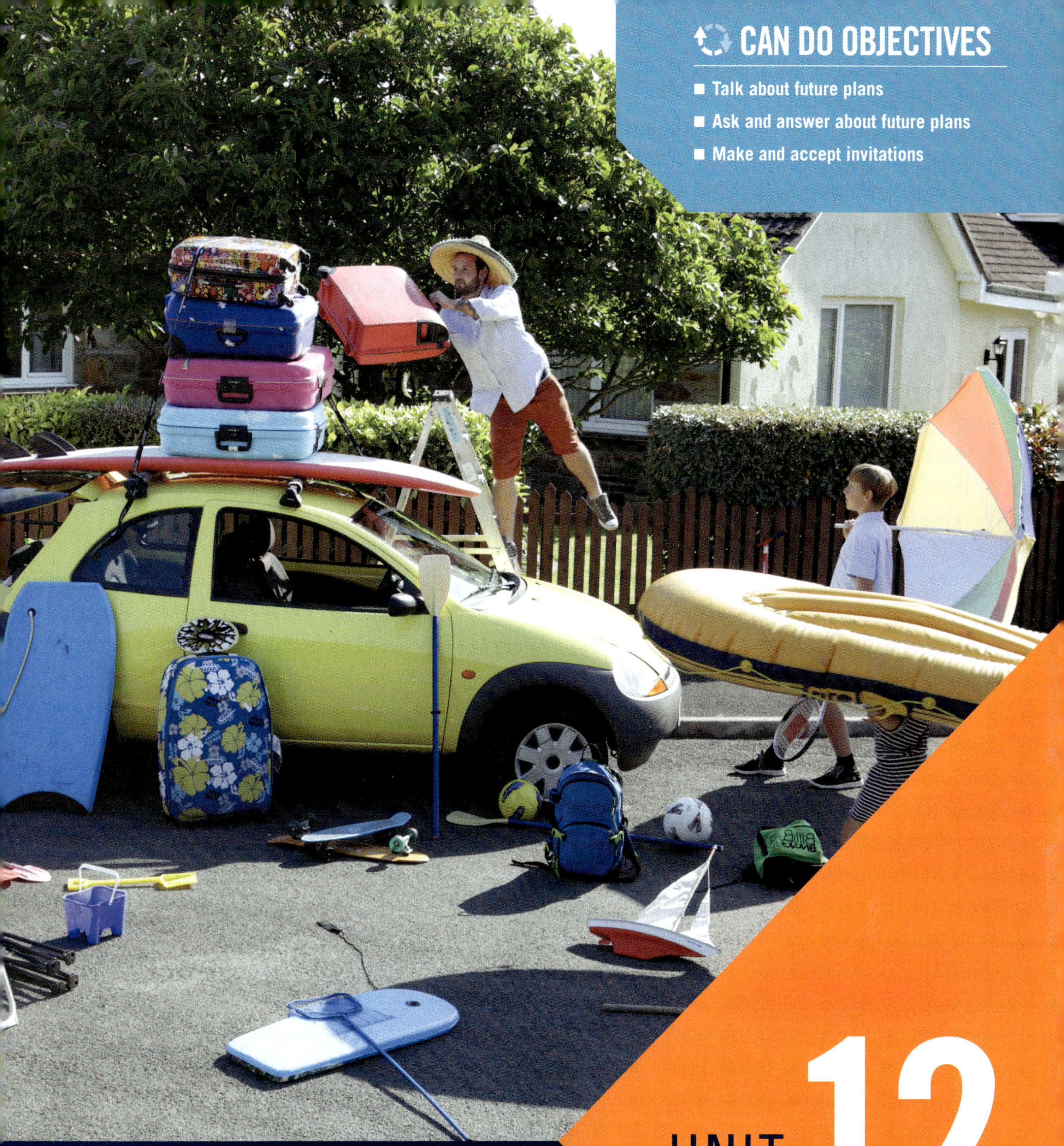

## CAN DO OBJECTIVES

- Talk about future plans
- Ask and answer about future plans
- Make and accept invitations

UNIT 12

# PLANS

## GETTING STARTED

**a** Look at the picture and answer the questions.

1 Do you think this family are going to … ?
- go on a long or short holiday
- go somewhere near or far
- go somewhere hot or cold
- go by car or drive to the airport

Why?

2 What did the man do … ?
- the day before the trip
- the morning of the trip
- a month before the trip

3 What do you think this family is going to do on the trip? Why?

**b** Talk about the questions.

1 When you go on holiday, do you pack too much or not enough?
2 What do you sometimes forget to take when you go on holiday?

# 12A I'M GOING TO HAVE A LONG HOT BATH

**Learn to talk about future plans**

- **G** *be going to*: positive and negative
- **V** Months and future time expressions; Ordinal numbers

## 1 READING

**a** Talk about everyday objects and activities that are important to you. Think about:

- food and drink (*my morning coffee …*)
- your things (*my sofa …*)
- things you do (*listen to music …*)

> Every day I play video games – I really like them.

**b** Read about *Danger Zone*. Is it about … ?

1 a fun holiday  2 a dangerous competition

**c** Read about the TV programme again. Answer the questions.

1 Where do people on the TV programme go?
2 Do they have an easy time? Why / Why not?
3 What do the two best people get?

**d** Read the people's ideas for after the TV programme. Which is the best idea? Tell a partner.

## 2 GRAMMAR *be going to*: positive

**a** 12.01 Complete Mick's sentences with the words in the box. Listen and check.

| to are going |
|---|

1 I'm ________ to sleep for a long time.
2 Melissa's going ________ have a long hot bath.
3 Joel and Shelley ________ going to have their favourite food and drink.

**b** Underline the correct answer in the rule.

We use *be* + *going to* to talk about *now* / *the future*.

**c** 12.01 **Pronunciation** Listen to the sentences in 2a again. Notice the sentence stress and the pronunciation of *going to*. Answer the questions.

1 Do we stress *going*, the main verb or both?
2 Can we hear the words *going to* clearly?

Practise saying the sentences.

**d** Now go to Grammar Focus 12A Part 1 on p. 134.

**e** Write three sentences about something you're going to do after class.

*After class, I'm going to meet my friend Diego.*

**f** Tell other students your sentences in 2e.

> I'm going to study in the Learning Centre. What about you?

> I'm going to get some coffee.

## DANGER ZONE

In this exciting new TV programme, ten people go and live in the mountains for ten days. Every day they do something difficult and sometimes dangerous. It's usually cold and wet and they don't have a lot of food. They need to stay safe and comfortable (if possible!), but it's not easy. The two people who do the best win a prize of €25,000!

**It starts on Channel Six next Tuesday at 8:30 pm**

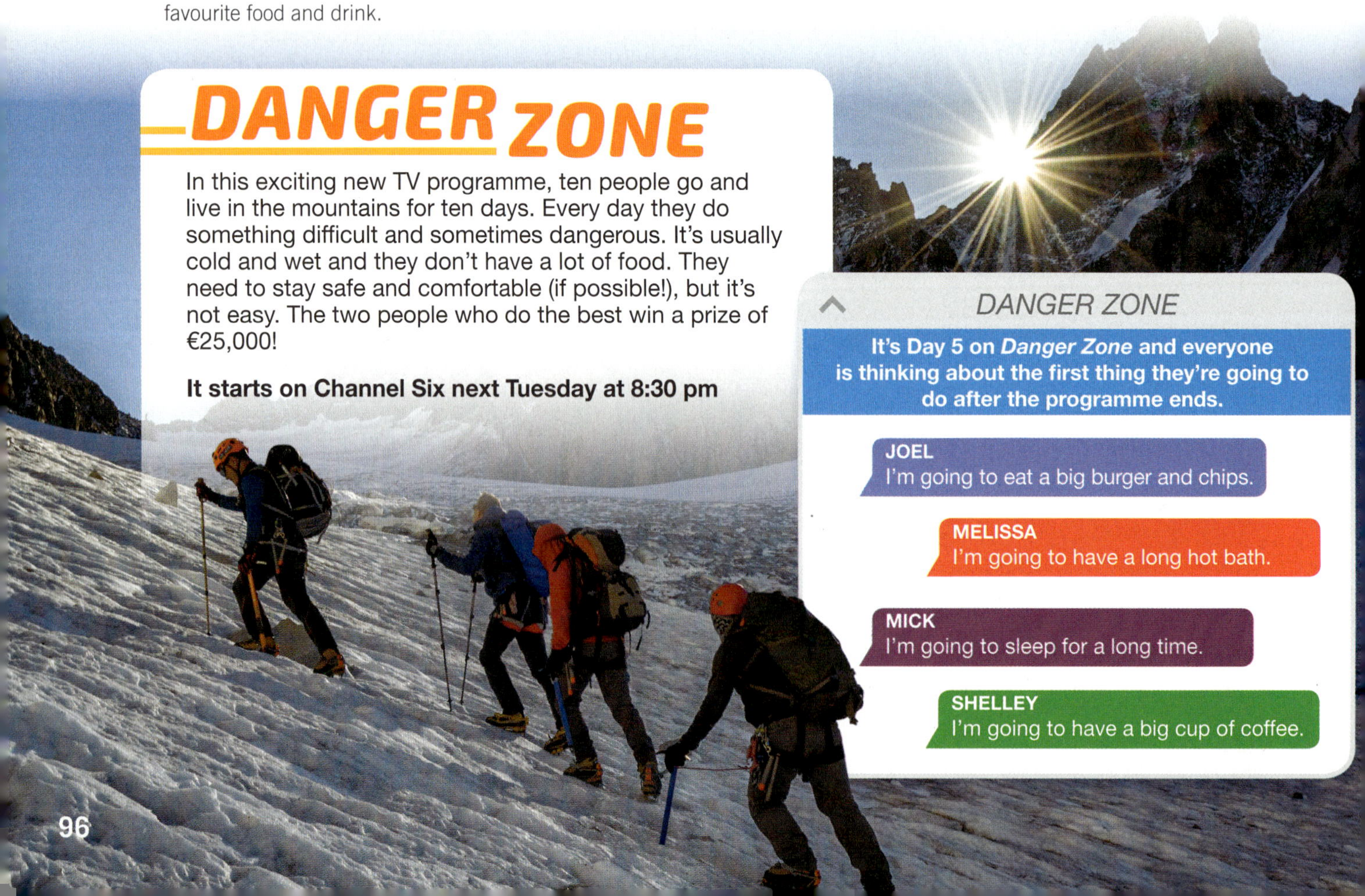

### DANGER ZONE

**It's Day 5 on *Danger Zone* and everyone is thinking about the first thing they're going to do after the programme ends.**

**JOEL** I'm going to eat a big burger and chips.

**MELISSA** I'm going to have a long hot bath.

**MICK** I'm going to sleep for a long time.

**SHELLEY** I'm going to have a big cup of coffee.

## 3 VOCABULARY Months and future time expressions; Ordinal numbers

**a** It's Monday morning. Put time expressions 1–6 in the correct place on the timeline.

1 this evening 2 on Friday 3 next Monday 4 tomorrow 5 at the weekend 6 this Wednesday

| MONDAY | | TUESDAY | | WEDNESDAY | | THURSDAY | | FRIDAY | | SATURDAY | | SUNDAY | | MONDAY | |
|---|---|---|---|---|---|---|---|---|---|---|---|---|---|---|---|
| am | pm | am | pm | am | pm | am | pm | am | pm | am | pm | am | pm | am | pm |

**Language Plus** The date

*What's the date today? It's* ***the fifth of August****.*
*When's your birthday? It's* ***on the twentieth of March****.*
**Note:** With dates we use ordinal numbers:
*first, second, third, fourth …*

**b** Now go to Vocabulary Focus 12A on p. 156.

## 4 LISTENING

**a** 12.06 Listen to Paola (*P*), Yaz (*Y*) and Nikita (*N*) talk about their holiday plans this summer. Match them with pictures a–c.

**b** 12.06 Listen again. Are the sentences true (*T*) or false (*F*)?

1 Paola often goes to a cooking school for her holiday.
2 The trip to Norway is a different kind of holiday for Yaz.
3 Nikita doesn't want to make money on the farm.

**c** Which holiday plan do you like? Which don't you like? Why?

a

b

c

**c** Ask and answer the questions with a partner. Use time expressions in your answers.

1 When's your next English class?
2 When's your next English test?
3 When's your birthday?

It's on the fifteenth of November.

## 5 GRAMMAR *be going to*: negative

**a** 12.07 Listen and complete the sentences.

1 **PAOLA** I ______ ______ going ______ have a normal holiday.
2 **YAZ** We ______ going ______ do that this year.

**b** Now go to Grammar Focus 12A Part 2 on p. 134.

**c** 12.09 Complete the conversations. Listen and check.

1 **A** After class, I'______ not ______ to do my homework.
**B** Why not?
**A** I'm tired. I'm going ______ do it tomorrow.
2 **C** After class, I'______ not ______ to go home.
**D** Why not?
**C** I'm going ______ meet friends in a café.

**d** Practise the conversations in 5c. Use your own ideas to have similar conversations.

## 6 SPEAKING

**a** Write two things you're going to do on your next holiday. Think about:

- places
- things to buy
- activities
- sports
- places to stay
- people

**b** Write two things from your everyday life you aren't going to do on your holiday.

- things you do at school / work
- things you do at home

**c** Talk to other students about your ideas in 6a and 6b. Do you all have the same ideas?

I'm going to go to the beach.

I'm not going to read work emails.

# 12B WHAT ARE YOU GOING TO DO THIS WEEKEND?

**Learn to ask and answer about future plans**

**G** *be going to*: questions

**V** Common verbs and collocations

## ONLY 4,000 WEEKENDS IN YOUR LIFE!
### So, What Are You Going To Do With Them?

**What's your answer to this question? Perhaps it's 'I don't know' or 'Not a lot'. In her new book, *What the Most Successful People Do on the Weekend*, Laura Vanderkam says these are bad answers. She says the weekend is a time to relax, but also a time to do interesting things. With only 4,000 weekends in our life, each one is important. So don't just sit on the sofa and watch TV. It's a good idea to plan the weekend – then you can use the time well. Here are some of her ideas:**

1 Plan three to five activities to do at the weekend and write them down. Be sure you do these things.

2 Plan to read a book. Buy a book for the weekend and then plan a time to read it.

3 Write a list of 100 'big' things you'd like to do in your life. Choose one to do this weekend.

4 Get up early. Between 6:00 and 8:00 in the morning is the best time to do things. Plan to wake up early and do something before breakfast!

5 Turn off your phone and don't use your computer. You can read your emails on Monday. On Sunday evening, go for a run, play some music or do yoga so you relax and don't think about work.

6 Don't clean your house or flat at the weekend. It's a time to do things you like!

d

e

a

b

c

## 1 READING

**a** Talk about sentences 1–3 in small groups. Which are true for you?

1 Weekends are too short and we don't have many of them.
2 It's not a good idea to do a lot at the weekend.
3 It's important to use the time well at the weekend.

**b** Read about Laura Vanderkam's new book. Which sentence in 1a is her main idea?

**c** Look at pictures a–e. Which does Laura say are good things to do at the weekend? Which aren't good?

**d** Look at Wendy's, David's and Rachel's plans for the weekend. Match them with ideas 1–3 in the text.

**e** What do you think of Laura's ideas? Which do you like? Which don't you like? Why / Why not?

Great ideas! I'd like to try them.

That's not my idea of a good weekend.

Interesting ideas, but ...

**Wendy's big ideas**

I'd like to ...
- make a cheesecake
- visit Paris
- paint my room
- learn Chinese
- read a book by Stephen King
- start a blog
- go skydiving

**DAVID'S SCHEDULE**

| | SUNDAY |
|---|---|
| 10:00 | |
| 11:00 | |
| 12:00 | Sit in the park and read my new book. |
| 1:00 | |
| 2:00 | Play football with friends. |

**Rachel's weekend to-do list**

This weekend I'm going to:
1 go for a long run (10 km or more!).
2 invite some friends for dinner.
3 have my first tennis lesson.

## 2 VOCABULARY Common verbs and collocations

**a** 12.10 Match the verbs in the box with the words and phrases in 1–8. Listen and check.

paint clean use make invite visit go do

1 ________ sport / your homework
2 ________ someone to a party
3 ________ a friend
4 ________ a list / lunch
5 ________ a picture / a wall
6 ________ your flat / your windows
7 ________ your phone / the Internet
8 ________ for a walk / shopping / to a museum

**b** Find examples of each verb on page 98. Add them to 1–8 in 2a.

**c** Tell a partner which activities in 2a and 2b you do at the weekend.

I always ... I often ...
I sometimes ... I never ...

**d** Now go to Vocabulary Focus 12B on p. 157.

**e** **Sound and spelling** /v/ and /w/

1 12.12 Listen and practise these sounds.
1 /v/ **v**isit 2 /w/ **w**eekend

2 12.13 Listen to these words and practise saying them.

in**v**ite **v**erb **w**atch **w**ith e**v**ening **w**ell ne**v**er

## 3 LISTENING AND GRAMMAR *be going to*: questions

**a** 12.14 Listen to Lee and Marcus talk to a friend about their weekend plans. Write their names on the line.

NO PLAN ⟷ CLEAR PLAN

**b** 12.14 Listen again. Tick (✓) the things you know after listening to the conversations.

1 ☐ the name of the film Lee's going to see
2 ☐ Lee's plans for Sunday
3 ☐ Marcus's shopping plans
4 ☐ the name of the restaurant Marcus is going to go to
5 ☐ Marcus's plans for Sunday

**c** 12.15 Tick (✓) the correct questions in 1–2. Listen and check.

1 a ☐ What are you going to do on Saturday?
b ☐ What you are going to do on Saturday?
2 a ☐ You going to go shopping?
b ☐ Are you going to go shopping?

**d** Now go to Grammar Focus 12B on p. 134.

**e** 12.18 Put the words in the correct order to make questions. Listen and check.

1 what / you / this weekend / do / going to / are ?
2 go out / you / are / going to ?
3 what / going to / film / see / are / you ?
4 you / are / buy / going to / what ?
5 go / going to / where / you / are ?

**f** Have two conversations with a partner.

1 Student A: You're Lee.
Student B: Ask questions 1, 2 and 3 in 3e.
2 Student B: You're Marcus.
Student A: Ask questions 1, 4 and 5 in 3e.

## 4 SPEAKING

**a** Write questions to ask your partner about their plans. Use the ideas below and *be going to*.

- this evening
- the weekend
- on your next birthday

**b** Ask your partner your questions in 4a. Listen to the answers and write your partner's name on the line in 3a.

**c** Compare your line with other students. Who has clear plans for the future?

# 12C EVERYDAY ENGLISH
## Would you like to come for dinner?

Learn to make and accept invitations

- P Sound and spelling: *oo*
- W An invitation

## 1 LISTENING

**a** You invite friends for a meal. Which of these things do you do? Write *Yes*, *No* or *Sometimes*.

- make special food
- wear your best clothes
- eat at a fixed time
- use the best plates
- play music when you eat
- cook with your friends

**b** Talk about your ideas in 1a with a partner.

**c** Look at pictures a and b. Why do you think James calls Sophia?

**d** 12.19 Watch or listen to Part 1. Check your answer in 1c.

**e** 12.19 Watch or listen to Part 1 again. Underline the correct answer.

1 Sophia's plates are *new* / *old*.
2 Sophia wants to *help James* / *thank James*.
3 James *is* / *isn't* happy about the invitation.

a

b

## 2 USEFUL LANGUAGE Making and accepting invitations

**a** Look at the expressions. Do we use them to ... ?

a make an invitation
b accept an invitation
c say no to an invitation

1 Would you like to come for dinner?
2 I'd love to, but ...
3 I'd love to come. Thank you.
4 Are you free on Friday?
5 Sorry, I'm busy then.
6 Saturday's OK.

12.20 Listen and check your answers.

**b** 12.21 Complete the conversation with the words in the box. Listen and check.

sorry thank love like OK free busy

**A** Would you [1]______ to come to the cinema?
**B** Yes, I'd [2]______ to come. [3]______ you.
**A** Are you [4]______ on Saturday?
**B** No, [5]______, I'm [6]______ on Saturday. But Sunday's [7]______.
**A** OK, we can go on Sunday.

**c** Practise the conversation in 2b with a partner.

## 3 LISTENING

**a** Look at picture c and talk about the questions.

1 Where is James going?
2 Why did he buy flowers?

**b** 12.22 Watch or listen to Part 2. Check your answers in 3a.

**c** 12.22 Watch or listen to Part 2 again. What is Sophia's news? Tick (✓) the correct answer.

1 ☐ She's going to leave her job.
2 ☐ She's going to go back to Canada.
3 ☐ She's going to stay in London.

**d** Match 1–4 with a–d.

| | | |
|---|---|---|
| 1 James is surprised<br>2 Sophia wants to say thank you<br>3 Sophia wasn't happy in London<br>4 Now she wants to stay | because | a James and Megan helped her.<br>b Megan is there too.<br>c she has new friends.<br>d she missed her friends in Canada. |

## 4 PRONUNCIATION Sound and spelling: *oo*

**a** 12.23 Listen to these sentences. When is *oo* an /uː/ sound? When is it an /ʊ/ sound?

1 G**oo**d – now you're both here.
2 I'll bring the f**oo**d.

**b** 12.24 Listen to these words. Put them in the correct place in the table.

cool cook spoon look book soon football

| Sound 1 /ʊ/ | Sound 2 /uː/ |
| --- | --- |
| *good* | *food* |

**c** Practise saying the words in 2b with a partner.

## 5 SPEAKING

Communication 12C
Student A: Go to p. 110.
Student B: Go to p. 115.

## 6 WRITING

**a** James and Megan wrote invitations to friends. Read the invitations and the replies. Do Jon and Emma say yes or no? Why?

**Birthday on Saturday**

Hi Jon,

It's my birthday on Saturday. Would you like to come to my party? It's at my flat and it starts at 9:00.

See you then, I hope.

James

**RE: Birthday on Saturday**

Hi James,

Thanks, I'd love to come, but I'm not in London. I'm in Sheffield and I'm staying here till Sunday.

Hope you have a great time! See you next week.

Jon

**Let's meet up**

Hi Emma,

I'm in town this afternoon. Would you like to meet for coffee?

We could go to Café Roma. It's just near your office. I'm free at 4:00. Is that OK for you?

Megan

**RE: Let's meet up**

Hi Megan,

Sorry, I'm working till 6:30.

Café Roma's a great idea. Maybe we could meet there tomorrow for lunch. Are you in town then?

Emma

**b** Now go to Writing Plus 12C on p. 163 for Paragraphs.

**c** You want to meet a friend. Think of a place and time. Write an invitation. Here are some ideas:

Would you like to … ?
I'm free at …
See you …
We could …
Is that OK for you?

**d** Read another student's invitation. Write a reply.

## UNIT PROGRESS TEST

### CHECK YOUR PROGRESS

You can now do the Unit Progress Test.

# UNIT 12
## Review

## 1 GRAMMAR

**a** Complete Emily's email with *be going to* and the verbs in brackets.

> Hi Mia,
>
> I have so many plans for this week! This afternoon I [1]__________ (study), and then I [2]__________ (work) from Tuesday to Thursday. On Wednesday evening I [3]__________ (cook) for my parents and then on Thursday evening Marco [4]__________ (cook) dinner for me!
>
> I [5]__________ (not / work) on Friday morning because you [6]__________ (arrive) at lunchtime! James [7]__________ (have) a party on Friday evening. Do you want to go? He [8]__________ (not / invite) a lot of people.
>
> It's a busy week for me! So I [9]__________ (not / do) any work or housework at the weekend and we [10]__________ (not / go) to a lot of different places! I hope that's OK.
>
> See you on Friday!
>
> Emily

**b** Correct the sentences.

> 'Is your friend going to have lunch with us?' 'No, she not.'
*No, she isn't.*
1 'You are going to watch TV this evening?' 'No, I'm not.'
2 Are your mum going to cook your dinner this evening?
3 'Are you going to clean your bedroom?' 'Yes, I'm going.'
4 What do you going to wear tomorrow?
5 'Are your friends going to visit you today?' 'Yes, they're.'
6 What you going to do next summer?

**c** Ask and answer the questions in 1b. Use *be going to.*

## 2 VOCABULARY

**a** ~~Cross out~~ the answers that are NOT possible.

1 *tomorrow / on tomorrow*
2 *this / in / next / on* Friday
3 *at / in* the weekend
4 *on / this / in / next* June
5 *next / at* weekend
6 *on / in* Sunday
7 *in / on* three weeks
8 *this / at* afternoon

**b** Complete the ordinal numbers.

> 6th s *i* *x* *t* h
1 2nd s _ _ _ _ d
2 30th t _ _ _ _ _ _ _ _ h
3 21st t _ _ _ _ y-f _ _ _ t
4 3rd t _ _ _ d
5 15th f _ _ _ _ _ _ _ _ h
6 9th n _ _ _ h

**c** Complete the questions with the words in the box.

clean do invite make use go

1 Do you often ______ to museums?
2 Are you going to ______ a cake this weekend?
3 Did you ______ any sport yesterday?
4 Are you going to ______ your bedroom today?
5 Do you ______ your computer every day?
6 Are you going to ______ someone for lunch next week?

**d** Ask and answer the questions in 2c.

## 3 SOUND AND SPELLING

**a** 12.25 Circle the /v/ sounds in the phrases and <u>underline</u> the /w/ sounds. Practise saying the phrases and sentences.

1 visit in the evening
2 We never invite Wendy.
3 I love weekends in winter.
4 win video games every week
5 watch TV with Vicky and William
6 on Wednesday, the twelfth of November

**b** 12.26 Complete the table with the words in the box. Practise saying the words.

g**oo**d b**oo**k f**oo**tball b**oo**ts
c**oo**l l**oo**k sch**oo**l s**oo**n

| /ʊ/ | /uː/ |
|---|---|
| *cooking* | *spoon* |

## REVIEW YOUR PROGRESS

**How well did you do in this unit? Write 3, 2 or 1 for each objective.**
3 = very well 2 = well 1 = not so well

| I CAN ... | |
|---|---|
| talk about future plans | ☐ |
| ask and answer about future plans | ☐ |
| make and accept invitations. | ☐ |

# Phonemic symbols

## Vowel sounds

**Short**

| /ə/ breakfast | /æ/ man | /ʊ/ put | /ɒ/ got | /ɪ/ chip | /i/ happy | /e/ men | /ʌ/ up |
|---|---|---|---|---|---|---|---|

**Long**

| /ɜː/ shirt | /ɑː/ part | /uː/ who | /ɔː/ walk | /iː/ cheap |
|---|---|---|---|---|

## Diphthongs (two vowel sounds)

| /eə/ hair | /ɪə/ near | /ʊə/ tour | /ɔɪ/ boy | /aɪ/ nine | /eɪ/ eight | /əʊ/ window | /aʊ/ now |
|---|---|---|---|---|---|---|---|

## Consonants

| /p/ picnic | /b/ book | /f/ face | /v/ very | /t/ time | /d/ dog | /k/ cold | /g/ go |
|---|---|---|---|---|---|---|---|
| /θ/ think | /ð/ the | /tʃ/ chair | /dʒ/ job | /s/ sea | /z/ zoo | /ʃ/ shoe | /ʒ/ television |
| /m/ me | /n/ now | /ŋ/ sing | /h/ hot | /l/ late | /r/ red | /w/ went | /j/ yes |

# Irregular verbs

| Infinitive | Simple past |
|---|---|
| be | was |
| begin | began |
| buy | bought |
| catch | caught |
| choose | chose |
| come | came |
| do | did |
| drink | drank |
| drive | drove |
| eat | ate |
| feel | felt |
| find | found |
| fly | flew |
| forget | forgot |
| get | got |
| give | gave |
| go | went |
| grow up | grew up |
| have | had |
| hear | heard |
| know | knew |
| learn | learned / learnt |
| leave | left |
| lose | lost |

| Infinitive | Simple past |
|---|---|
| meet | met |
| pay | paid |
| put | put |
| read | read |
| ride | rode |
| run | ran |
| say | said |
| see | saw |
| sell | sold |
| send | sent |
| sing | sang |
| sit | sat |
| sleep | slept |
| speak | spoke |
| spell | spelled / spelt |
| swim | swam |
| take | took |
| teach | taught |
| tell | told |
| think | thought |
| understand | understood |
| wake up | woke up |
| wear | wore |
| write | wrote |

# COMMUNICATION PLUS

## 1A STUDENT A

**a** You're Yoshi from Japan. You're a student. Complete the conversation.

**A** Hello, I'm ____________.
**B** Hi, I'm Bella. Nice to meet you.
**A** Are you from the UK?
**B** No, I'm not. I'm from the USA. And you?
**A** I'm from ____________.
**B** Are you a teacher?
**A** No, I'm a ____________. And you?
**B** I'm a teacher.

**b** Have a conversation with Student B.

**c** Choose a name and a country and have another conversation.

## 1B STUDENT A

Jenna = British  Doruk = Turkish  Sandra = Italian

**a** Look at the picture and the information box. Then cover the box.

**b** Tell Student B the names of the people and answer Student B's questions.

This is …

**c** Listen to Student B talk about the people in the picture. Then ask Student B about the nationalities of the people.

Are they Spanish?

No, they aren't. They're Brazilian.

## 2A STUDENT A

**a** Read the information about Kate.

**Name:** Kate
**Town/city:** Ely – small city near Cambridge, in England
**Home:** beautiful, old house

**b** Tell Students B and C about Kate.

Her name's …

She's from …

Her home is …

**c** Listen to Students B and C talk about two people. What information is the same about all three people?

## 2B STUDENT A

**a** Look at the picture. Student B has a similar picture. Ask and answer questions to find seven differences.

Do you have a phone in your picture?

I have two phones.

**b** Now go back to p. 19.

## 4C STUDENT A

**a** Look at the pictures. The two people are your friends. You want to show the pictures to Student B. Think about what you want to say.

Rob, teacher, interesting

Carla, hotel manager, happy

**b** Cover the information under the pictures. Show them to Student B and talk about your friends.

> These are my friends Rob and Carla.

**c** Ask Student B about his/her two friends.

> Do you have photos of your friends?

**d** Now go back to p. 37.

## 4A STUDENT A

**a** Read the information.

- You live in Paris, France, but you work three days a week in London, in the UK.
- You work two days a week at home.
- You study French and you go to lessons on Friday.

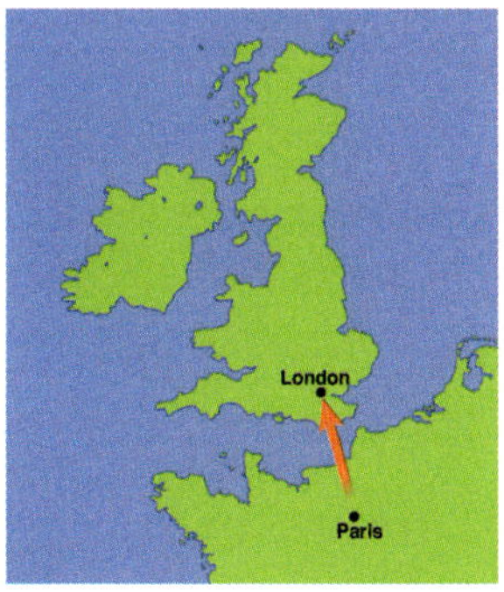


**b** Start a conversation with Student B about their life. Use the questions below to help you.

> Where do you live?

> Do you work in … ?

> Do you speak … ?

**c** Listen to Student B and reply.

> I live in …

> I speak a little …

## 2C STUDENT A

**a** Ask Student B about his/her:

- surname
- address
- phone number
- email address

> What's your surname?

**b** Read the information on your card. Answer Student B's questions.

**Surname:** Ramirez
**Address:** 5 High Street
**Phone number:** (714) 555-4321
**Email address:** toniramirez@travelmail.com

**c** Now go back to p. 20.

## 3B STUDENT A

**a** Ask Student B the time in these cities:

- Paris
- Rio de Janeiro
- Beijing
- Los Angeles

**b** Answer Student B's questions about the time in these cities.

Tokyo New York Mexico City Berlin

**c** Now go back to p. 27.

## 4B STUDENT A

**a** Read the information about Omar on your card.

'I'm a student. I'm 19 and I study English at Cairo University, in Egypt. I live at home with my parents. My mother is a teacher and my father works at the Bank of Cairo. He's a bank manager. I have one brother. He's married and he lives in Dubai. He works at Dubai Airport.'

**b** Tell Student B about Omar.

> He's a student. He studies English …

**c** Listen to Student B talk about Monica. Find six things that are the same about Omar and Monica.

1 *They're both students.*

**d** Now go back to p. 35.

## 1A STUDENT B

**a** You're Bella from the USA. You're a teacher. Complete the conversation.

**A** Hello, I'm Yoshi.
**B** Hi, I'm ____________. Nice to meet you.
**A** Are you from the UK?
**B** No, I'm not. I'm from ____________. And you?
**A** I'm from Japan.
**B** Are you a ____________?
**A** No, I'm a student. And you?
**B** I'm a ____________.

**b** Have a conversation with Student A.

**c** Choose a name and a country and have another conversation.

## 1B STUDENT B

Sara = Spanish   Luis and Marta = Brazilian   Thomas = French

**a** Look at the picture and the information in the box. Then cover the box.

**b** Listen to Student A talk about the people in the picture. Then ask Student A about the nationalities of the people.

Is he British?

No, he isn't. He's Turkish.

**c** Tell Student A the names of the people and answer Student A's questions.

This is …

## 2A STUDENT B

**a** Read the information about Carla.

**Name:** Carla
**Town/city:** Hamilton – small city near Toronto, in Canada
**Home:** nice, new flat

**b** Listen to Student A.

**c** Tell Students A and C about Carla.

Her name's …

She's from …

Her home is …

**d** Listen to Student C talk. What information is the same about all three people?

## 2B STUDENT B

**a** Look at the picture. Student A has a similar picture. Ask and answer questions to find seven differences.

Do you have keys in your picture?

I have one key.

**b** Now go back to p. 19.

## 5C STUDENT B

**a** **Conversation 1.** You're on a street you know. Use the information to answer Student A's questions.

a hotel: not near here – near the train station
cafés: Black Cat Café on this street

**b** **Conversation 2.** Now you're on a street you don't know. Ask Student A about:

- a bank
- shops

**c** Now go back to p. 45.

## 5B STUDENT B

**a** Read the information about a hotel on your card.

### Hotel Helena

- Rooms with showers and TVs
- Restaurant
- Swimming pool
- Car park

***Note:*** *There isn't free wi-fi in the hotel. You pay for it.*

**b** Student A has information about a hostel. Ask and answer questions to find what things are the same and what things are different at the hotel and the hostel.

Is there free wi-fi at the hostel?

Yes, there is.

## 6A STUDENT B

**a** Look at the information about Sarah and Hassan. Make positive (+) and negative (–) sentences.

+ meet a lot of people
+ work in a restaurant
→ a waitress

– work in the morning
– sit a lot

+ meet a lot of of people
+ like his job
→ a taxi driver

– work during the day
– work very hard

**b** Ask Student A about Rosa and Franco.
Say: *Tell me about … .*
Can you guess their jobs?

**c** Tell Student A about Sarah and Hassan. Don't say their jobs.

Sarah meets a lot of people.

## 3B STUDENT B

**a** Answer Student A's questions about the time in these cities.

Paris

Rio de Janeiro

Beijing

Los Angeles

**b** Ask Student A the time in these cities:

- Tokyo
- New York
- Mexico City
- Berlin

**c** Now go back to p. 27.

## 6B STUDENT B

**a** Peter and Gamal live in the same flat. Read about Peter's daily routine.

Peter works at a bank. He always wakes up at 6:30. He gets up at 7:00, has a coffee and goes to work. He starts work at 8:30 and he finishes at 5:30. He gets home at 6:00, has dinner and watches TV. Sometimes he goes out, but he always goes to bed at 10:30.

**b** Answer Student A's questions about Peter.

**c** Ask Student A questions about Gamal. Then write the answers.

When does he go to class?

What does he do in the afternoon?

- When / get up? *9:00*
- When / go to class?
- What / do in the afternoon?
- When / get home?
- What / do in the evening?
- When / start work?
- When / finish work?
- When / go to bed?

**d** When does Peter see Gamal?

## 4A STUDENT B

**a** Read the information.

- You live in Monterrey, Mexico, but you work four days a week in Austin, Texas, in the USA.
- You work one day a week at home.
- You study Spanish and you go to lessons on Saturday.

**b** Listen to Student A and reply.

I live in …

I speak a little …

**c** Start a conversation with Student A about their life. Use the questions below to help you.

Where do you live?

Do you work in … ?

Do you speak … ?

## 4C STUDENT B

**a** Look at the pictures. The two people are your friends. You want to show the pictures to Student A. Think about what you want to say.

Haley, student, kind

Will, bank manager, funny

**b** Ask Student A about his/her two friends.

Do you have photos of your friends?

**c** Cover the information under the pictures. Show them to Student A and talk about your friends.

These are my friends Haley and Will.

**d** Now go back to p. 37.

## 2A STUDENT C

**a** Read the information about Dave.

**Name:** Dave
**Town/city:** Newcastle – small city near Sydney, in Australia
**Home:** big, new flat

**b** Listen to Students A and B talk about two people.

**c** Tell Students A and B about Dave. What information is the same about all three people?

His name's …

He's from …

His home is …

## 2C STUDENT B

**a** Read the information on your card. Answer Student A's questions.

**Surname:** Adams
**Address:** 8 Park Road
**Phone number:** (714) 555-9876
**Email address:** alexadams@travelmail.com

**b** Ask Student A about his/her:

- surname
- address
- phone number
- email address

What's your surname?

**c** Now go back to p. 20.

## 4B STUDENT B

**a** Read the information about Monica on your card.

> 'I'm Spanish. I'm 20. I live in Madrid and I study English at university. I live at home with my parents. I have a brother and two sisters. My brother works at the airport. He's married and he has two children.'

**b** Listen to Student A talk about Omar.

**c** Tell Student A about Monica. Find six things that are the same about Omar and Monica.

She's a student.
She studies English …

1 *They're both students.*

**d** Now go back to p. 35.

## 5B STUDENT A

**a** Read the information about a hostel on your card.

> **HARRY'S HOSTEL**
> - Big rooms with no shower
> - Small rooms with a shower
> - Free wi-fi
> - A small café
>
> ***Note:*** *There isn't a swimming pool or a car park.*

**b** Student B has information about a hotel. Ask and answer questions to find what things are the same and what things are different at the hotel and the hostel.

Is there a swimming pool at the hotel?

Yes, there is.

## 6B STUDENT A

**a** Gamal and Peter live in the same flat. Read about Gamal's daily routine.

Gamal is a student. He usually gets up at 9:00 and has breakfast. Then he goes to class at 10:00. In the afternoon, he studies in the library and he gets home at 5:00. In the evening, he works in a café near their flat. He starts work at 7:00 and finishes at 11:00. He goes to bed at 12:00.

**b** Ask Student B questions about Peter. Then write the answers.

When does he get up?

What does he do then?

- When / wake up? *6:30*
- When / get up?
- What / do then?
- When / start work?
- When / finish work?
- When / get home?
- What / do in the evening?
- When / go to bed?

**c** Answer Student B's questions about Gamal.

**d** When does Gamal see Peter?

## 6A STUDENT A

**a** Look at the information about Rosa and Franco. Make positive (+) and negative (–) sentences.

\+ work very hard
\+ work at a hospital
→ a doctor
– have a lot of free time
– sit a lot

\+ work long hours
\+ like his job
→ a teacher
– sit a lot
– work in the summer

**b** Tell Student B about Rosa and Franco. Don't say their jobs.

Rosa works very hard.

**c** Ask Student B about Sarah and Hassan. Say: *Tell me about … .* Can you guess their jobs?

## 7B STUDENT A

**a** Look at picture 1. Make notes about their clothes.

**b** Tell Student B about the clothes the people in picture 1 are wearing. Find out their names and write them under each picture.

> This person has a blouse and a skirt. What's this person's name?

**c** Listen to Student B talk about the clothes in picture 2. Tell him/her the people's names.

**d** Now go back to p. 58.

## 9A STUDENT B

**a** Read notes about your trip to Dubai, in the UAE. Make sentences from the notes. Use the past simple.

- in the north of the UAE
- plane to Dubai …
- didn't stay in a hotel …
- … my brother's flat (he lives in Dubai)
- … then taxi around the city
- a lot of photos
- shopping – a lot of clothes
- restaurants – very good food

**b** Listen to Student A talk about a trip to Seville.

**c** Tell Student A about your trip. Find four things you both did on your trips.

## 12C STUDENT A

**a** You want to invite Student B to:

1 go for a walk at the weekend.
2 meet for coffee.

Think about what you want to say. Start the conversation with Student B. Try to find times when you're both free.

> Do you want to go for a walk at the weekend?

**YOUR DIARY**

| | | | |
|---|---|---|---|
| SUN | *visiting parents 12:00–5:00* | THURS | *work 8:00–6:00* |
| MON | *work 8:00–6:00* | FRI | *work 8:00–6:00*<br>*yoga 7:00–8:30* |
| TUES | *work 8:00–6:00* | SAT | *concert 7:00 pm* |
| WED | | | |

**b** Now go back to p. 101.

## 10C STUDENT A

**a** **Conversation 1.** Read your first card. Think about what you want to say. Then start the conversation with Student B with *Excuse me*.

**1** You want to go to Manchester.

- Time now: 11:15 am
- Ask about the next train.
- Ask about the platform.
- You have a big suitcase – it's difficult to run.

**b** **Conversation 2.** Now read your second card. Think about what you want to say. Listen to Student B and reply.

**2** You're a ticket agent at a bus station.

- Time now: 2:45 pm

| | Time | Bus stop | Price |
|---|---|---|---|
| Oxford | 3:00 pm | 4 | £16 |
| Oxford | 4:00 pm | 3 | £11 |

**c** Now go back to p. 85.

## 7A STUDENT B

**a** You have a stall at a flea market. You sell the objects in the box.

pictures clocks lamps chairs old books

Write a price for each object.

**b** At Student A's stall, you see three things you like:

- some beautiful plates
- an interesting plant
- a good knife for your kitchen

Try to buy them for a good price.

> They're expensive. Is £2 OK?

**c** Try to sell things to Student A.

> They're £10 each. They're very old.

> It's only £5 – it's very cheap.

## 8A STUDENT B

**a** Answer Student A's questions about Morgan.

| 1 year ago | last weekend | on Monday |
|---|---|---|
| in Germany | at a party at her home | at university |

**b** Ask Student C about Marcella.

> Where was she a year ago?

> Where was she last weekend?

> Was she at work on Monday?

**c** Listen to Students A and C talk about Henri.

**d** What is the same for all three people?

## 7C STUDENT A

**a** **Conversation 1.** You're a shop assistant. Student B is your customer. You have six glasses and they are £2.00 each. Your customer can pay by card. Start a conversation with *Hello, can I help you?*

**b** **Conversation 2.** You're a customer in a shop. Student B is a shop assistant. You want to buy four plates. Ask how much they are.

**c** ≫ Now go back to p. 61.

## 8B STUDENT B

**a** Look at the pictures of Charlotte's day yesterday. Make notes about what she did.

**b** Listen to Student A talk about what Leo did yesterday.

**c** Tell Student A what Charlotte did yesterday. What activities are the same?

## 9B STUDENT A

**a** Read the information about the weather in Mumbai, in India. Listen to Student B and reply.

| Weather in Mumbai | |
|---|---|
| Yesterday | hot, sunny |
| Today | cloudy, warm |
| Summer | a lot of rain, hot |

**b** Ask Student B these questions about the weather in Berlin, in Germany.

> What was the weather like yesterday?

> What's the weather like today?

> What's the weather like in winter?

**c** ≫ Now go back to p. 75.

## 10A STUDENT B

**a** Listen to Student A. Are they talking about picture 1, 2 or 3?

**b** Ken is in picture 6. Tell Student A:

- where he is (*He's sitting in …* )
- what's in the next room (*There's a … next door.*)
- what he's doing (*He's …* )

**c** Listen to Student A again. Which picture are they talking about now?

**d** Choose picture 1 or 3. Describe it to Student A.

## 7C STUDENT B

**a** **Conversation 1.** You're a customer in a shop. Student A is a shop assistant. You want to buy four glasses. Ask how much they are. You'd like to pay by card.

**b** **Conversation 2.** You're a shop assistant. Student A is your customer. You have four plates and they are £3 each. Your customer can pay by card. Start a conversation with *Hello, can I help you?*

**c** »» Now go back to p. 61.

## 10C STUDENT B

**a** **Conversation 1.** Read your first card. Think about what you want to say. Listen to Student A and reply.

1 You're a ticket agent at a train station.

- Time now: 11:15 am
- Platform 6 is a two-minute walk.

| | Time | Platform |
|---|---|---|
| Manchester | 11:17 am | 6 |
| Manchester | 11:35 am | 6 |

**b** **Conversation 2.** Now read your second card. Think about what you want to say. Then start the conversation with Student A with *Excuse me.*

2 You want to go to Oxford.

- Time now: 2:45 pm
- Ask about the next bus.
- Ask about the bus stop.
- Ask about the price. (You only have £15 with you.)

**c** »» Now go back to p. 85.

## 10B STUDENT B

**a** Look at the picture. What are the people doing? Make notes.

**b** Student A has a similar picture. Ask and answer questions to find five differences. Student A starts.

Is Ali in the kitchen?

Yes, he is.

Is he eating?

No, he isn't. He's …

**c** »» Now go back to p. 83.

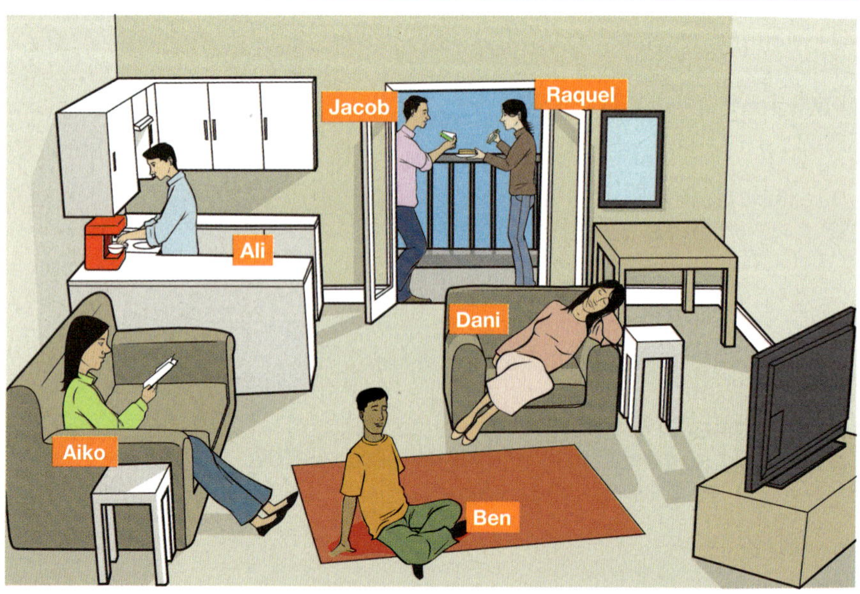

## 7A STUDENT A

**a** You have a stall at a flea market. You sell the objects in the box.

cups glasses plates plants knives

Write a price for each object.

**b** Try to sell things to Student B.

It's only £5 – it's very cheap.

They're £3 each. They're very beautiful.

**c** At Student B's stall, you see three things you like:

- a beautiful old picture
- a lamp
- some interesting old books

Try to buy them for a good price.

It's very expensive. Is £10 OK?

## 8A STUDENT A

**a** Ask Student B about Morgan.

Where was she a year ago?

Where was she last weekend?

Was she at work on Monday?

**b** Listen to Students B and C talk about Marcella.

**c** Answer Student C's questions about Henri.

| **1 year ago** | **last weekend** | **on Monday** |
|---|---|---|
| in Chile | at a party in Paris | at work in Germany |

Henri

**d** What is the same for all three people?

## 11C STUDENT A

**a** You and Student B live in the same city. Talk about good places for tourists to visit. This is what you think of the four main places to visit:

the Museum of History – very interesting
Central Park – OK, nice
the Old Town – a bit boring
the Mega Department Store – very expensive

What do you think of Central Park?

I think Central Park is OK.

Really? I don't think so.

**b** Now go back to p. 93.

## 9B STUDENT B

**a** Ask Student A these questions about the weather in Mumbai, in India.

What was the weather like yesterday?

What's the weather like today?

What's the weather like in summer?

**b** Read the information about the weather in Berlin, in Germany. Listen to Student A and reply.

| Weather in Berlin | |
|---|---|
| Yesterday | wet, windy |
| Today | sunny, cold |
| Winter | snows, cold |

**c** Now go back to p. 75.

## 8B STUDENT A

**a** Look at the pictures of Leo's day yesterday. Make notes about what he did.

**b** Tell Student B what Leo did yesterday.

**c** Listen to Student B talk about what Charlotte did yesterday. Which activities are the same?

## 7B STUDENT B

a Look at picture 2. Make notes about their clothes.

b Listen to Student A talk about the clothes in picture 1. Tell him/her the people's names.

c Tell Student A about the clothes the people in picture 2 are wearing. Find out their names and write them under each picture.

This person has a coat and trousers. What's the person's name?

d Now go back to p. 58.

## 9A STUDENT A

a Read notes about your trip to Seville, in Spain. Make sentences from the notes. Use the past simple.

- in the south of Spain
- plane to Madrid …
- … then train to Seville
- small hotel – city centre
- a lot of photos
- shopping – didn't buy anything
- restaurants – very good food
- a concert – you liked it!

b Tell Student B about your trip.

c Listen to Student B talk about a trip to Dubai. Find four things you both did on your trips.

## 11C STUDENT B

a You and Student A live in the same city. Talk about good places for tourists to visit. This is what you think of the four main places to visit:

the Museum of History – OK
Central Park – boring
the Old Town – beautiful
the Mega Department Store – a lot of fun

What do you think of the Museum of History?

I think the museum is OK.

Really? I don't think so.

b Now go back to p. 93.

## 10B STUDENT A

a Look at the picture. What are the people doing? Make notes.

b Student B has a similar picture. Ask and answer questions to find five differences. You start. Ask about Ali.

Is Ali in the kitchen?

Yes, he is.

Is he eating?

No, he isn't. He's …

c Now go back to p. 83.

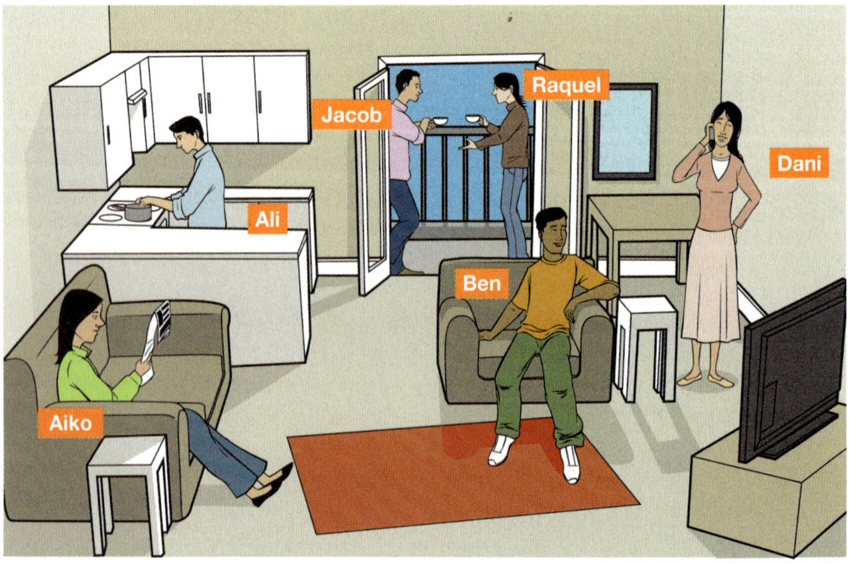

## 8A STUDENT C

**a** Listen to Students A and B talk about Morgan.

**b** Answer Student B's questions about Marcella.

| **1 year ago** | **last weekend** | **on Monday** |
|---|---|---|
| in Greece | at a party<br>in Venice | in a meeting<br>at work |

Marcella

**c** Ask Student A about Henri.

Where was he a year ago?

Where was he last weekend?

Was he at work on Monday?

**d** What is the same for all three people?

## 12C STUDENT B

**a** You want to invite Student A to:

1 go out for dinner one evening.
2 go shopping for clothes.

Think about what you want to say. Listen to Student A and reply. Try to find times when you're both free.

Do you want to go out for dinner?

YOUR DIARY

| | |
|---|---|
| SUN | |
| MON | work 8:00–6:00<br>theatre 8:00 pm |
| TUES | |
| WED | work 8:00–6:00<br>Spanish lesson 7:00–8:30 |
| THURS | on holiday – not here |
| FRI | on holiday – not here |
| SAT | football 9:00–2:00 |

**b** Now go back to p. 101.

## 10A STUDENT A

**a** Ken is in picture 2. Tell Student B:

- where he is (*He's sitting in …* )
- what's in the next room (*There's a … next door.*)
- what he's doing (*He's …* )

**b** Listen to Student B. Are they talking about picture 4, 5 or 6?

**c** Choose picture 4 or 5. Describe it to Student B.

**d** Listen to Student B again. Which picture are they talking about now?

## 1A be: I / you / we

### Part 1: Positive and questions

01.03

| | **Positive (+)** |
|---|---|
| **I** | ***I'm*** *fine.* |
| **you** | ***You're*** *right.* |
| **we** | ***We're*** *from the USA.* |
| **you** | ***You're*** *John and Hannah.* |

**Tip**

I **am** → I'**m**
You **are** → You'**re**
We **are** → We'**re**

01.05

| | ***Wh-* questions (?)** |
|---|---|
| **I** | *Where* ***am*** *I?* |
| **you** | *How* ***are*** *you?* |
| **we** | *Where* ***are*** *we?* |
| **you** | *Where* ***are*** *you?* |

01.04

| ***Yes/No*** **questions (?)** | | **Short answers** | |
|---|---|---|---|
| ***Am*** *I* | *at home?* | *Yes, I* ***am****.* | *No,* ***I'm not****.* |
| ***Are*** *you* | *OK?* | *Yes, you* ***are****.* | *No, you* ***aren't****.* |
| ***Are*** *we* | *in London?* | *Yes, we* ***are****.* | *No, we* ***aren't****.* |
| ***Are*** *you* | *students?* | *Yes, you* ***are****.* | *No, you* ***aren't****.* |

***Are you*** *from Spain?* NOT ~~*You are from Spain?*~~
*Yes,* ***I am****.* NOT ~~*Yes, I'm.*~~

### Part 2: Negative

01.08

| | **Negative (–)** |
|---|---|
| **I** | ***I'm not*** *from Italy.* |
| **you** | *You* ***aren't*** *a teacher.* |
| **we** | *We* ***aren't*** *from the USA.* |
| **you** | *You* ***aren't*** *teachers.* |

**Tip**

I **am not** → I'**m not**
You **are not** → You **aren't** / You'**re not**
We **are not** → We **aren't** / We'**re not**

***I'm not*** *from Brazil.* NOT ~~*I amn't from Brazil*~~.

## 1B be: he / she / they

### Part 1: Positive

01.16

| | **+** |
|---|---|
| **he** | *He****'s*** *Japanese.* |
| **she** | *She****'s*** *Mexican.* |
| **they** | *They****'re*** *American.* |

**Tip**

He **is** → He'**s**
She **is** → She'**s**
They **are** → They'**re**

### Part 2: Negative and questions

01.18

| | **–** |
|---|---|
| **he** | *He* ***isn't*** *Japanese.* |
| **she** | *She* ***isn't*** *Mexican.* |
| **they** | *They* ***aren't*** *American.* |

**Tip**

He **is not** → He **isn't** / He'**s not**
She **is not** → She **isn't** / She'**s not**
They **are not** → They **aren't** / They'**re not**

01.19

| ***Yes/No*** **questions (?)** | | **Short answers** | |
|---|---|---|---|
| **he** | ***Is*** *he Japanese?* | *Yes, he* ***is****.* | *No, he* ***isn't****.* |
| **she** | ***Is*** *she Mexican?* | *Yes, she* ***is****.* | *No, she* ***isn't****.* |
| **they** | ***Are*** *they American?* | *Yes, they* ***are****.* | *No, they* ***aren't****.* |

01.20

| | ***Wh-* questions (?)** |
|---|---|
| **he/she** | *Where****'s*** *he/she from?*<br>*Who****'s*** *he/she?* |
| **they** | *Where* ***are*** *they from?*<br>*Who* ***are*** *they?* |

***Is he*** *Japanese?* NOT ~~*Is Japanese?*~~ OR ~~*He is Japanese?*~~
***Are they*** *American?* NOT ~~*Are American?*~~ OR ~~*They are American?*~~
*Yes,* ***he is****.* NOT ~~*Yes, he's.*~~

**Tip**

*Where* ***is*** *he from?* → *Where****'s*** *he from?*
*Who* ***is*** *she?* → *Who****'s*** *she?*

## 1A *be*: *I / you / we*

### Part 1: Positive and questions

**a** Write sentences with *'re* or *'m*.

1 I am from New York. *I'm from New York.*
2 We are students.
3 You are Roberto.
4 I am fine, thanks.
5 We are from Mexico.

**b** Put the words in the correct order to make questions.

1 you / are / how ? *How are you?*
2 are / from / the USA / you ?
3 we / in / Turkey / are ?
4 OK / I / am ?
5 name / your / what's ?

**c** Now go back to p. 8.

### Part 2: Negative

**a** Write one positive (+) and one negative (–) sentence for 1–5.

1 We / from Brazil
*We're from Brazil. We aren't from Brazil.*
2 You / Rebecca
3 I / a teacher
4 We / in Paris
5 I / OK

**b** Write short answers.

1 **A** Are you from the USA?
**B** No, *I'm not*.
2 **A** Are you Eric?
**B** Yes, ______________.
3 **A** Are we in Spain?
**B** No, ______________.
4 **A** Are you students?
**B** Yes, ______________.

**c** Now go back to p. 9.

## 1B *be*: *he / she / they*

### Part 1: Positive

**a** Complete the sentences with *he's*, *she's* or *they're*.

1 ______________ Italian.

2 ______________ Chinese.

3 ______________ Brazilian.

4 ______________ Mexican.

5 ______________ Spanish.

6 ______________ British.

**b** Now go back to p. 11.

### Part 2: Negative and questions

**a** Complete the sentences with *isn't* or *aren't*.

1 She ______________ Italian. She's Brazilian.
2 They ______________ American. They're English.
3 He ______________ Chinese. He's American.
4 They ______________ Turkish. They're English.
5 He ______________ Spanish. He's Italian.
6 She ______________ Brazilian. She's Mexican.

**b** Tick (✓) the correct questions. Correct the wrong questions.

1 ☐ He is Turkish?
2 ☐ Is she Brazilian?
3 ☐ Are English they?
4 ☐ Are he Italian?
5 ☐ She is Chinese?
6 ☐ Are they Japanese?

**c** Complete the conversations with *is*, *isn't*, *'s*, *are*, *aren't* or *'re*.

**A** Who is this?
**B** He [1]______________ my friend Lee.
**A** [2]______________ he Chinese?
**B** No, he [3]______________. He [4]______________ from the USA.

**A** Who are they?
**B** They [5]______________ my friends Nick and Anna.
**A** [6]______________ they from England?
**B** No, they [7]______________. They [8]______________ Brazilian.

**d** Now go back to p. 11.

## 2A *be: it's / it isn't*; Possessive adjectives

### Part 1: *it's / it isn't*

*it* = a place/thing

*they* = 2+ places/things

▶ 02.04

| | + | – |
|---|---|---|
| **it** | *It**'s** an old hotel.* | *It **isn't** a new hotel.* |
| **they** | *They**'re** old houses.* | *They **aren't** big houses.* |

▶ 02.05

| | *Yes/No* questions | Short answers | |
|---|---|---|---|
| **it** | ***Is** it a big hotel?* | *Yes, it **is**.* | *No, it **isn't**.* |
| **they** | ***Are** they new houses?* | *Yes, they **are**.* | *No, they **aren't**.* |

***Is it** in Japan?* NOT ~~*Is in Japan?*~~ OR ~~*It is in Japan?*~~
*Yes, **it is**.* NOT ~~*Yes, it's.*~~

**Tip**
*It **is** in Spain.* → *It**'s** in Spain.*
*It **is not** in Italy.* → *It **isn't** in Italy.*

### Part 2: Possessive adjectives

| Pronoun | Possessive adjective | ▶ 02.10 |
|---|---|---|
| I | **my** | ***My** flat is small.* |
| you | **your** | *Is this **your** book?* |
| he | **his** | ***His** home is old and beautiful.* |
| she | **her** | *She's here with **her** friend.* |
| we | **our** | *This is **our** home in Madrid.* |
| they | **their** | *Is that **their** home?* |

***your*** *bag* NOT ~~*you're bag*~~
***their*** *house* NOT ~~*they're house*~~

## 2B Plural nouns

**SPELLING: Plural nouns**

| | |
|---|---|
| most words → add *-s* | *book* → *book**s***<br>*boy* → *boy**s***<br>*house* → *house**s*** |
| consonant + *-y* → ~~*-y*~~ add *-ies* | *city* → *cit**ies***<br>*baby* → *bab**ies*** |
| ends in *-o*, *-ch*, *-ss*, *-s*, *-sh* and *-x* → add *-es*<br>Exception: For some *-o* words, add *-s*. | *watch* → *watch**es***<br>*glass* → *glass**es***<br>*photo* → *photo**s*** |
| irregular | *knife* → ***knives*** |

*books* NOT ~~*a books*~~

a book

a ticket

an apple

book**s**

two ticket**s**

apple**s**

## 3A Present simple: *I / you / we / they*

▶ 03.09

| | + | | – | |
|---|---|---|---|---|
| **I** | *I **like*** | *fish.* | *I **don't like*** | *fish.* |
| **you** | *You **eat*** | *meat.* | *You **don't eat*** | *meat.* |
| **we** | *We **eat*** | *a lot of vegetables.* | *We **don't eat*** | *a lot of vegetables.* |
| **they** | *They **like*** | *eggs.* | *They **don't like*** | *eggs.* |

*I **don't like** fish.* NOT ~~*I not like fish.*~~

**Tip**
*I **do not** like rice.* → *I **don't like** rice.*

▶ 03.10

| *Yes/No* questions | Short answers | |
|---|---|---|
| ***Do** I **like** fish?* | *Yes, I **do**.* | *No, I **don't**.* |
| ***Do** you **eat** meat?* | *Yes, you **do**.* | *No, you **don't**.* |
| ***Do** we **eat** a lot of vegetables?* | *Yes, we **do**.* | *No, we **don't**.* |
| ***Do** they **like** eggs?* | *Yes, they **do**.* | *No, they **don't**.* |

***Do you** eat meat?* NOT ~~*You eat meat?*~~
*Yes, **I do**.* NOT ~~*Yes, I like.*~~
*No, **we don't**.* NOT ~~*No, we don't like.*~~

## 2A *be*: *it's / it isn't*; Possessive adjectives

### Part 1: *it's / it isn't*

**a** Complete the sentences with *it's* or *they're*.

1 ____________ a beautiful town near Barcelona.
2 São Paulo and Rio de Janeiro are big cities. ____________ in Brazil.
3 My flat is small. ____________ in a new part of town.
4 Our homes are old. ____________ in a nice part of town.
5 The flats are in an old part of town. ____________ big and beautiful.
6 They're from a small town in China. ____________ near Beijing.

**b** Complete the sentences with *it isn't* or *they aren't*.

1 The houses are in Ravello. ____________ in Naples.
2 'Is this your flat?' 'No, ____________.'
3 Mumbai is a big city. ____________ small.
4 They are from Switzerland. ____________ a big country.
5 They are from Sydney. ____________ from Melbourne.
6 Their flats are very old. ____________ in a new part of town.

**c** Now go back to p. 16.

### Part 2: Possessive adjectives

**a** Complete the sentences.

1 'Hi, I'm Jack. What's ____________ name?' 'I'm Selim.'
2 She's from Brazil and ____________ name's Maria.
3 They're from the UK, and ____________ names are Sam and Erica.
4 We live in Bangkok. ____________ flat is in an old part of town.
5 'Is this ____________ book?' 'Yes, it is. Thank you.'
6 They're from London, but ____________ parents are from Mumbai.

**b** Now go back to p. 17.

## 2B Plural nouns

**a** Write the plurals.

1 an egg ________
2 a knife ________
3 a girl ________
4 a country ________
5 a town ________
6 a phone ________
7 a house ________
8 a city ________

**b** Underline the correct words.

1 Rome is *big city / a big city*.
2 Villajoyosa is *a town / towns* in Spain.
3 It's *small / a small* house.
4 They're new *flat / flats*.
5 Two *bottle / bottles* of water, please.
6 He's a big *baby / babies*.
7 New York and Washington are *cities / citys* in the USA.
8 Two *tickets / ticketes* to London, please.

**c** Now go back to p. 19.

## 3A Present simple: *I / you / we / they*

**a** Complete the sentences with the words in the box.

do (x2) don't (x3) eat

1 I like rice, but I ____________ like bread.
2 ____________ you like fruit?
3 **A** Do they eat meat? **B** Yes, they ____________.
4 We ____________ fruit every day.
5 I eat rice, but I ____________ like it.
6 **A** Do you like fish? **B** No, I ____________.

**b** Look at the information about the Brown family. Write five sentences about them.

| | |
|---|---|
| meat | ✓ |
| fish | ✗ |
| vegetables | ✓ |
| rice | ✓ |
| bread | ✗ |

*They eat … They don't eat …*

**c** Write sentences about things you eat and drink.

*I eat rice. I eat vegetables every day. I don't like coffee …*

**d** Now go back to p. 25.

## 3B Adverbs of frequency

03.20

We **always** have breakfast at 7:00.

I **usually** have a sandwich for lunch.

We **sometimes** eat fish for dinner.

I **never** eat cake.
NOT ~~*I never don't eat cake.*~~

> **Tip**
> Adverbs of frequency go **before** the verb.
> NOT ~~***Always we have** breakfast at 7:00.*~~ OR ~~***We have always** breakfast at 7:00.*~~
> The adverb of frequency ***sometimes*** can go **at the beginning of the sentence**, too.
> ***We sometimes eat** fish for dinner.* OR ***Sometimes we eat** fish for dinner.*

## 4A Present simple: *Wh-* questions

04.05

| ***Wh-* questions with *be*** | |
|---|---|
| *What**'s** your name?* | *My name**'s** Lucia.* |
| *When **are** you at home?* | *We**'re** at home this evening.* |
| *Where **are** they from?* | *They**'re** from Brazil.* |

NOT ~~*What **your name is**?*~~ OR ~~*Where **you are** from?*~~

> **Tip**
> *Wh-* word + *is*/*are* + person (*you*, *they*, etc.)?

04.06

| ***Wh-* questions with other verbs** | |
|---|---|
| *Where **do** you **live**?* | *I **live** in Barcelona.* |
| *What **do** you **study**?* | *We **study** Italian.* |
| *When **do** they **go** to school?* | *They **go** to school at 8:00.* |

NOT ~~*Where **you live**?*~~ OR ~~*Where **live you**?*~~

> **Tip**
> *Wh-* word + *do* + person (*you*, *they*, etc.) + verb?

## 4B Present simple: *he / she / it* positive

04.14

| | + | |
|---|---|---|
| **he** | *My brother **works***<br>*He **lives*** | *in a hotel.*<br>*in a small house.* |
| **she** | *Ingrid **lives***<br>*She **works*** | *in Berlin.*<br>*in an office.* |
| **it** | *My room **has***<br>*It **has*** | *a big window.*<br>*a big table.* |

> **Tip**
> *I/You/We/They **work** in a hotel.*
> *He/She **works** in a hotel.*

**SPELLING: verb + *-s***

| | |
|---|---|
| most verbs<br>→ add ***-s*** | *work* → *work**s***<br>*live* → *live**s*** |
| consonant + ***-y***<br>→ ~~***-y***~~ add ***-ies*** | *study* → *stud**ies*** |
| ends in ***-o***, ***-ch***, ***-ss***, ***-s***, ***-sh*** and ***-x***<br>→ add ***-es*** | *go* → *go**es***<br>*do* → *do**es***<br>*teach* → *teach**es*** |
| irregular | *have* → ***has*** |

*He **studies*** NOT ~~*He **studys***~~
*She **has*** NOT ~~*She **haves***~~

## 3B Adverbs of frequency

**a** Put the words in the correct order to make sentences.

1 sometimes / at 10:00 / have dinner / we
2 I / in the evening / have coffee / never
3 have a sandwich / I / for lunch / usually
4 we / at home / always / have dinner
5 at lunchtime / always / eat fruit / I
6 usually / in a café / I / have lunch

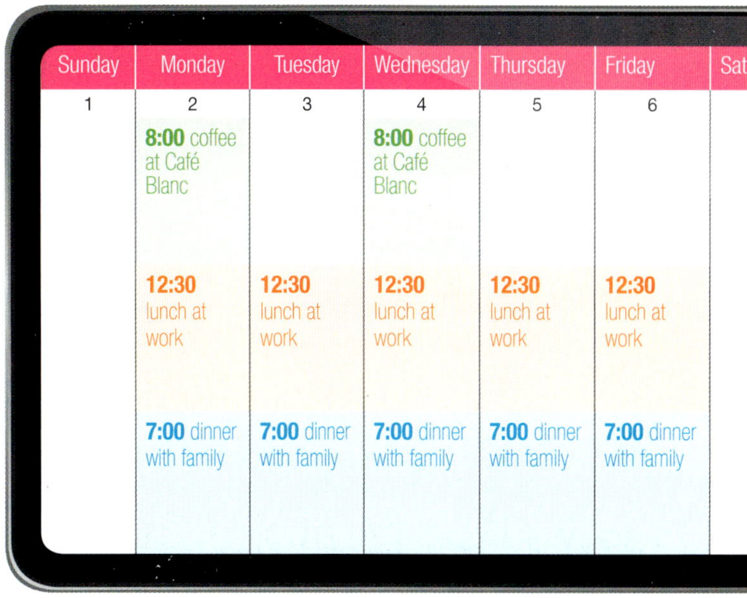


**b** Look at Monica's diary. Complete her sentences with adverbs of frequency.

1 'I ____________ have coffee in a small café.'
2 'I ____________ eat breakfast.'
3 'My friends and I ____________ have lunch at work.'
4 'We ____________ have dinner at home.'

**c** Now go back to p. 27.

## 4A Present simple: *Wh-* questions

**a** Complete the questions with *'s*, *are* or *do*.

1 Where ____________ they work?
2 What ____________ you eat for breakfast?
3 Where ____________ your home?
4 When ____________ you at university?
5 Where ____________ you study English?
6 Where ____________ you from?
7 What time ____________ you go to university every day?
8 What ____________ your address?

**b** Write questions for the sentences. Use the question word in brackets.

1 I work in Madrid. (where)
*Where do you work?*
2 We go to work at 7:00 in the morning. (when)
3 I eat a sandwich for lunch. (what)
4 We study at a big language school in Madrid. (where)
5 I study business at university. (what)
6 I go to my lesson at 6:00 in the evening. (when)

**c** Now go back to p. 33.

## 4B Present simple: *he / she / it* positive

**a** Underline the correct words.

1 She always *drink* / *drinks* tea for breakfast.
2 My son *studies* / *studys* Spanish at university.
3 He *works* / *workes* in a supermarket.
4 The car *have* / *has* new lights.
5 She has breakfast and then she *gos* / *goes* to school.
6 The dog *play* / *plays* in the garden.

**b** Look at the picture. Complete the sentences about Carmen with the verbs in the box.

| have | drink | eat | live | study |
|---|---|---|---|---|

1 She ____________ in Madrid.
2 She ____________ English.
3 She ____________ bananas.
4 She ____________ coffee.
5 She ____________ a computer.

**c** Now go back to p. 35.

## 5A *there is* / *there are*: positive

On Regent Street, …
… **there's** a cinema.
… **there are** two cafés.
… **there are** a lot of people.

*There's = There is*
***There's** a café.* NOT ~~***There** a café.*~~
***There are** three cafés.*
NOT ~~***There's three** cafés.*~~

05.02

| | + | |
|---|---|---|
| **Singular** | ***There's*** | *a café.*<br>*one café.* |
| **Plural** | ***There are*** | *cafés.*<br>*three cafés.* |

## 5B *there is* / *there are*: negative and questions

05.16

| | – | | – | |
|---|---|---|---|---|
| **Singular** | ***There isn't*** | *a shower.*<br>*a blanket.* | ***There's no*** | *shower.*<br>*blanket.* |
| **Plural** | ***There aren't*** | *any pillows.*<br>*any rooms.* | ***There are no*** | *pillows.*<br>*rooms.* |

NOT ~~***There's isn't** shower.*~~ OR ~~***There's no** a shower.*~~
NOT ~~***There are no** any pillows.*~~

**Tip**
*There **is not** a hotel.* → *There **isn't** a hotel.* → *There**'s no** hotel.*
*There **are not** any cafés.* → *There **aren't** any cafés.* → *There **are no** cafés.*
Use *any* after *there are not* and *there aren't.*

05.17

| | *Yes/No* questions | | Short answers | |
|---|---|---|---|---|
| **Singular** | ***Is there*** | *a café?* | *Yes, **there is**.* | *No, **there isn't**.* |
| **Plural** | ***Are there*** | *any small rooms?* | *Yes, **there are**.* | *No, **there aren't**.* |

NOT ~~***There is** a café?*~~ OR ~~***There are** small rooms?*~~
NOT ~~*Yes, there**'s**.*~~ OR ~~*No, there **not**.*~~

**Tip**
Use *any* after *Are there … ?*

## 5A *there is / there are*: positive

**a** Write three more sentences about Regent Street on page 122. Use *there's* or *there are* and the words in the box.

flat car supermarket

1 ______________________________
2 ______________________________
3 ______________________________

**b** Look at the picture. Change the sentences to make them true.

1 There's a taxi.
2 There are two restaurants.
3 There's one shop.
4 There are three women.
5 There are three girls.
6 There's a boy.
7 There are two schools.

**c** Now go back to p. 40.

## 5B *there is / there are*: negative and questions

**a** Complete the sentences with a negative (–) or question (?) form of *there is* or *there are*.

1 ____________ any cafés on my street.
2 ____________ a cinema in this part of town.
3 ____________ a hotel near the underground station?
4 ____________ any shops near the hotel?
5 ____________ any restaurants on High Street.
6 ____________ a café near here?
7 ____________ a restaurant near the cinema.
8 ____________ any supermarkets near the hostel?

**b** Add *any* to the sentences if possible.

1 There aren't good restaurants in this town.
2 Are there shops near the hotel?
3 Is there a TV in the room?
4 Sorry, there aren't free rooms.
5 There's a café on the first floor.
6 There are two cinemas near here.

**c** Complete the conversation with the correct form of *there is / there are*.

**A** Excuse me, ____________ ____________ any hotels near here?
**B** No, ____________ ____________. But ____________ one near the train station.
**A** And ____________ ____________ a restaurant near the hotel?
**B** Yes, ____________ ____________. It's a very good one.

**d** Rewrite the sentences using *there's no* or *there are no*.

1 There isn't a TV in the room. There's no TV in the room.
2 There aren't hotels on this street. ____________
3 There aren't any pillows in the room. ____________
4 There isn't a swimming pool. ____________
5 There isn't a school in the town. ____________
6 There aren't petrol stations on this road. ____________

**e** Now go back to p. 43.

## 6A Present simple: *he / she / it* negative

06.05

| | – | |
|---|---|---|
| **he** | *He **doesn't work*** | *on Monday.* |
| **she** | *She **doesn't study*** | *Spanish.* |
| **it** | *The village **doesn't have*** | *a school.* |

*He **doesn't work** on Monday.* NOT ~~*He doesn't work**s** on Monday.*~~
OR ~~*He **don't works** on Monday.*~~
OR ~~*He **not works** on Monday.*~~

**Tip**

*I **do not work** at night.* → *I **don't work** at night.*
*He **does not work** at night.* → *He **doesn't work** at night.*

## 6B Present simple: *he / she / it* questions

06.13

| | *Yes/No* questions | | Short answers | |
|---|---|---|---|---|
| **he** | ***Does** he* | ***work** at a bank?* | *Yes, he **does**.* | *No, he **doesn't**.* |
| **she** | ***Does** she* | ***get up** early?* | *Yes, she **does**.* | *No, she **doesn't**.* |
| **it** | ***Does** the party* | ***start** at 9:00?* | *Yes, it **does**.* | *No, it **doesn't**.* |

***Does he work** in a bank?* NOT ~~*Does he work**s** … ?*~~
*Yes, **she does**.* NOT ~~*Yes, she **works**.*~~
*No, **she doesn't**.* NOT ~~*No, she **doesn't work**.*~~

06.14

| | *Wh-* questions | | |
|---|---|---|---|
| **he** | *Where* | ***does** he* | ***work**?* |
| **she** | *When* | ***does** she* | ***get up**?* |
| **it** | *What time* | ***does** it* | ***start**?* |

*Where **does she** work?* NOT ~~*Where **she does** work?*~~
OR ~~*Where **she works**?*~~

Does she get up early?

## 6A Present simple: *he / she / it* negative

**a** Complete the sentences with *don't* or *doesn't*.

1 They __don't__ speak French.
2 He ______ like chocolate cake.
3 She ______ eat eggs for breakfast.
4 We ______ go to work early.
5 Eva and Ben ______ like their jobs.
6 Penelope and her sister ______ live in Spain.
7 Her brother ______ work in a bank.
8 My sister, Lucia, and I ______ eat fish.

**b** Make the sentences negative.

1 Pia works in a shop. *Pia doesn't work in a shop.*
2 My brother works in a car factory.
3 My parents like coffee.
4 We live near the station.
5 He studies Italian.
6 They go to work early.
7 Akira lives in Tokyo.
8 Their son works in a bank.

**c** Now go back to p. 49.

## 6B Present simple: *he / she / it* questions

**a** Complete the questions.

1 **A** He works in a restaurant.
**B** ______ he like it?
2 **A** I'm a taxi driver.
**B** ______ you meet interesting people?
3 **A** My brother's in London.
**B** ______ he live there?
4 **A** My children go to school at 7:30.
**B** What time ______ they get up?
5 **A** She often works in the evenings.
**B** When ______ she get home?

**b** Underline the correct words.

1 **A** Does your daughter like school?
**B** Yes, she *likes / does*. She thinks it's great.
2 **A** Do you like ice cream?
**B** *Yes / No*, I don't. I never eat it.
3 **A** Does he watch football?
**B** No, he *don't / doesn't*. He only likes tennis.
4 **A** Do you start work early?
**B** Yes, we *are / do*. We start at 5:00 in the morning!
5 **A** Does your wife work in a restaurant?
**B** No, she *doesn't work / doesn't*. She's a hotel receptionist.

**c** Now go back to p. 51.

## 7A *this, that, these, those*

07.06

*this, these* = here, near me

*'My brother wants* ***this*** *car.'*

*'I love* ***these*** *flowers.'*

*that, those* = there, not near me

*'My sister wants* ***that*** *car.'*

*'I love* ***those*** *flowers.'*

| | | |
|---|---|---|
| **Singular** | ***this*** *car* | ***that*** *car* |
| **Plural** | ***these*** *flowers* | ***those*** *flowers* |

| ***this / that / these / those* + *be*** |
|---|
| ***That's*** *my car.* |
| ***These are*** *your flowers.* |
| ***Those are*** *my books.* |
| ***Is this*** *your bag?* |

| ***this / that / these / those* + noun** |
|---|
| *I like* ***that car****.* |
| ***These flowers*** *are beautiful.* |
| ***Those books*** *are big.* |
| ***This bag*** *is red.* |

## 7B Possessive *'s*

07.17

Kristina's Zane**'s** sister. → Kristina is Zane**'s** sister.
Millie's Kristina**'s** friend. → Millie is Kristina**'s** friend.
**KRISTINA** My brother**'s** jeans are light blue. NOT ~~***The jeans of my brother*** *are light blue.*~~
The girls**'** dresses are beautiful.

Zane and Kristina**'s** parents are Lara and Jim.

> **Tip**
>
> We use **'** after the *-s* for plural nouns ending in *-s*.
> → *The* ***girls'*** *dresses are beautiful.* (2+ girls)
>
> We use ***'s*** after a singular noun.
> → *The* ***girl's*** *dresses are beautiful.* (1 girl)

## 7A *this, that, these, those*

**a** Underline the correct words.

1 Excuse me, is *this / these* your coat?
2 Who's *this / that* man in the next room?
3 How much are *those / that* watches?
4 This *is / are* my wife, Tammy.
5 Are *this / these* your glasses?

**b** Complete the sentences with *this*, *that*, *these* or *those*.

1 'Look at ___________ beautiful house.'

2 '___________ are our tickets.'

3 'Who are ___________ people?'

4 'Is ___________ your phone?'

**c** Now go back to p. 57.

## 7B Possessive *'s*

**a** Complete the sentences with the words in brackets.

1 It's Mara's skirt. (Mara / skirt)
2 It's ___________. (Steven / shirt)
3 It's ___________. (Beth / dress)
4 They're ___________. (Luke / jeans)
5 They're ___________. (Sara / shoes)
6 It's ___________. (Matthew / jacket)

**b** Write new sentences. Use the names in brackets.

1 **His** new jeans are dark blue. (Sam)
*Sam's new jeans are dark blue.*
2 **His** house is near the train station. (Jacob)
3 **Her** shoes are brown. (Vanessa)
4 I like **her** new coat. (my friend)
5 **Their** new car is blue. (Rob and Emma)
6 **Her** new dress is pretty. (Penelope)
7 He's **his** best friend. (Ryan)
8 **Their** room is on the first floor. (the boys)

**c** Now go back to p. 59.

## 8A Past simple: *be*

### Part 1: Positive

08.02

| | + | |
|---|---|---|
| **I/you/he/she/it** | *I* **was**<br>*You* **were**<br>*He/She* **was**<br>*It* **was** | *in Munich yesterday.*<br>*in Madrid yesterday.*<br>*in Rome yesterday.*<br>*fun.* |
| **we/you/they** | *We* **were**<br>*You* **were**<br>*They* **were** | *in Istanbul last weekend.*<br>*in Moscow last weekend.*<br>*in Paris last weekend.* |

*She* **was** *in Rome yesterday.* NOT ~~*She* **is** *in Rome yesterday.*~~
OR ~~*She* **were** *in Rome yesterday.*~~

> **Tip**
> We often use past forms of *be* with past time expressions like *yesterday, last night, two days ago, on Saturday, this morning.* (See Vocabulary Focus 8A on p. 149.)

### Part 2: Negative and questions

08.08

| | – | |
|---|---|---|
| **I/you/he/she/it** | *I* **wasn't**<br>*You* **weren't**<br>*He/She* **wasn't**<br>*It* **wasn't** | *in Munich yesterday.*<br>*in Madrid yesterday.*<br>*in Rome yesterday.*<br>*fun.* |
| **we/you/they** | *We* **weren't**<br>*You* **weren't**<br>*They* **weren't** | *in Istanbul last weekend.*<br>*in Moscow last weekend.*<br>*in Paris last weekend.* |

*I* **wasn't** *at home yesterday.* NOT ~~*I'm not at home yesterday.*~~
OR ~~*I* **not was** *home yesterday.*~~

> **Tip**
> *I* **was not** *in Munich yesterday.* → *I* **wasn't** *in Munich yesterday.*
> *You* **were not** *in Madrid yesterday.* → *You* **weren't** *in Madrid yesterday.*

08.09

| *Yes/No* questions | | Short answers | |
|---|---|---|---|
| **Were** *you* | *in Madrid yesterday?* | *Yes, I* **was**. | *No, I* **wasn't**. |
| **Was** *she* | *in Rome yesterday?* | *Yes, she* **was**. | *No, she* **wasn't**. |
| **Were** *they* | *in Paris yesterday?* | *Yes, they* **were**. | *No, they* **weren't**. |

08.10

| *Wh-* questions | | |
|---|---|---|
| *Where* | **was** *she* | *yesterday?* |
| *When* | **was** | *the meeting?* |
| *Where* | **were** *you* | *yesterday?* |
| *When* | **were** *they* | *in Milan?* |

*Where* **were you** *yesterday?* NOT ~~*Where* **you were** *yesterday?*~~

## 8B Past simple: positive

08.15

| Regular verbs | + | |
|---|---|---|
| **talk** | *I* **talked** | *to Sue yesterday.* |
| **play** | *They* **played** | *tennis on Saturday.* |
| **like** | *He was nice – I* **liked** | *him.* |
| **arrive** | *They* **arrived** | *last night.* |

*I* **talked** *to her.* NOT ~~*I* **was talk** *to her.*~~

### SPELLING: *-ed* endings

| | |
|---|---|
| most verbs<br>→ add ***-ed*** | *talk* → *talk**ed***<br>*play* → *play**ed*** |
| verb ends in ***-e***<br>→ add ***-d*** | *like* → *like**d*** |

08.16

| Irregular verbs | + | |
|---|---|---|
| **go** | *I* **went** | *to a party on Friday.* |
| **have** | *We* **had** | *sandwiches for lunch.* |
| **see** | *I* **saw** | *Peter yesterday.* |

*I* **went** *to a party.* NOT ~~*I* **goed** *to a party.*~~
*We* **had** *sandwiches.* NOT ~~*We* **did** *have sandwiches.*~~

See Irregular verbs on p. 103.

> **Tip**
> The past simple form is the same for all persons, e.g. *I played tennis., He played tennis., We played tennis.*, etc.

## 8A Past simple: *be*

### Part 1: Positive

**a** Complete the sentences with *was* or *were*.

1 I ____________ at home yesterday.
2 He ____________ in the office in the morning, but not in the afternoon.
3 We ____________ at the cinema last night.
4 They ____________ in Bangkok last month.
5 Two nights ago you ____________ at your sister's house.
6 The film ____________ really good.
7 You ____________ at school last week.
8 Ben and Jorge ____________ at the football match on Saturday.
9 The concert ____________ very good.
10 This morning I ____________ at a café.

**b** Now go back to p. 65.

### Part 2: Negative and questions

**a** Complete the text with *was*, *were*, *wasn't* or *weren't*.

'It [1]____________ Saturday yesterday, but I [2]____________ at work all morning. I [3]____________ (not) at my desk – I [4]____________ in a meeting. It [5]____________ very boring. In the afternoon I [6]____________ at home with a book – it [7]____________ great. In the evening my friend Michelle and I [8]____________ at the cinema, but the film [9]____________ (not) very good. We [10]____________ tired, so I [11]____________ (not) out late.'

**b** Put the words in the correct order to make questions.

1 last night / were you / at the cinema ?
*Were you at the cinema last night?*
2 football match / was / on Saturday / he at the ?
3 were / the supermarket / they at / yesterday ?
4 you three / where were / years ago ?
5 interesting / film / was the ?
6 China / you in / when were ?
7 was the / concert / where ?
8 a boring / was it / meeting ?

**c** Now go back to p. 65.

## 8B Past simple: positive

**a** Match verbs 1–6 with the past forms in the box.

arrived had watched saw stayed went

1 go ____________
2 have ____________
3 stay ____________
4 see ____________
5 watch ____________
6 arrive ____________

**b** Underline the correct words.

1 She *goed* / *went* to Spain last week.
2 I *was sees* / *saw* my sister last weekend.
3 It wasn't a very interesting evening. Everyone *talkd* / *talked* about work.
4 I *staied* / *stayed* in a cheap hotel near the train station.
5 We *watch* / *watched* Germany vs Uruguay last night.
6 She *read* / *readed* a magazine in the garden.

**c** Complete the text with the past form of the verbs in the box.

have (x2) go (x2) stay read talk watch ~~get~~

Last Saturday, Mr Jones [1]*got* up late and he [2]____________ a big breakfast. Then he [3]____________ shopping. He [4]____________ a pizza for lunch and in the afternoon, he [5]____________ to his mother on the phone for an hour. In the evening he [6]____________ at home and he [7]____________ football on TV. He [8]____________ to bed at 10:30 and [9]____________ a book until 11:00.

**d** Complete the sentences about you or your friends. Use the past simple.

1 Last weekend, ______________________________.
2 Yesterday, ______________________________.
3 This morning, ______________________________.
4 Last Monday, ______________________________.

**e** Now go back to p. 67.

## 9A Past simple: negative

She **didn't get** a taxi to the airport.

09.07

| | – | |
|---|---|---|
| **stay** | *We **didn't stay*** | *at a hostel.* |
| **finish** | *They **didn't finish*** | *work early.* |
| **see** | *I **didn't see*** | *them at the party.* |
| **get** | *She **didn't get*** | *a taxi to the airport.* |

*I **didn't see** them.* NOT ~~*I don't saw them.*~~
*We **didn't stay**.* NOT ~~*We didn't stayed.*~~

**Tip**
In the negative:
- add *didn't* before the verb
- the verb doesn't change

## 9B Past simple: questions

09.19

| *Yes/No* questions | | Short answers | |
|---|---|---|---|
| ***Did** you* | ***see** the concert?* | *Yes, you **did**.* | *No, you **didn't**.* |
| ***Did** she* | ***work** in a café?* | *Yes, she **did**.* | *No, she **didn't**.* |
| ***Did** they* | ***go** to the party?* | *Yes, they **did**.* | *No, they **didn't**.* |

***Did** you **work** … ?* NOT ~~***Did** you **worked** … ?*~~
***Did** she **go** … ?* NOT ~~***Did** she **went** … ?*~~
*Yes, she **did**.* NOT ~~*Yes, she **worked**.*~~
*No, she **didn't**.* NOT ~~*No, she **didn't work**.*~~

09.20

| *Wh-* questions | | |
|---|---|---|
| *Where* | ***did** you* | ***work**?* |
| *Where* | ***did** she* | ***go**?* |
| *When* | ***did** they* | ***arrive**?* |

*Where **did** you **work**?* NOT ~~*Where you **worked**?*~~
OR ~~*Where did you **worked**?*~~
*Where **did** she **go**?* NOT ~~*Where did she **went**?*~~

## 10A Present continuous: positive

We use the present continuous to talk about now.

10.07

| | + |
|---|---|
| **I** | ***I'm writing** an email.* |
| **you** | ***You're working** a lot.* |
| **he/she** | ***He's**/**She's studying**.* |
| **it** | ***It's raining**.* |
| **we** | ***We're watching** TV.* |
| **they** | ***They're eating** a big dinner.* |

***I'm working** hard.* NOT ~~*I working hard.*~~ OR ~~*I'm work hard.*~~
***I'm having** breakfast.* NOT ~~*I'm haveing breakfast.*~~
***I'm sitting** in the car.* NOT ~~*I'm siting in the car.*~~

"It's **raining** and I'm **writing** this email ..."

**Tip**
*I'**m writing** an email.* → *I **am writing** an email.*
*We'**re watching** TV.* → *We **are watching** TV.*
*He'**s studying**.* → *He **is studying**.*

## 9A Past simple: negative

**a** Complete the sentences with the past simple negative form of the verbs in brackets.

1 I _didn't play_ football. (play)
2 I ______ early. (get up)
3 I ______ cereal for breakfast. (have)
4 I ______ my phone. (use)
5 I ______ my emails. (read)
6 I ______ a friend. (visit)
7 I ______ shopping. (go)
8 I ______ any photos. (take)
9 I ______ to the radio. (listen)

**b** Look at the pictures. Complete the sentences with the verbs in the box. Make one positive and one negative sentence.

arrive play go (x2) have ~~get up~~

1 Last week, John _didn't get up_ at 6:00. He _got up_ at 7:00.

2 He ______ to work by bus. He ______ to work by train.

3 He ______ at work at 9:00. He ______ at work at 10:00.

4 He ______ pizza for lunch. He ______ spaghetti.

5 After work, he ______ football. He ______ tennis.

6 In the evening, he ______ to the cinema. He ______ to a restaurant.

**c** Now go back to p. 73.

## 9B Past simple: questions

**a** Put the words in the correct order to make questions.

1 you go / where did / on holiday ?
2 see / what did / you ?
3 you have / did / a good time ?
4 you / meet / who did ?
5 you / what did / eat ?
6 like it / you / did ?

**b** Complete the questions with *did* or *do/does*.

1 Where ______ you go last night?
2 ______ you see Jim yesterday?
3 What time ______ he go to work every day?
4 ______ they go to the cinema every Saturday?
5 What ______ you do after class last week?
6 What time ______ their lessons usually start?
7 What time ______ she start work yesterday?
8 Who ______ you see at the party last night?

**c** Complete the answers to the questions.

1 **A** Did you go home early?
**B** Yes, _I_ _did_. I left at 4:00.
2 **A** Did they enjoy their holiday?
**B** No, ______ ______. It was boring.
3 **A** Did he watch the football match?
**B** No, ______ ______. He was at the cinema.
4 **A** Did you go to the supermarket?
**B** Yes, ______ ______. We got some bread and cheese.
5 **A** Did your sister work in a restaurant?
**B** No, ______ ______. She worked in a café.

**d** Now go back to p. 75.

## 10A Present continuous: positive

**a** Write the *-ing* forms of the verbs.

1 eat ______
2 cook ______
3 talk ______
4 listen ______
5 get ______
6 have ______
7 wear ______
8 go ______

**b** Complete the sentences with the present continuous form of the verbs in brackets.

1 I (wear) jeans and a T-shirt.
2 We (listen) to Drake's new song.
3 Lee (study) in her bedroom.
4 They (have) dinner at the moment.
5 Rob and Ben (play) football in the park.
6 He (watch) a film in the living room.
7 Our children (cook) dinner for us.
8 I (write) this email at work.

**c** Now go back to p. 81.

## 10B Present continuous: negative and questions

10.15

| | – |
|---|---|
| I | *I'm* ***not waiting*** *for the bus.* |
| you | *You* ***aren't listening****!* |
| he/she | *She* ***isn't reading*** *a book.* |
| it | *It* ***isn't raining****.* |
| we | *We* ***aren't staying*** *in a hostel.* |
| they | *They* ***aren't working****.* |

*She* ***isn't reading****.* NOT ~~*She not reading.*~~ OR ~~*She's not read.*~~

10.16

| ***Yes/No*** **questions** | | **Short answers** | |
|---|---|---|---|
| ***Are*** *you* | ***waiting*** *for the bus?* | *Yes, you* ***are****.* | *No, you* ***aren't****.* |
| ***Is*** *she* | ***reading*** *a book?* | *Yes, she* ***is****.* | *No, she* ***isn't****.* |
| ***Is*** *it* | ***raining****?* | *Yes, it* ***is****.* | *No, it* ***isn't****.* |
| ***Are*** *they* | ***working****?* | *Yes, they* ***are****.* | *No, they* ***aren't****.* |

***Are you*** *waiting?* NOT ~~*You waiting? You are waiting?*~~

10.17

| | ***Wh-*** **questions** | | |
|---|---|---|---|
| you | *What* | ***are*** *you* | ***doing****?* |
| he/she | *Where* | ***is*** *he* | ***going****?* |
| it | *Why* | ***is*** *it* | ***raining****?* |
| they | *What* | ***are*** *they* | ***watching****?* |

*What* ***are you*** *doing?* NOT ~~*What you are doing?*~~

## 11A Object pronouns

10.08

| Subject pronouns | Object pronouns | |
|---|---|---|
| I | me | ***I*** *talked to Mark last night. He called* ***me****.* |
| you | you | ***You*** *were in town yesterday. I saw* ***you****.* |
| he | him | ***He****'s a great singer. I like* ***him****.* |
| she | her | ***She*** *lives nearby. I often visit* ***her****.* |
| it | it | *I live near Henley.* ***It****'s a nice town. I like* ***it****.* |
| we | us | ***We*** *were at the party. Did you see* ***us****?* |
| they | them | *These shoes are nice, but* ***they****'re expensive. I can't buy* ***them****.* |

*He called* ***me****.* NOT ~~*He called I.*~~

**Tip**

We use *it* and *them* to talk about things and places.

***It*** *isn't a very interesting book. I don't want to finish* ***it****.*

NOT ~~***She*** *isn't an interesting book. I don't want to finish* ***her****.*~~

***It****'s a nice town. I like* ***it****.*

NOT ~~***He****'s a nice town. I like* ***him****.*~~

## 10B Present continuous: negative and questions

**a** Complete the sentences using the negative form of the present continuous.

1 She isn't studying (study). She's watching TV.
2 They ____________ (have) lunch. They're having breakfast.
3 I ____________ (work). I'm at home.
4 He ____________ (play) football. He's watching the match.
5 We ____________ (stay) in a hotel. We're camping.
6 Are you OK? You ____________ (eat).

**b** Put the words in the correct order to make questions.

1 wearing / a coat / you / why / are ?
2 working / she / is ?
3 you / doing / are / what ?
4 are / where / going / you ?
5 she / is / texting / who ?
6 a video game / playing / he / is ?

**c** Write two questions to ask your partner about now. Use the present continuous. Ask and answer your questions.

**d** Now go back to p. 83.

## 11A Object pronouns

**a** Underline the correct words.

1 We're waiting at the station. Please come and meet *we* / *us*.
2 She was in town. We saw *her* / *him* there.
3 My parents live in London. *It* / *They* have a small flat.
4 I bought a pizza. Do you want to have *it* / *her* for dinner?
5 Where are my keys? Do you have *they* / *them* in your bag?
6 Here's a photo of my new boyfriend. I met *it* / *him* two months ago at a party.

**b** Complete the text with the words in the box.

he she it we me him her us

**c** Write sentences about your favourite things and people. Use pronouns in your sentences.

**d** Now go back to p. 89.

### JULIE THOMPSON, ACTOR

MY FAVOURITE THINGS AND PEOPLE ...

**1 My car**

It's a very old Volkswagen, but I use [1]____________ every day.

**2 My brother**

[2]____________ works in Japan, so we don't see [3]____________ very often, but he always stays with [4]____________ on New Year's Eve.

**3 The singer Lana Del Rey**

I think [5]____________'s a wonderful singer. I can listen to [6]____________ for hours.

**4 My husband, Paul**

We got married 30 years ago and [7]____________'re very happy. He always listens to [8]____________ when I have problems.

## 11B *can* for ability

### Part 1: Positive and negative

We use *can* to talk about things we know how to do.

11.09

| | | | |
|---|---|---|---|
| + | I/You/He/She/It/We/They | ***can*** | ***swim.*** |
| – | | ***can't*** | ***swim.*** |

*I* ***can swim*** *well.* NOT ~~*I can to swim well.*~~
*She* ***can swim*** *well.* NOT ~~*She cans swim well.*~~
*He* ***can't swim*** *well.* NOT ~~*He not can swim well.*~~

**Tip**
*I* ***cannot*** *swim.* → *I* ***can't*** *swim.*
For all persons (*I/you/he/she/it/we/they*), *can/can't* and the verb don't change.

### Part 2: Questions

11.14

| *Yes/No* questions | + | – |
|---|---|---|
| ***Can*** *you* ***swim****?* | *Yes, I* ***can****.* | *No, I* ***can't****.* |
| ***Can*** *she* ***swim****?* | *Yes, she* ***can****.* | *No, she* ***can't****.* |
| ***Can*** *they* ***swim****?* | *Yes, they* ***can****.* | *No, they* ***can't****.* |

***Can you*** *swim?* NOT ~~*You can swim?*~~
*Yes,* ***I can****.* NOT ~~*Yes, I swim.*~~
*No,* ***I can't****.* NOT ~~*No, I not swim.*~~

## 12A *be going to*: positive and negative

### Part 1: Positive

We use *be + going to* to talk about things we plan to do in the future.

12.02

| | + | | |
|---|---|---|---|
| **I** | ***I'm*** | ***going to*** | ***have*** *a cup of coffee.* |
| **you/we/they** | ***You're*** | | ***go*** *shopping.* |
| **he/she/it** | ***She's*** | | ***have*** *chicken tonight.* |

***I'm going to have*** *a bath.* NOT ~~*I going to have a bath.*~~
OR ~~*I'm going have a bath.*~~
OR ~~*I'm go to have a bath.*~~

### Part 2: Negative

12.08

| | – | | |
|---|---|---|---|
| **I** | ***I'm not*** | ***going to*** | ***go*** *on holiday.* |
| **you/we/they** | ***You aren't*** | | ***read*** *a book.* |
| **he/she/it** | ***She isn't*** | | ***visit*** *her sister.* |

***We're not going to have*** *a bath.*
NOT ~~*We're going not to have a bath.*~~

## 12B *be going to*: questions

12.16

| *Yes/No* questions | | | Short answers | |
|---|---|---|---|---|
| ***Am*** *I* | ***going to*** | ***see*** *you soon?* | *Yes, I* ***am****.* | *No,* ***I'm not****.* |
| ***Are*** *you* | | ***go*** *out?* | *Yes, you* ***are****.* | *No, you* ***aren't****.* |
| ***Is*** *he* | | ***leave*** *home?* | *Yes, he* ***is****.* | *No, he* ***isn't****.* |

***Are you going to*** *… ?* NOT ~~*You are going to … ?*~~
*Yes,* ***I am****.* NOT ~~*Yes, I'm going.*~~

12.17

| | *Wh-* questions | | | |
|---|---|---|---|---|
| **I** | *When* | ***am*** *I* | ***going to*** | ***see*** *you?* |
| **you/we/they** | *What* | ***are*** *you* | | ***do****?* |
| **he/she/it** | *Where* | ***is*** *he* | | ***live****?* |

*What* ***are you going to*** *do?* NOT ~~*What you going to do?*~~
OR ~~*What you are going to do?*~~

## 11B *can* for ability

### Part 1: Positive and negative

**a** Complete the sentences with *can* or *can't*.

1 I studied Spanish at university for three years. I ____________ speak with Spanish people.
2 Her meals are terrible. She ____________ cook!
3 My brother and I don't like the sea or swimming pools. We ____________ swim.
4 I went to guitar lessons. Now I ____________ play some easy songs.
5 I don't have a bike, but I ____________ ride one.
6 I don't like that band. They ____________ sing.

**b** Now go to p. 91.

### Part 2: Questions

**a** Put the words in the correct order to make questions.

1 you ride / can / a horse ?
2 well / cook / can he ?
3 sing and / can / play the guitar / they ?
4 can / draw pictures / she ?
5 speak / both Japanese / can you / and Mandarin ?
6 he drive / a car and / can / a bus ?

**b** Now go back to p. 91.

## 12A *be going to*: positive and negative

### Part 1: Positive

**a** Complete the sentences with *going to* and the verb in brackets.

1 I'm hungry. I'm ____________ (eat) a sandwich.
2 The house is dirty. He's ____________ (clean) it today.
3 We're bored. We're ____________ (watch) a film.
4 It's very cold today. I'm ____________ (wear) a coat.
5 She's tired. She's ____________ (go) to bed.

**b** Now go back to p. 96.

### Part 2: Negative

**a** Put the words in the correct order to make sentences.

1 his homework at / he's going / the weekend / to do
2 visit my parents / aren't / next week / we / going to
3 going to / Friday night / I'm / party on / have a
4 they aren't / to play football / going / on Saturday
5 not / cook dinner / she's / going to / this evening
6 to meet / tomorrow evening / we're going / some friends

**b** Complete the conversation with the correct form of *be going to* and the verb in brackets.

**A** What are your plans for this evening?
**B** I [1]____________ (stay) home.
**A** That's not very interesting.
**B** Maybe not. But I [2]____________ (cook) a nice dinner.
**A** OK, and then maybe watch a film?
**B** No, I [3]____________ (not / watch) a film. I [4]____________ (read) a book. And you?
**A** Well, I [5]____________ (not / cook) dinner. I [6]____________ (get) a pizza and then I [7]____________ (go) to a party. Do you want to come?
**B** No, thanks. I [8]____________ (have) a quiet evening.

**c** Now go back to p. 97.

## 12B *be going to*: questions

**a** Make questions with *be going to*.

1 you / watch / a film / tonight?
Are you going to watch a film tonight?
2 what / you / do / this evening?
3 they / go / Italy / next summer?
4 when / you / have / lunch?
5 how / she / get to / the airport?
6 when / we / clean / the flat?

**b** Complete the questions with *be going to* and the words in brackets.

1 **A** ____________ home tonight? (you / stay)
**B** No, we aren't. We're going to go out.
2 **A** What ____________? (she / buy)
**B** A new coat.
3 **A** ____________ shopping? (you / go)
**B** Yes, I am. Do you want to come with me?
4 **A** Who ____________? (they / invite)
**B** Oh, just a few friends. They don't want to have a big party.
5 **A** ____________ TV? (he / watch)
**B** No, he isn't. He's going to work.

**c** Now go back to p. 99.

## 1A Countries

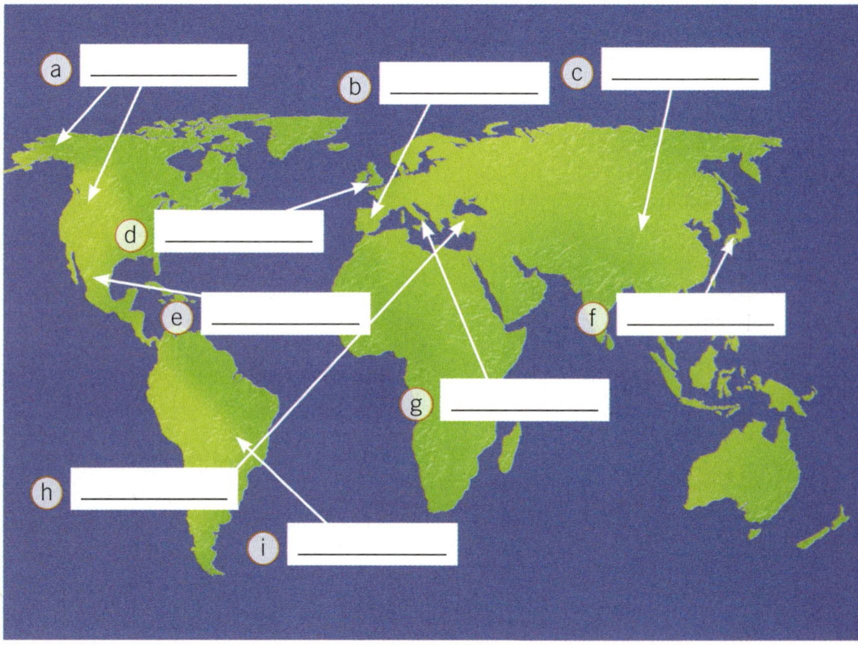


**a** 01.11 Listen and write the countries on the map.

the USA Brazil the UK / Britain
Turkey Spain Mexico Italy
China Japan

> **Tip**
> the USA = the United States of America
> the UK = the United Kingdom

**b** 01.11 Listen again and practise saying the countries.

**c** Add the name of your country in English to the list in a. Practise saying it.

**d** Now go back to p. 9.

## 1B Nationalities

**a** Complete the tables with countries from page 9.

| Country | Nationality |
|---|---|
| | *-ian* |
| 1 ____________ | Brazilian |
| Australia | Australian |
| Italy | Italian |
| | *-an* |
| 2 ____________ | Mexican |
| 3 ____________ / The United States of America | American |

| Country | Nationality |
|---|---|
| | *-ish* |
| 4 ____________ | Spanish |
| 5 ____________ / The United Kingdom | British |
| 6 ____________ | Turkish |
| | *-ese* |
| 7 ____________ | Chinese |
| 8 ____________ | Japanese |

**b** 01.14 Listen and repeat the countries and nationalities.

**c** Write your nationality.

I'm ____________.

**d** Work in pairs.

Student A: Say a country.
Student B: Say the nationality.

Then swap roles.

Brazil

Brazilian

**e** Now go back to p. 10.

## 2A Common adjectives

**a** 02.09 Listen and repeat the adjectives.

1 small

big

2 old

new

3 good

bad

4 happy

sad

5 interesting

boring

6 easy

difficult

7 right

wrong

8 beautiful

9 funny

**b** Work in pairs.

Student A: Say an adjective.
Student B: Say the opposite.

happy

sad

**c** Complete the sentences with an adjective. There is no correct answer.

1 New York is a ____________ city.
2 Harry Potter books are ____________.
3 My house is very ____________.
4 The English language is ____________ for me.
5 My best friend is ____________.

Tell a partner your sentences. Are the adjectives the same?

**d** Now go back to p. 17.

## 2B Common objects 1

a book (books)

a bottle of water (bottles of water)

a computer (computers)

a key (keys)

a newspaper (newspapers)

a knife (knives)

a phone (phones)

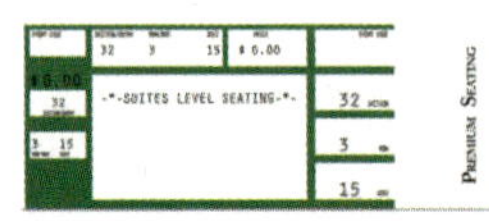
a ticket (tickets)

a watch (watches)

an umbrella (umbrellas)

**a** 02.12 Listen and repeat the objects.

**b** Write three objects on three pieces of paper. Don't show your partner!

*a phone* *an umbrella* *a book*

**c** Guess your partner's words.

Is it a watch?
No.
Is it a book?
Yes.

**d** Now go back to p. 18.

## 5B Hotels

**a** 05.11 Listen and repeat the words.

bath

room

bed

pillow

shower

wi-fi

blanket

car park

TV

towel

*There's wi-fi in the room.* NOT ~~There's a wi-fi in the room.~~ OR ~~There are wi-fi in the room.~~

**b** Which word is different in each group? Compare your answers with your partner.

1 shower pillow bath
2 TV wi-fi room
3 shower blanket pillow
4 car park towel blanket
5 bed room bath

**c** Now go back to p. 42.

## 3A Food 1

**a** 03.04 Listen and repeat the words.

fruit

vegetables

meat

fish

eggs

bread

rice

**b** Talk to a partner. What food is in the pictures?

1

2

3

4

5

6

**c** Match pictures 1–6 with the words in the box.

coffee cola fruit juice milk tea water

1

2

3

4

5

6

**d** 03.05 Listen and check your answers in c. Practise saying the words.

**e** Talk to your partner. Which drinks are in the pictures?

**f** Now go back to p. 24.

## 3B Food 2

**a** 03.11 Listen and repeat the words.

breakfast

lunch

dinner

*I have breakfast at 7:30.* NOT ~~*I have a breakfast at 7:30.*~~
*She has lunch at 12:30.* NOT ~~*She has a lunch at 12:30.*~~
*We have dinner at 7:00.* NOT ~~*We have a dinner at 7:00.*~~

**b** 03.12 Match the words in the box with pictures 1–12. Listen and check your answers. Then listen and repeat.

| orange | sandwich | butter | biscuit | banana | pizza | potato | tomato | apple | ice cream | cheese | cake |
|---|---|---|---|---|---|---|---|---|---|---|---|

**c** Which food in b do you eat for … ?

- breakfast
- lunch
- dinner

**d** Now go back to p. 27.

## 2B Numbers 1

**a** 02.19 Listen and repeat the numbers.

| 1 | 2 | 3 | 4 | 5 | 6 | 7 | 8 | 9 | 10 |
|---|---|---|---|---|---|---|---|---|---|
| one | two | three | four | five | six | seven | eight | nine | ten |

| 11 | 12 | 13 | 14 | 15 | 16 | 17 | 18 | 19 |
|---|---|---|---|---|---|---|---|---|
| eleven | twelve | thirteen | fourteen | fifteen | sixteen | seventeen | eighteen | nineteen |

*thirteen* NOT ~~threeteen~~, *fifteen* NOT ~~fiveteen~~

| 20 | 30 | 40 | 50 | 60 | 70 | 80 | 90 |
|---|---|---|---|---|---|---|---|
| twenty | thirty | forty | fifty | sixty | seventy | eighty | ninety |

*thirty* NOT ~~threety~~, *forty* NOT ~~fourty~~, *fifty* NOT ~~fivety~~

**b** 02.20 Listen to a–g. Underline the number you hear.

a 13 / 30
b 14 / 40
c 15 / 50
d 16 / 60
e 17 / 70
f 18 / 80
g 19 / 90

**c** Now go back to p. 19.

## 3B Time

**a** 03.15 Match the clocks with the times in the box. Listen and check.

two o'clock   twenty past two   (a) quarter past two
half past two   (a) quarter to two   twenty to two

**b** 03.15 Listen again and repeat the times.

**c** Complete the sentences.

1 My English class is at ________________.
2 My favourite TV programme is at ________________.
3 My school / job starts at ________________.

Tell a partner your sentences.

**d** Now go back to p. 27.

## 4B Numbers 2

**a** 04.13 Listen and repeat the numbers.

| 21 | 34 | 42 | 57 | 63 | 79 | 85 | 99 | 100 |
|---|---|---|---|---|---|---|---|---|
| twenty-one | thirty-four | forty-two | fifty-seven | sixty-three | seventy-nine | eighty-five | ninety-nine | a hundred |

*thirty-four* NOT ~~thirty and four~~ OR ~~four and thirty~~

**b** Work with a partner.
Student A: Say a number in the box.
Student B: Say the next two numbers.

52 41 29 68 98 36 82 75 59

fifty-two

fifty-three, fifty-four

**c** Now go back to p. 35.

## 4A Common verbs

**a** 04.02 Listen to the sentences. Repeat the verbs.

1 We **live** in a big house.

2 I **work** in a factory.

3 I **speak** Spanish.

4 We **study** at school.

5 I **go** to the cinema every weekend.

6 I **teach** young children.

7 We **play** tennis on Saturdays.

8 I **meet** my friends for coffee every day.

**b** Complete the phrases with verbs in a.

1 ___work___ in an office / in a bank
2 ________ football / the guitar
3 ________ in a flat / in New York
4 ________, 5 ________ and 6 ________ Italian
7 ________ at university
8 ________ people / a friend
9 ________ to the gym / home

**c** Write two sentences about you with phrases in a and b.

*I study English. I play football.*

Tell a partner your sentences.

**d** Now go back to p. 32.

# 4B Family and people

**a** 04.09 Listen and repeat the words.

**b** Look at the words in a. Complete 1–10.

**c** 04.10 Listen and repeat the words.

**d** Complete the sentences with words from a and c.

1 They have three c________n, a b________y and two g________s.
2 I'm Olivia and this is David. He's my h________d.
3 That w________n is my s________r.
4 They have a new b________y. It's a g________l. Her name's Lucia.
5 My yoga class has ten p________e: nine w________n and only one m________n!

**e** Now go back to p. 34.

## 5A Places in a town

a 05.04 Listen and repeat the places.

station

supermarket

school

hotel

hospital

cinema

restaurant

bank

shop

café

swimming pool

park

museum

beach

b Talk to your partner. Where are these signs?

*I think 1 is at a swimming pool, or maybe a beach.*

1 

2 

3 

4 

5 

6 

7 

8 

c Now go back to p. 41.

# 6A Jobs

**a** 06.03 Listen and repeat the jobs.

football player

student

receptionist

waiter / waitress

taxi driver

factory worker

bank worker

shop assistant

businessman / businesswoman

chef

office worker

IT worker

teacher

doctor

**b** Cover the words and pictures in a. Correct the spelling in each job. Then check your answers.

1 studint
2 waitres
3 factery worker
4 shop asistant
5 taxi drivar
6 fotball player
7 receptonist
8 bank woker
9 ofice worker

**c** Do you know people who do the jobs in a? Tell your partner.

My father is a taxi driver.

My friend Kumiko is a chef.

**d** Now go back to p. 49.

## 6B Daily routine

**a** 06.08 Listen to Danny's daily routine and complete the times.

1 Danny **wakes up** at __________.

2 He **gets up** at __________.

3 He **has breakfast** at __________.

4 He **goes to work** at __________.

5 He **starts work** at __________.

6 He **has lunch** at __________.

7 He **finishes work** at __________.

8 He **gets home** at __________.

9 He **has dinner** at __________.

10 He **goes to bed** at __________.

**b** 06.09 Listen and repeat the verb phrases.

| wake<br>get | up |
|---|---|

| have | a shower<br>breakfast<br>lunch<br>dinner<br>coffee |
|---|---|

| go | to school<br>to work<br>to bed |
|---|---|

| start<br>finish | work |
|---|---|

| get<br>arrive | home |
|---|---|

*have breakfast/lunch/dinner* NOT ~~*have the breakfast, have a lunch*~~
*go to work* NOT ~~*go to the work*~~
*go to bed* NOT ~~*go in the bed*~~

**c** Read about Pablo's daily routine. Then complete the sentences about him with words in a and b.

> I sleep from 11:00 to 7:00 every night.
> In the morning, I get up and have breakfast. I finish at 7:30.
> It's 30 minutes by bus to go to work.
> I work from 8:30 until 12:30, then I have lunch for half an hour.
> Then I work for three hours until I go home.

1 He ______________ at 7:00.
2 He ______________ at 7:30.
3 He ______________ at 8:00.
4 He ______________ at 8:30.
5 He ______________ at 12:30.
6 He ______________ at 4:00.
7 He ______________ at 11:00 at night.

**d** Now go back to p. 50.

## 7A Common objects 2

**a** 07.01 Listen and repeat the objects.

a bag (bags)

a chair (chairs)

a clock (clocks)

a cup (cups)

a glass (glasses)

a guitar (guitars)

a lamp (lamps)

a picture (pictures)

a plant (plants)

a plate (plates)

a football (footballs)

a speaker (speakers)

a suitcase (suitcases)

**b** Work in groups of three. Cover the pictures and make sentences. Add one more object each time.

At home, I have a guitar.

At home, I have a guitar and ten plates.

At home, I have a guitar, ten plates and three big plants.

**c** Now go back to p. 56.

## 10B Place phrases with prepositions

**a** 10.08 Listen and repeat the phrases.

**in** the car

**in** a taxi

**in** a hotel

**in** bed

**in/at** a restaurant

**in/at** a café

**at** the station

**at** the airport

**at** the bus stop

**at** the cinema

**at** a party

**at** home

**at** work

**at** school

**on** a bus

**on** a train

**on** a plane

**on** holiday

**b** Correct the phrases with prepositions.

1 It's 10:00, but he's still at the bed.
2 I'm waiting for the plane on the airport.
3 I can't talk now. I'm on the car. I'm driving home.
4 Are you in home or are you at the work?
5 I'm having coffee on a café.
6 John's not here. He's still in the holiday.

**c** Think about people you know. Where are they now?

I think my sister is on a plane.

My husband is at work.

**d** Now go back to p. 82.

# 7B Clothes and colours

**a** 07.13 Listen and repeat the clothes.

1

2

3

4

5
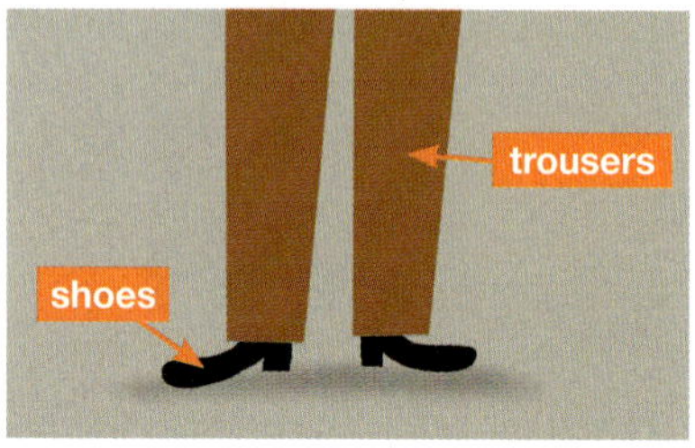


6

**b** 07.14 Listen and repeat the colours.

| light blue | dark blue | light brown | dark brown | light green | dark green | light grey | dark grey | red | black | white | yellow |
|---|---|---|---|---|---|---|---|---|---|---|---|

**c** What do the people usually wear? Write sentences.

1 *Enrico usually wears a dark grey jacket and a light blue shirt.*

2 ______________________

3 ______________________

4 ______________________

5 ______________________

6 ______________________

**d** Now go back to p. 59.

## 8A Past time expressions

**a** ▶ 08.03 Listen and repeat the days of the week.

**b** Complete the sentences.

1 Today is ____________.
2 Yesterday was ____________.
3 My favourite day is ____________, because ______________________________.

Tell a partner your answer in 3.

My favourite day is …

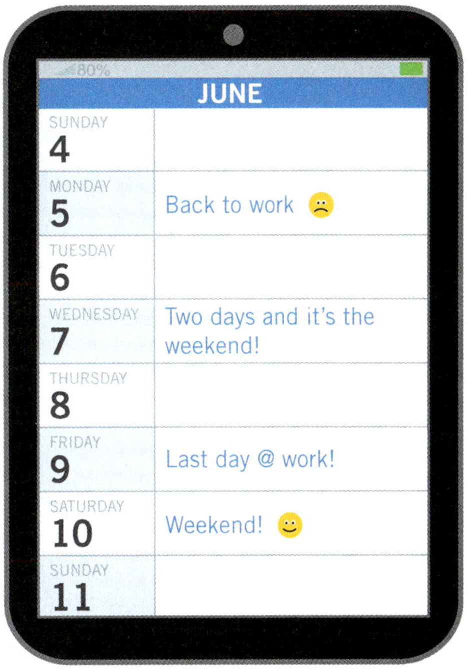


**c** ▶ 08.04 Listen and repeat the past time expressions.

yesterday

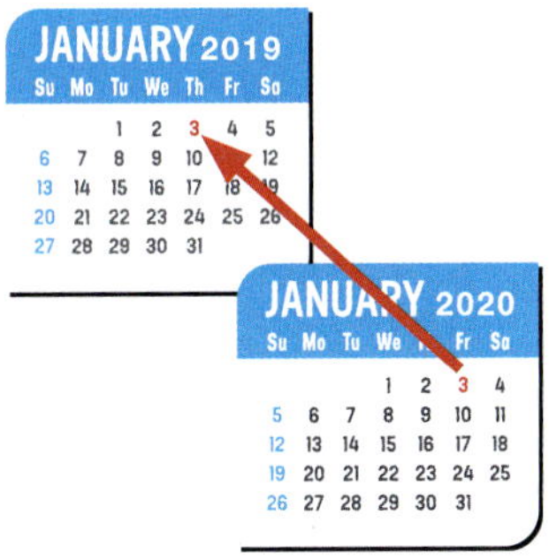


a year ago

last weekend

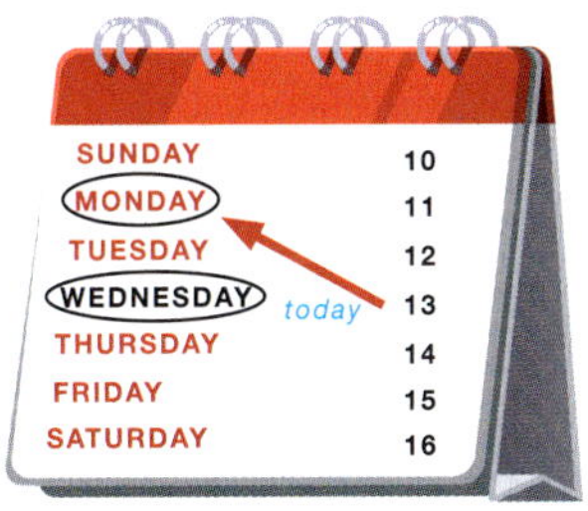


two days ago *or* on Monday

last night

this morning

**d** ▶ 08.05 Complete the table with words in the box. Listen and check.

ago last on this

| | |
|---|---|
| 1 ______ | night<br>Sunday<br>month |
| a week<br>two months<br>ten years | 2 ______ |
| 3 ______ | morning<br>afternoon |
| 4 ______ | Monday<br>Friday |

*two months ago* NOT ~~*before two months ago*~~
*on Monday* NOT ~~*at Monday*~~

**e** Complete the sentences with words from c and d.

1 I was in Barcelona ____________ weekend.
2 They were at the World Cup ____________ year ago.
3 Were you at home ____________ morning?
4 I was at a meeting two days ____________.
5 We were at work ____________ Friday.
6 He was at his friend's house ____________ night.

**f** Now go back to p. 65.

## 8B Free time activities

**a** 08.20 Listen to five people talk about free time activities. Put their activities in the correct order.

1 go (**past simple**: *went*)

☐ I went to the cinema.

☐ I went to a party.

☐ I went shopping.

☐ I went to a café.

2 have (**past simple:** *had*)

☐ I had a pizza.

☐ I had a glass of water.

☐ I had a coffee.

☐ I had a shower.

3 listen (**past simple:** *listened*); watch (**past simple:** *watched*)

☐ I listened to music.

☐ I watched a football match.

☐ I listened to the radio.

☐ I watched a film on TV.

4 read (**past simple:** *read* (/red/))

☐ I read a book.

☐ I read a magazine.

☐ I read the newspaper.

5 play (**past simple:** *played*)

☐ I played the guitar.

☐ I played a video game.

☐ I played football.

**b** 08.21 Listen and repeat the present and past verbs in a.

**c** Complete the sentences with the correct past simple verb.

1 We ____________ football on TV last night.
2 He had breakfast and ____________ the newspaper.
3 I ____________ to a party last night until 2:00.
4 I ____________ to music on the bus this morning.
5 We went to a café and ____________ a pizza.

**d** Write two true sentences about a free time activity in a.

*On Friday, I went to a party.*

**e** Read the first part of your sentences in d. Stop at the verb! Your partner guesses the second part of the sentence.

On Friday, I went ...

... to the cinema ... ?

No, try again!

**f** Now go back to p. 67.

# 9A Transport

**a** 09.02 Listen and repeat the words.

**b** Cover the transport pictures in a. What do these signs show?

1 

2 

3 

4 

5 

6 

7 

8 

**c** Which kind of transport do you prefer? Why?

**d** Notice how we use *go by*, *get* and *take* with different kinds of transport.

| | | | |
|---|---|---|---|
| go by | bus<br>train<br>plane<br>tram | get<br>take | a bus<br>a train<br>a taxi<br>a tram |

*go by bus* NOT ~~*go with bus, go by the bus*~~
We can also use *get the bus*, *get the train* or *get the tram*. NOT ~~*get the taxi*~~

**e** 09.03 Tick (✓) the activity you see. Then listen and check.

1 

☐ I go to work by train.
☐ I drive to work.

2 

☐ He takes a taxi to school.
☐ He takes a bus to school.

3 

☐ She drives to work.
☐ She takes a tram to work.

4 

☐ She takes the underground to see her parents.
☐ She goes by plane to see her parents.

5 

☐ They always walk to school.
☐ They take the metro to school.

**f** Think of three places you went to in the last year. Write how you got there.

*I drove to a friend's house yesterday.*
*I flew to Turkey last summer.*

Tell a partner your sentences.

**g** Now go back to p. 72.

## 9B The seasons and the weather

**a** 09.12 Listen and repeat the seasons.

spring

summer

autumn

winter

**b** Look at pictures 1–5 below. Which season do you think it is in each picture?

**c** 09.13 Complete the sentences with the words in the box. Listen and check.

windy sunny snowy rainy cloudy

1 It often **rains** in England. (verb)
There's a lot of **rain** in England. (noun)
It's often ___________ in England. (adjective)

2 It often **snows** in Antarctica. (verb)
There's always **snow** in Antarctica. (noun)
It's always ___________ in Antarctica. (adjective)

3 There's a lot of **wind** in my town. (noun)
It's often ___________ in my town. (adjective)

4 It's very **sunny** and **hot** today. (adjectives)
It was ___________ and **warm** yesterday. (adjectives)

5 There are a lot of **clouds** today. (noun)
It's ___________ and **cold** today. (adjectives)

**d** Underline the correct words.

1 Do you like hot and *sun* / *sunny* weather?
2 Is the weather *cloudy* / *cloud* today?
3 Is winter cold and *snow* / *snowy* in your country?
4 Is summer hot and *sunny* / *sun* in your country?
5 Does it *rainy* / *rain* in the autumn in your country?

**e** Ask and answer the questions in d with a partner.

**f** Now go back to p. 75.

# 10A The home

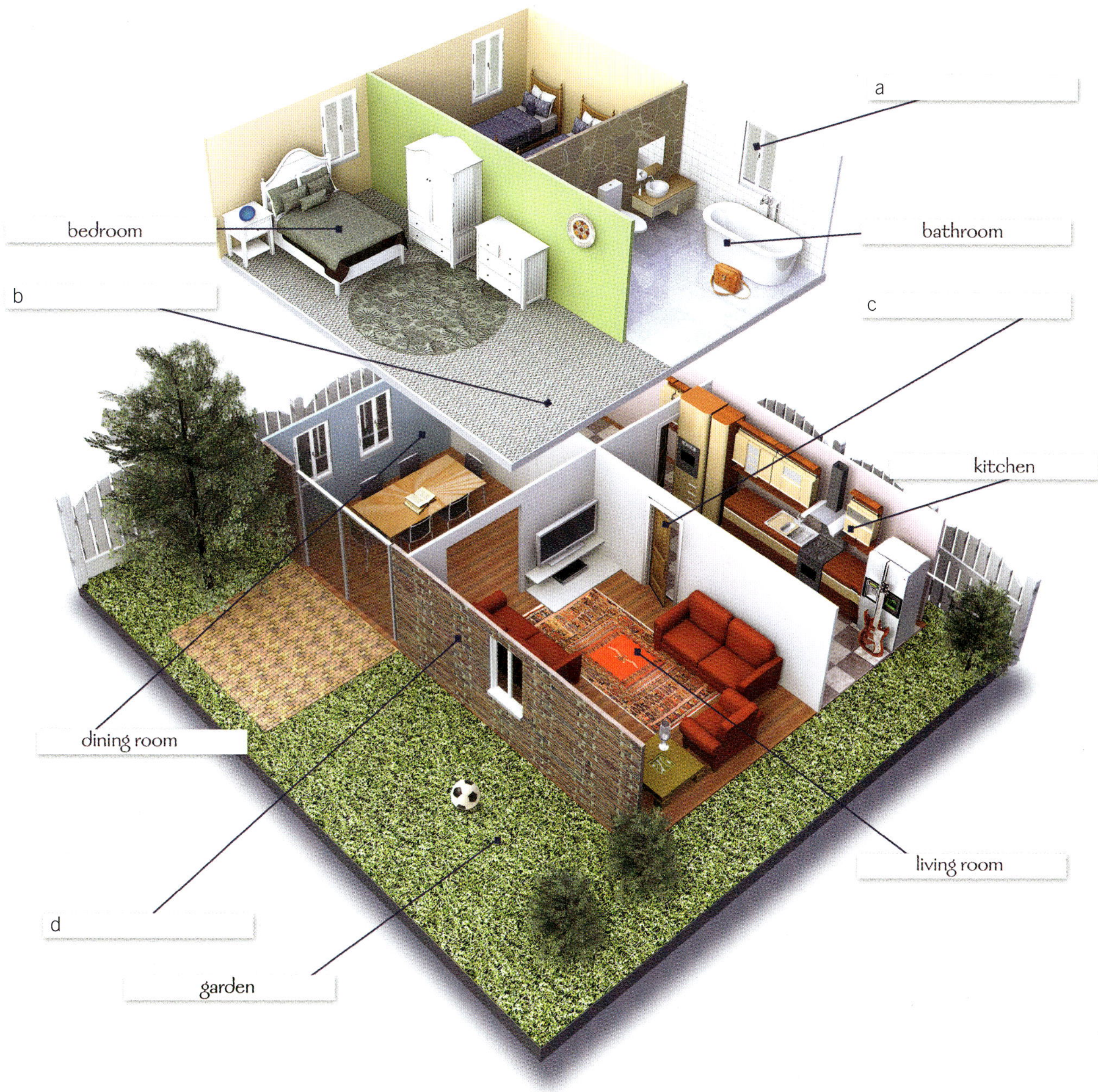


**a** Look at the picture. Where are objects 1–6? Ask and answer questions with a partner.

| | | |
|---|---|---|
| 1 the glass | 3 the book | 5 the guitar |
| 2 the bag | 4 the football | 6 the plate |

Where's the glass?

It's in the living room.

**b** 10.02 Match the words in the box with a–d in the picture. Listen and check.

wall window floor door

**c** Complete the sentences with the correct words.

1 My family has dinner in the d__________ r__________ every evening.
2 We have a small g__________ behind our house. We often sit there on summer evenings.
3 My bedroom has a large w__________ and I can see the mountains.
4 I don't need a chair – I can sit on the f__________.
5 There are a lot of pictures on the w__________ in the dining room.
6 After dinner I like to read in the l__________ r__________.
7 My brother is always in the b__________ – he likes long showers.
8 There are two d__________s in the dining room – one goes to the kitchen, the other to the living room.

**d** Now go back to p. 80.

# 11A Life events

**a** Put the life events in the order you think is correct.

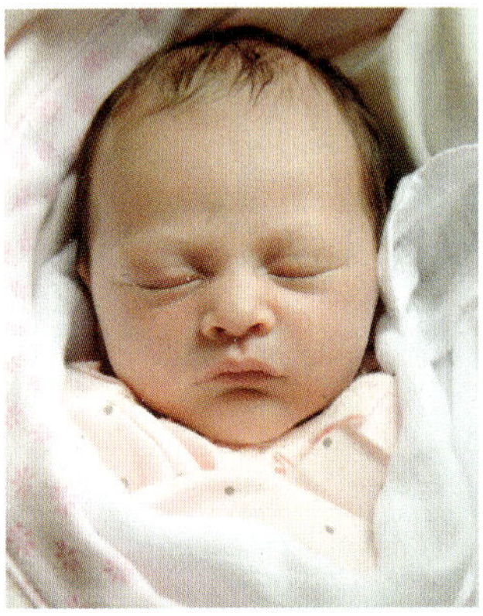

☐ be born
(**past simple:** *was born*)

☐ finish university
(**past simple:** *finished*)

☐ grow up
(**past simple:** *grew up*)

☐ get married
(**past simple:** *got*)

☐ go to school
(**past simple:** *went*)

☐ have a baby
(**past simple:** *had*)

☐ finish school
(**past simple:** *finished*)

☐ stop working
(**past simple:** *stopped*)

☐ go to university
(**past simple:** *went*)

☐ die
(**past simple:** *died*)

**b** 11.04 Listen and repeat the verb phrases in a.

**c** Complete the sentences with the verbs in brackets.

1 I ____________ (go to) university when I was 18 and I ____________ (finish) university when I was 24.
2 Nelson Mandela ____________ (be born) in 1918 and he ____________ (die) in 2013.
3 My father ____________ (stop) working when he was 68.
4 She ____________ (get married) when she was 25 and she ____________ (have) a baby two years later.
5 I ____________ (finish) school when I was 16 and I ____________ (get) a job in a car factory.
6 Michelle Obama ____________ (be born) in 1964 and she ____________ (grow up) in Chicago.

**d** 11.05 Look at the answers and complete the questions. Listen and check.

1 **Q** ________________ go to school? **A** In Valencia.
2 **Q** ________________ finish? **A** In 2012.
3 **Q** ________________ do after that?
**A** I went to Canada.
4 **Q** ________________ go there?
**A** My brother lives there.
5 **Q** ________________ like it? **A** Yes, I had a great time.

**e** Ask and answer the questions in d with a partner. Say answers that are true for you.

**f** Now go back to p. 89.

# 11B Abilities

**a** 11.10 Listen and repeat the verbs.

swim
(**past simple:** *swam*)

cook
(**past simple:** *cooked*)

paint
(**past simple:** *painted*)

sing
(**past simple:** *sang*)

dance
(**past simple:** *danced*)

drive a car
(**past simple:** *drove*)

play volleyball
(**past simple:** *played*)

play cards

ride a horse
(**past simple:** *rode*)

ride a bike

run
(**past simple:** *ran*)

**b** 11.11 Complete the phrases with verbs in a. Listen and check.

1 ____________ a picture

2 ____________ a motorbike

3 ____________ a song

4 ____________ dinner

5 ____________ basketball

6 ____________ to work

**c** Write four sentences about what you did:

- yesterday
- last night
- last weekend
- last Monday

*Yesterday I drove my car to work.*
*I danced at a party last weekend.*

Tell a partner your sentences.

Last night …

**d** Now go back to p. 91.

## 12A Months and future time expressions

**a** 12.03 Listen and repeat the months.

1 December, January, February
2 March, April, May
3 June, July, August
4 September, October, November

**b** Which seasons are 1–4 in **a** in your country?

**c** 12.04 Listen and repeat the time expressions.

tomorrow

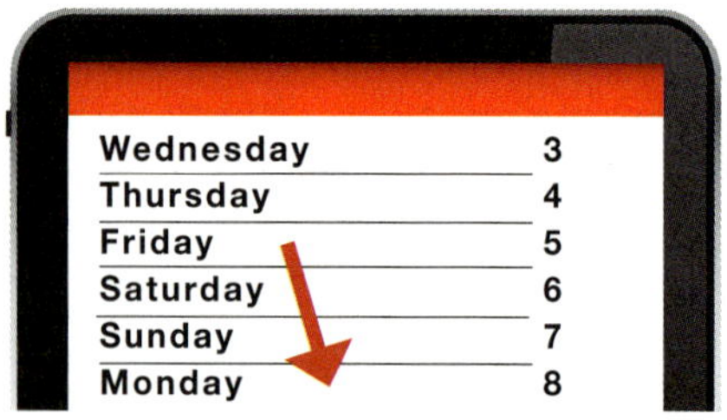

on Monday

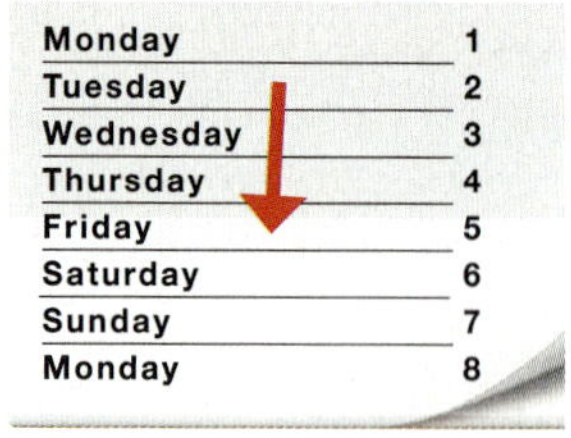

this Friday

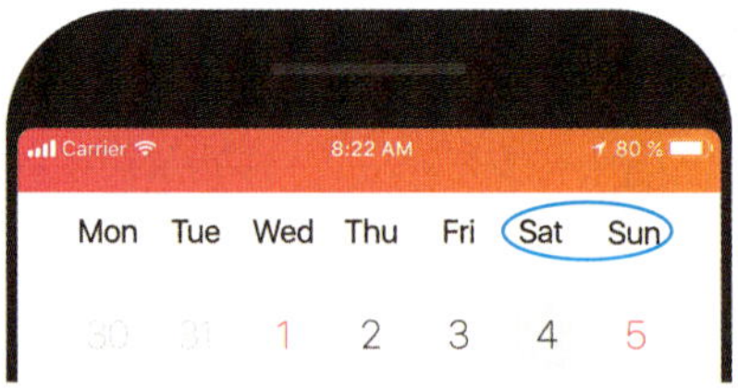

at the weekend

next Tuesday

in two weeks

**d** Complete groups 1–4 with words and phrases in the box. Some of them can go in more than one group.

| Thursday three months June winter year the winter |
|---|

1 **on** Monday, Tuesday, Wednesday …
2 **this** afternoon, Monday, week, March, month, summer …
3 **in** March, the summer, two weeks …
4 **next** Monday, week, March, month, summer …

**e** Complete the sentences with a time expression.

1 I'm going to have (*meal*) ______________________.
2 I'm going to go on holiday ______________________.
3 I'm going to visit a friend ______________________.
4 I'm going to buy a new (*object*) ______________________.

Tell a partner your sentences.

I'm going to visit a friend tomorrow.

## Ordinal numbers

**a** 12.05 Listen and repeat the ordinal numbers.

1 first
2 second
3 third
4 fourth
5 fifth
6 sixth
7 seventh
8 eighth
9 ninth
10 tenth
11 eleventh
12 twelfth
13 thirteenth
14 fourteenth
20 twentieth
21 twenty-first
22 twenty-second
30 thirtieth
31 thirty-first

**b** Work with a partner.
Student A: Say a number.
Student B: Say the ordinal number.

fifteen

fifteenth

**c** Now go back to p. 97.

## 12B Common verbs and collocations

**a** 12.11 Listen and repeat the phrases.

**clean** (**past simple:** *cleaned*)

clean a room / your flat

**exercise** (**past simple:** *exercised*)

exercise at the gym

**go** (**past simple:** *went*)

go to the beach

go to a museum

**make** (**past simple:** *made*)

make a cake

**visit** (**past simple:** *visited*)

visit a friend

visit Paris

**invite** (**past simple:** *invited*)

invite someone to a party

invite someone for a meal

**use** (**past simple:** *used*)

use a computer

use the Internet

**do** (**past simple:** *did*)

do yoga

do your homework

do the washing

do sport

**b** Underline the correct words.

1 He eats a lot and he never *does* / *makes* sport.
2 It's my birthday next week. I'm going to *visit* / *invite* some friends to my flat for dinner.
3 She's going to *paint* / *draw* the walls of her room dark green. Don't ask me why!
4 We were in Mexico and we *visited* / *went* Palenque.
5 I'm going to *do* / *make* some coffee.
6 A woman comes on Wednesday. She cleans our flat and *does* / *makes* the washing for us.
7 Excuse me, can I *clean* / *use* your phone? I need to call my sister.

**c** Write three sentences with the phrases in a.

*I'm going to clean my bedroom tomorrow.*

Tell a partner your sentences.

**d** Now go back to p. 99.

# WRITING PLUS

## 1C Capital letters and full stops

**a** Look at the sentence. Read the information about capital letters and full stops.

My name's Sophia Taylor.

**Capital letters**

We use capital letters (*A, B, C, D …* ):

- for names (***S**ophia **T**aylor, **B**en **W**ilson, **M**aria **G**onzález*)
- for names of places (***T**oronto, **C**anada, **H**igh **S**treet*)
- for nationalities (***I**talian, **B**ritish, **C**hinese*)
- at the beginning of a sentence (***M**y name's …* )

**Full stops**

. = full stop

We usually use full stops at the end of sentences.

*My name's Sophia Taylor.*

**b** Write the capital letters.

| | | |
|---|---|---|
| 1 a A | 4 e | 7 q |
| 2 b | 5 g | 8 r |
| 3 d | 6 h | 9 t |

**c** Add capital letters and full stops to each sentence.

> they're married. (T)
1 we're from brazil
2 he's a student
3 this is ruben
4 i'm in a class with amy lee
5 my name is sandro
6 their flat is in mexico city it's small

**d** Now go back to p. 13.

## 2C The alphabet and spelling

**Part 1: The alphabet**

**a** 02.26 Listen to how we say the letters of the alphabet.

| /eɪ/ (*day*) | /iː/ (*we*) | /e/ (*ten*) | /aɪ/ (*hi*) | /əu/ (*no*) | /uː/ (*you*) | /ɑː/ (*car*) |
|---|---|---|---|---|---|---|
| Aa /eɪ/<br>Hh /eɪtʃ/<br>Jj /dʒeɪ/<br>Kk /keɪ/ | Bb /biː/<br>Cc /siː/<br>Dd /diː/<br>Ee /iː/<br>Gg /dʒiː/<br>Pp /piː/<br>Tt /tiː/<br>Vv /viː/ | Ff /ef/<br>Ll /el/<br>Mm /em/<br>Nn /en/<br>Ss /es/<br>Xx /eks/<br>Zz /zed/ | Ii /aɪ/<br>Yy /waɪ/ | Oo /əu/ | Qq /kjuː/<br>Uu /juː/<br>Ww /dʌbəljuː/<br>('double u') | Rr /ɑː/ |

**b** Add the letters to the group with similar sounds. Say the letters.

R H ~~Q~~ O Z Y C F

1 (**you**) U, Q, W
2 (**day**) J, __, A, K
3 (**hi**) I, __
4 (**we**) T, __, B, D, E, G, P, V
5 (**ten**) N, L, __, M, S, X, __
6 (**car**) __
7 (**no**) __

**c** Now go back to p. 20.

**Part 2: Spelling**

Some words in English have double letters in their written form.

*umbre**ll**a*

Other words in English have letters in their written form that might seem different from what you hear.

*c**i**ty*

**d** 02.30 Correct the spelling. Listen and check. Then practise spelling the words.

| | | |
|---|---|---|
| 1 adress | 5 smal | 9 rong |
| 2 bok | 6 dificult | 10 nife |
| 3 umbrela | 7 intresting | |
| 4 hapy | 8 rite | |

**e** Now go back to p. 21.

## 3C Contractions

**a** Look at the sentences and read about contractions.

**I'm** in a café with Sophia. **She's** my friend from work.

*I'm* (contraction) = *I am*   *She's* (contraction) = *She is*
We use contractions in speaking and writing, usually in informal situations.

***be*: positive and negative**

| + | | – | |
|---|---|---|---|
| **Full form** | **Contraction** | **Full form** | **Contraction** |
| *I am* | *I'm* | *I am not* | *I'm not* |
| *you are* | *you're* | *you are not* | *you aren't / you're not* |
| *we are* | *we're* | *we are not* | *we aren't / we're not* |
| *he is* | *he's* | *he is not* | *he isn't / he's not* |
| *she is* | *she's* | *she is not* | *she isn't / she's not* |
| *it is* | *it's* | *it is not* | *it isn't / it's not* |
| *they are* | *they're* | *they are not* | *they aren't / they're not* |

***It is** a pizza.* → ***It's** a pizza.*

**Present simple: negative**

| Full form | Contraction |
|---|---|
| *I / you / we do not* | *I / you / we don't* |

*I **do not** eat fish.* → *I **don't** eat fish.*

**b** Match the contractions in the box with 1–8.

we aren't   it isn't   don't   I'm   you're   she's
they're   we're

1 you are ____________
2 she is ____________
3 I am ____________
4 do not ____________
5 they are ____________
6 we are not ____________
7 we are ____________
8 it is not ____________

**c** Add the words in brackets to each sentence. Use contractions.

1 ____________ from Sweden. (He is)
2 ____________ tomatoes. (They are)
3 ____________ five o'clock. (It is not)
4 I ____________ have a big meal in the evening. (do not)
5 ____________ a teacher. (You are not)
6 ____________ OK. (I am)
7 We ____________ eat meat. (do not)
8 ____________ Spanish. (I am not)

**d** Now go back to p. 29. Try to use contractions in your text message.

## 4C Word order

**a** Look at the examples and the word order.

**Word order**

- **subject + verb**
*I work.*
*You don't work.*
- **subject + verb + object**
*Emma and Charlotte don't have a brother.*
*They speak Spanish.*
- **subject + verb + preposition + noun**
*My daughters study at university.*
*They don't live in a flat.*
- **subject + verb + object + preposition + noun**
*I don't have a phone in my bag.*
*I like milk in my coffee.*

We can use *here* or *there* after a verb.
*I live **there**.*
*You don't work **here**.*

**b** Tick (✓) the correct sentences.

1 a ☐ Tennis we play.
  b ☐ We play tennis.
2 a ☐ I don't teach children.
  b ☐ Don't teach children I.
3 a ☐ They there don't study.
  b ☐ They don't study there.
4 a ☐ My sister in Japan lives.
  b ☐ My sister lives in Japan.
5 a ☐ These are my friends.
  b ☐ These my friends are.
6 a ☐ I have a flat in New York.
  b ☐ I in New York have a flat.

**c** Put the words in the correct order to make sentences. Remember to use capital letters and full stops.

1 don't speak / they / German
2 there / have coffee / you
3 we / in a factory / don't work
4 teaches / at the university / my dad / Italian
5 the computer / I / at the office / don't like
6 have / in New Zealand / a nice house / they

**d** Now go back to p. 37.

## 5C *and* and *but*

**a** Look at the sentences and read about *and* and *but*.

There's a beautiful park near the hotel **and** there are shops in the next street.
Our hotel is in a nice part of town, **but** it's really small.

| ☺ | *and* | ☺ |
|---|---|---|
| *There's a beautiful park near the hotel* | *and* | *there are shops in the next street.* |

| ☹ | *and* | ☹ |
|---|---|---|
| *The hotel's not very big* | *and* | *it's not near Sebastien's flat.* |

| ☹ | *but* | ☺ |
|---|---|---|
| *The hotel is really small,* | *but* | *it's in a nice part of town.* |

| ☺ | *but* | ☹ |
|---|---|---|
| *His flat is nice,* | *but* | *it's not near our hotel.* |

**b** Underline the correct words.

1 I love London, but it's very *expensive / nice.*
2 The hotel has free wi-fi and *there's / it doesn't have* a TV in every room.
3 Libya is a very hot country, but *the old houses are always cool / it's sometimes 55°C.*
4 There are a lot of expensive hotels, but *there are a lot of / there aren't any* cheap hostels.
5 There are a lot of good books in the bookshop and *they are very boring / the shop assistants are very friendly.*
6 The Maris Hotel is beautiful and *it's near the sea / the restaurant isn't very good.*

**c** Add *and* or *but* to each sentence.

1 I live in Spain, ______ I don't speak Spanish.
2 The food is good, ______ it's very expensive!
3 Their house is nice ______ it's near the bus station.
4 This hotel room is small ______ the shower is cold.
5 The city has a good university ______ I'd like to study there.
6 There isn't a supermarket here, ______ there is a market in the next street.

**d** Now go back to p. 45. Try to use *and* and *but* in your writing.

## 6C *because* and *also*

**a** Look at the sentences and read about *because* and *also*.

I walk to work every day **because** my flat is near the office.
We go out to a café for coffee every day. We **also** have lunch there.

We use *because* and *also* to join ideas.

- *Because* joins two ideas in one sentence. We use *because* to give a reason. It answers the question *Why?*

  Why do you like your job?

  It's interesting.

  *I like my job* ***because*** *it's interesting.*
  *He sleeps in the morning* ***because*** *he works at night.*
- *Also* joins two ideas in two sentences. It means *and.*
  *He plays baseball and tennis. He plays football.*
  *He plays baseball and tennis. He* ***also*** *plays football.*
  (= He plays baseball, tennis and football.)
- We use *also* before the verb:
  *He sleeps in the morning. He* ***also*** *sleeps in the afternoon.*
- We use *also* after *be*:
  *I'm a doctor. I'm* ***also*** *a teacher.*

**b** Underline the correct answers.

1 She plays basketball *also she teaches basketball. / . She also teaches basketball.*
2 I feel good in the morning *because I sleep for seven hours at night. / . Because I sleep for seven hours at night.*
3 I speak English. I also speak Italian because my parents *Italian / are Italian.*
4 Michael works at night. His wife *also works / works also* at night.
5 We always eat at home because *like / we like* cooking.
6 He's a student. He *also is / 's also* a waiter.

**c** Use *because* and *also* to join the ideas.

> I want to go shopping. I need some cups. (because)
I want to go shopping because I need some cups.
> She teaches English at the school. She teaches Turkish. (also)
She teaches English at the school. She also teaches Turkish.

1 I don't like my job. It's boring. (because)
2 She doesn't have breakfast. She isn't hungry in the morning. (because)
3 I need to make lunch. I need to go to the supermarket. (also)
4 The children are nice. They're very funny. (also)

**d** Now go back to p. 53. Try to use *because* and *also* in your writing.

## 7C Commas, exclamation marks and question marks

**a** Look at the sentences and read about commas, exclamation marks and question marks.

*Women's coats, blouses, jeans, bags – all in good condition.*
*Not expensive!*
*How much are they?*

, = comma  ! = exclamation mark  ? = question mark

**Commas**

- We use commas in lists of nouns (things or people).
  *Beautiful things for your home –* ***chairs, lamps, small tables***
- We often finish a list with *and* + noun. We don't use a comma before *and* in lists.
  *I'd like a bag, a coat* ***and a blouse****.*

**Exclamation marks**

- We use exclamation marks to mean *Look at this* or *This is important.*
  *Not expensive!*

**Question marks**

- We use question marks at the end of questions.
  *How much are they?*

**b** Add commas to each list.

1 For sale: old books newspapers magazines.
2 I love old cups plates and glasses.
3 She's wearing black trousers a white shirt a grey jacket and black shoes.
4 They sell radios clocks pictures lamps tables chairs …
5 For sale: coats jackets hats shoes shirts dresses …
6 We need bread milk cheese and apples.

**c** Add a question mark (?) or an exclamation mark (!) to each sentence.

1 How old are these things
2 Thank you
3 Write soon
4 New bookshop
5 Can I pay by credit card
6 How much are they

**d** Now go back to p. 61. Try to use commas, exclamation marks and question marks in your email.

## 8C Writing short emails, notes and texts

**a** Look at the text and read about writing short emails, notes and texts.

SOPHIA >

Hi Megan!
Thank you for your help on Saturday. It was fun to go shopping with you and you helped me find some good shops. I hope we can go shopping again some time soon.
See you soon.

1 We start **emails and notes** like this:
- *Dear* (name),
- *Hi* (name),

We are usually less formal in **texts**:
- *Hi* (name)*!*
- *Hey* (name).

2 In the main part, we use phrases like these:
- *I want to say …*
- *Thanks for your email/note/text.*
- *Thank you for …*
- *Here is/are …*
- *I was …*
- *It was …*
- *I hope …*

We often use the past simple, e.g., *I* ***had*** *lots of fun. I* ***stayed*** *at home. I* ***went*** *into town.*

3 We finish **emails and notes** like this:
- *Best,* (name)
- *Thanks,* (name)
- *See you soon,* (name)

We don't usually finish a **text** with our name.
- *See you soon.*
- *Talk to you later!*

**b** Put a–e in the correct order to make a note.

a The food was great and it was good to talk! I went home and watched a film in the afternoon.
b I hope we can go to the concert on Friday.
c Hi Laura,
d See you soon,
Matt
e I want to say thank you very much for lunch yesterday.

**c** Complete the email with the words and phrases in the box.

| hope | wishes | sorry | It was | Here are | Dear | talked |
|---|---|---|---|---|---|---|

Reply Forward

1 ________ Allie,
2 ________ some photos of the party on Saturday night. I'm 3 ________ I was late!
4 ________ good to meet your friends. I
5 ________ to Emma and Marco – they're really nice!
I 6 ________ we can meet for coffee next week.
Best 7 ________,
Janelle

**d** Now go back to p. 69.

## 9C Making the order clear

**a** Look at part of Sophia's online post and read about making the order clear with *first*, *next*, *then*.

***First**, we went for a walk by the river. It was beautiful.*
***Next**, we went to a small museum and had lunch.*
***Then**, we went shopping and I saw a lovely clock.*

When we write about events in the past, it's good to make the order clear. We use phrases like:

- *First, ...*
  ***First**, we flew to Berlin.*
- *Next, ...  Then, ...  After that, ...*
  ***After that**, we took a bus to Claudia's village.*
  ***Then**, we went shopping.*

We usually use *Next* for the middle event, not the last event.
*First, we went to the zoo. **Next**, we had lunch. Then, we went shopping.*

**b** Underline the correct words.

The weather was very bad! [1] *Then, / First,* it rained. [2] *First, / Next,* it was very windy. [3] *Then, / After,* it snowed!

[4] *First, / Next,* we camped in Anton's garden. [5] *First, / After that,* we stayed in a hotel.

Last summer I went to the UK with Sasha and Yuri. [6] *First, / Then,* we went to London. It was great. [7] *Next, / First,* we went to Scotland for three days. [8] *After this, / After that,* we stayed with Yuri's family in Cambridge.

**c** Add the words and phrases in brackets in the correct place to make the order clear.

> We visited Emma's family in the country. We went to the city. (*then, first,*)
First, we visited Emma's family in the country. Then, we went to the city.

1 I went to a café. I went to the park. (*first, after that,*)
2 It was sunny and warm. It was sunny and cold. (*then, first,*)
3 We went to a restaurant. We saw a film. We went home. (*next, first, then,*)
4 I finished work. I went for a walk by the river. I met Terry at the station. (*first, after that, next,*)

**d** Now go back to p. 77. Try to make the order clear in your online post.

## 10C Word order in questions

**a** Look at part of Amelia's message to Megan and read about word order in questions.

*First, where can I find a taxi at the train station? And how much is it from the station to the hotel?*

| *Yes/No* questions | | |
|---|---|---|
| Do | they | have a garden? |
| Did | Eduardo | visit you? |
| Can | you | call me, please? |
| Is | she | working? |

| *Wh-* questions | | | |
|---|---|---|---|
| How many rooms | does | your house | have? |
| Where | can | I | find a taxi? |
| When | did | the train | leave? |
| What | is | Selma | doing? |

Questions with *be* are different.

| *Yes/No* questions with *be* | |
|---|---|
| Is | Grace's flat big? |
| Were | you at work today? |

| *Wh-* questions with *be* | | |
|---|---|---|
| Where | was | your phone? |
| How much | is | it from the station to the hotel? |

**b** Underline the correct words.

1 Where *are you / you are* going?
2 Who *is that / that is*?
3 *Did you use / You did use* your phone on the plane?
4 *You can / Can you* help me?
5 How many taxis *there were / were there*?
6 What film *is your sister watching / is watching your sister*?
7 *There is / Is there* a garden?
8 How *you do often / often do you* watch TV?

**c** Put the words in the correct order to make questions. Add capital letters and question marks.

there / at the station / a café / is
Is there a café at the station?

1 where / the bus stop / is
2 do / when / start / work / you
3 you / the tickets / buy / did
4 some bread / you / buy / can
5 doing / what / you / are
6 the film / is / what time

**d** Now go back to p. 85.

## 11C Pronouns

**a** Look at part of Sophia's email to Lisa and read about subject and object pronouns.

*... I work in an office with a girl called Megan. She's from London and she's very friendly. ... I also know her cousin James. He's very kind. I often see them at the weekend.*

We use subject and object pronouns so that we don't repeat nouns and names.

*I work in an office with **a girl called Megan. She**'s from London and **she**'s very friendly.*

*I also know **her cousin James. He**'s very kind.*

*I work in an office with **a girl called Megan**...*
*I also know **her cousin James.** I often see **them** at the weekend.*

Read more about pronouns in Grammar Focus 11A on p. 132.

We often use *you* to mean 'people in general / everyone'.
***You** can study English online.*

**b** Underline the correct words.

Seema Bhadoria is a young woman from India. People call [1]*she / her* 'The Strong Woman'. [2]*She / Her* can pull a truck with her teeth.
The Bajau Laut people can swim underwater for a long time. [3]*They / Them* are amazing humans. Did you read about [4]*they / them*?
William Higinbotham was a scientist. [5]*It / He* lived from 1910 to 1994. At a science lab, [6]*it / he* invented a machine called 'Tennis for Two'. [7]*It / You* could play tennis! [8]*It / He* was the first video game in the world, but he didn't make any money from [9]*it / them*.

**c** Swap the underlined words with the subject and object pronouns in the box.

| he | her | him | him | it | it | me |
|---|---|---|---|---|---|---|
| us | she | she | ~~they~~ | they | we | |

\> I met a doctor and an IT worker. The doctor and the IT worker live in Madrid.
*They live in Madrid.*

1 Why is my sister eating that sandwich? My sister made that sandwich for me!
2 Do you like this picture of my wife and me? Valerie gave this picture to my wife and me.
3 My friends have a baby boy called Luke. My friends talk about the baby boy called Luke all the time!
4 Neil and Andy are students. Neil, Andy and I met at university.
5 I'm Tony Smith, from school. Do you remember Tony Smith?
6 That's Sophia and that's James. James likes Sophia, but Sophia doesn't like James!

**d** Now go back to p. 93. Try to use pronouns in your email.

## 12C Paragraphs

**a** Look at Megan's email to Emma and read about paragraphs.

> Reply
> Hi Emma,
>
> I'm in town this afternoon. Would you like to meet for coffee? ← **Paragraph 1 = invitation**
>
> We could go to Café Roma. It's just near your office. I'm free at 4:00. Is that OK for you? ← **Paragraph 2 = making plans for the time and place**
>
> Megan

Paragraphs divide writing into groups of ideas. We use them to make our writing clear. In Megan's email, she uses two paragraphs – one for the invitation and the other for making plans.
To start a new paragraph, write the next sentence on a new line, like this:

> Reply
> I'm sorry, I can't come this afternoon. I'm working today.
>
> Would you like to meet on Tuesday?

> Reply
> ~~I'm sorry, I can't come this afternoon. I'm working today. Would you like to meet on Tuesday?~~

**b** Match paragraphs a–b with 1–2.

> Reply
> 1 ______
> We could meet tomorrow. I'm free in the afternoon. What do you think?

> Reply
> There's a new restaurant in town. It looks really good.
> 2 ______

> a) Reply
> Thanks for the lunch invitation, but I can't come today. I'm busy.

> b) Reply
> Would you like to go there on Saturday?

**c** Rewrite the emails with two paragraphs.

1 Do you have any plans for the weekend? I'd like to see a film. We could meet at the cinema at 6:30. Is that OK for you?
2 It's my birthday next Friday. I'm going to be 25! Would you like to come here for dinner on Saturday? I'm going to invite a few friends.

**d** Now go back to p. 101. Try to use paragraphs in your invitations.

# Acknowledgements

The authors and publishers acknowledge the following sources of copyright material and are grateful for the permissions granted. While every effort has been made, it has not always been possible to identify the sources of all the material used, or to trace all copyright holders. If any omissions are brought to our notice, we will be happy to include the appropriate acknowledgements on reprinting and in the next update to the digital edition, as applicable.

**Key:**
U = Unit, CL = Classroom Language, C = Communication Plus, G = Grammar Focus, V = Vocabulary Focus

**Photographs:**
All the photographs are sourced from Getty Images.
**CL:** Alexis84/iStock/Getty Images Plus; Witthaya Prasongsin/Moment; Eric Audras/PhotoAlto; Image Source; Farknot_Architect/iStock/ Getty Images Plus; SDI Productions/E+; F. Lukasseck/Radius Images; **U1:** Oliver Burston/Ikon Images/Getty Images Plus; Alex Goodlett/Getty Images Sport; Sean M. Haffey/Getty Images Sport; Clive Brunskill/Getty Images Sport; Lucas Uebel/Getty Images Sport; Jordan Mansfield/ Getty Images Sport; Visual China Group; Clasos/LatinContent Editorial; Franckreporter/E+; **U2:** Jeff Kowalsky/AFP; Janoka82/iStock/ Getty Images Plus; Antonio Garrido Ramos/Moment; RolfSt/iStock/ Getty Images Plus; Saulgranda/Moment; Charlie Dean/Caiaimage; Fuse/Corbis; Thinkstock/Stockbyte; **U3:** Caiaimage; Mphillips007/ iStock/Getty Images Plus; AlexPro9500/iStock/Getty Images Plus; Anilakkus/iStock/Getty Images Plus; Baibaz/iStock/Getty Images Plus; Pidjoe/iStock/Getty Images Plus; Stockcam/E+; Dszc/iStock/ Getty Images Plus; Lane Oatey; Gurpal Singh Datta; Eli_asenova/ E+; Vitalina/iStock/Getty Images Plus; JohnGollop/E+; JoeGough/ iStock/Getty Images Plus; VvoeVale/iStock/Getty Images Plus; Atoss/ iStock/Getty Images Plus; Only_fabrizio/iStock/Getty Images Plus; Hispanolistic/E+; Skynesher/E+; Monkeybusinessimages/iStock/ Getty Images Plus; XiXinXing; Ridofranz/iStock/Getty Images Plus; Nadofotos/iStock/Getty Images Plus; **U4:** Michael Cogliantry/Taxi/ Getty Images Plus; Compassionate Eye Foundation/Robert Kent// DigitalVision; PeopleImages/E+; Kali9/E+; Efenzi/iStock/Getty Images Plus; Henryk Sadura/Moment; Sergio Monti/EyeEm; Bojan89/iStock/ Getty Images Plus; Sambrogio/E+; Albert L. Ortega/Getty Images Entertainment; Mike Coppola/WireImage; Christopher Polk/Getty Images Entertainment; Kevork Djansezian/Getty Images Entertainment; Quality Sport Images/Getty Images Sport; Dimitrios Kambouris/ WireImage; Aldomurillo/E+; Morsa Images/E+; **U5:** Oversnap/iStock/ Getty Images Plus; DuKai photographer/Moment/Getty Images Plus; IPGGutenbergUKLtd/iStock/Getty Images Plus; Andreka/iStock/Getty Images Plus; Monkeybusinessimages/Getty Images Plus; Patrick Foto/Moment; JackF/iStock/Getty Images Plus; Hispanolistic/E+; MangoStar_Studio/iStock/Getty Images Plus; Jupiterimages/Goodshoot/ Gett; Yogenyogeny/iStock/Getty Images Plus; Northlightimages/iStock/ Getty Images Plus; Jupiterimages/Stockbyte; Micah Wright/First Light/Getty Images Plus; Kitti Boonnitrod/Moment/; Tpopova/iStock/ Getty Images Plus; Anadolu Agency; **U6:** Westend61; Hugh Sitton/ Corbis/Getty Images Plus; Klaus Vedfelt/DigitalVision; FG Trade/E+; Philipp Nemenz/Cultura; Andresr/E+; Commercial Eye/Stone/Gett; TAGSTOCK1/iStock/Getty Images Plus; DragonImages/iStock/Getty Images Plus; Peopleimages/E+; Skynesher/E+; Jetta Productions Inc/ DigitalVision; Rowan Jordan/iStock/Getty Images Plus; Kurt Budiarto Photography/Moment Open; Niqin/E+/; Adamkaz/E+; **U7:** Cristina Arias/Cover; Danita Delimont; Dial-a-view/E+; Victor VIRGILE/ Gamma-Rapho; Stefania D'Alessandro/WireImage; JP Yim/Getty Images Entertainment; Michael Loccisano/Getty Images Entertainment; Stefanie Keenan/Getty Images Entertainment; Kali9/E+; Kettaphoto/ iStock/Getty Images Plus; **U8:** FEBRUARY/Moment; Doble.d/Moment Open; Bay Area News/MediaNews Group; KeithBinns/E+; Tier Und Naturfotografie J und C Sohns/Photographer's Choice RF; UrosPoteko/ iStock/Getty Images Plus; Mauriliers Schoenmaekers/500px; GK Hart/ Vikki Hart/Photodisc; Andrew_Howe/E+; Geoff Scott-Simpson/Moment Open; **U9:** Jeremy Maude/Photodisc; Kokkai Ng/Moment Open; Tatsiana Volskaya/Moment; StockstudioX/E+; GM Visuals/Royalty-free; Pigphoto/iStock/Getty Images Plus; Czekma13/iStock/Getty Images Plus; Allou/iStock/Getty Images Plus; J-wildman/Getty Images Plus; Jose Luis Pelaez Inc/DigitalVision; Simon Dux/iStock Editorial/Gett; Michael Lee/Moment; AntonioGuillem/iStock/Getty Images Plus; **U10:** Zero Creatives/Cultura; Cavan Images; KatarzynaBialasiewicz/ iStock/Getty Images Plus; Gerenme/E+; Russwitherington1/iStock/ Gett; Jacek Kadaj/Moment; John Keeble/Moment; JohnnyGreig/E+; Ppa5/iStock/Getty Images Plus; ExcellentPhoto/iStock/Getty Images Plus; FotoTravel/iStock/Getty Images Plus; Kohei Hara/DigitalVision; Flashpop/DigitalVision; PhotoAlto/Frederic Cirou; Luis Alvarez/ DigitalVision; **U11:** Greg Epperson/Photolibrary/Getty Images Plus; Sovfoto/Universal Images Group; Sven Creutzmann/Mambo Photo/ Hulton Archive; Hill Street Studios/DigitalVision; Timothy Allen/ Photolibrary/Getty Images Plus; OSTILL/iStock/Getty Images Plus; Kupicoo/E+; Vadimguzhva/iStock/Getty Images Plus; Artem Ermilov/ iStock/Getty Images Plus; **U12:** Peter Cade/The Image Bank/Getty Images Plus; Westend61; Holger Leue/The Image Bank; Simonkr/ E+; Mint Images; AJ_Watt/E+; Cavan Images; Tim Kitchen/The Image Bank/Getty Images Plus; Synergee/E+; Wavebreakmedia/ iStock/Getty Images Plus; Santypan/iStock/Getty Images Plus; **C:** Monkeybusinessimages/iStock; Vadimguzhva/iStock/Getty Images Plus; Ajr_images/iStock/Getty Images Plus; Adamkaz/iStock/Getty Images Plus; Juanmonino/E+; Drbimages/E+; Stevecoleimages/ E+; Juanmonino/iStock/Getty Images Plus; Maskot; Leland Bobbe/ Image Source; **G:** Eugenesergeev/iStock Editorial/Getty Images Plus; Chelsea Lauren/WireImage; **V:** Bravo1954/E+; Hyrma/iStock/ Getty Images Plus; Sohel Parvez Haque/EyeEm; Devonyu/iStock/ Getty Images Plus; Vofpalabra/iStock/Getty Images Plus; Eskymaks/ iStock/Getty Images Plus; Guvendemir/iStock; MicroStockHub/iStock/ Getty Images Plus; L_Mirror/iStock/Getty Images Plus; Carlosalvarez/ E+; Steve@Colorado/E+; Christina Lease/Lonely Planet Images/Getty Images Plus; Judd Pilossof/Photolibrary/Getty Images Plus; Andrea Bricco/StockFood Creative/Getty Images Plus; Gbh007/iStock/Getty Images Plus; Twomeows/Moment Open; Ma-k/E+; Pjohnson1/E+; Seregam/iStock/Getty Images Plus; Subjug/iStock/Getty Images Plus; Juanmonino/E+; Animaflora/iStock/Getty Images Plus; Kirin_photo/E+; LindasPhotography/iStock/Getty Images Plus; Akepong Srichaichana/ EyeEm; Chee Siong Teh/EyeEm; Ligorko/iStock/Getty Images Plus; Caziopeia/E+; Dimitris66/iStock/Getty Images Plus; Kutaytanir/E+; Hidesy/iStock/Getty Images Plus; Unpict/iStock/Getty Images Plus; RedHelga/iStock/Getty Images Plus; Bestfotostudio/iStock/Getty Images Plus; Gannet77/iStock/Getty Images Plus; Radionphoto/ iStock/Getty Images Plus; Ariel Skelley/DigitalVision; Monty Rakusen/ Cultura; Alvarez/E+; Monkeybusinessimages/iStock/Getty Images Plus; Image Source/DigitalVision; FatCamera/E+; PeopleImages/iStock/ Getty Images Plus; Hoxton/Tom Merton; Wavebreakmedia/iStock/ Getty Images Plus; Vav63/iStock/Getty Images Plus; Skrow/iStock/ Getty Images Plus; Monticellllo/iStock/Getty Images Plus; Classen Rafael/EyeEm; Dan Thornberg/EyeEm; CostinT/E+; MortenBjerregaard/ iStock/Getty Images Plus; Danielsbfoto/iStock/Getty Images Plus; Rosemary Calvert/The Image Bank/Getty Images Plus; Hudiemm/ iStock/Getty Images Plus; Suradech14/iStock/Getty Images Plus; Golibtolibov/iStock/Getty Images Plus; Yevgen Romanenko/Moment; MDHayes/iStock/Getty Images Plus; John Seaton Callahan/Moment; Tramino/iStock; Oliver Strewe/Lonely Planet Images/Getty Images Plus; FotografiaBasica/iStock/Getty Images Plus; Marin Tomas/ Moment; Rainer Grosskopf/Photolibrary/Getty Images Plus; John & Lisa Merrill/Photolibrary/Getty Images Plus; Jodie Wallis/Moment; Photographer Nick Measures/Moment; Fuse/Corbis; Real444/E+; IB/ iStock/Getty Images Plus; Iliana Mestari/Moment; Vanessa Davies/ Dorling Kindersley/Getty Images Plus; Skynesher/E+; Mark Williamson/ Photodisc; Mlenny/Stock/Getty Images Plus; Prasit photo/Moment; Eli_asenova/E+; Quim Llenas/Getty Images Entertainment; PeTer_Lau; RUSS ROHDE/Cultura; Image Source; Shapecharge/E+; Lukasz Olek/ Caiaimage; Jupiterimages/Stockbyte; UntitledImages/E+.

The following photographs are sourced from other sources/libraries. **U3:** Danita Delimont/Alamy Stock Photo; **U4:** Maryna Kulchytska/ Shutterstock; **U5:** © Gehry Partners, LLP, © Frank O. Gehry and © Iwan Baan 2014; **U7:** LOOK Die Bildagentur der Fotografen GmbH/Alamy Stock Photo; Bennyartist/Shutterstock; StudioSmart/ Shutterstock; Raulin/Shutterstock; PodPad/Shutterstock; Ruslan Semichev/Shutterstock; **U11:** Emilio Segre Visual Archives/American Institute of Physics/Science Photo Library; Courtesy Brookhaven National Laboratory; CB2/ZOB/Wenn/Newscom; Sanjeev Gupta/EPA/ Shutterstock.

Cover photography by Brandon Colbert Photography/Moment/ Getty Images.

Commissioned photography by Gareth Boden: U1; U2; U8.

We are grateful to The Stephen Perse 6th Form College, Cambridge, for their help with the commissioned photography.

Commissioned video stills by Mike Stone: U1; U2: U3: U4; U5; U5; U6; U7; U8; U9; U10; U11; U12

**Illustrations**
QBS Learning; Mark Bird; Mark Duffin; Sally Elford; John Goodwin (Eye Candy Illustration); Dusan Lakicevic (Beehive Illustration); Roger Penwill; Gavin Reece (New Division); Martin Sanders (Beehive Illustration); Sean 290 (KJA Artists); David Semple; Marie-Eve Tremblay (Colagene); Andrea Turvey (Eye Candy Illustration); Gary Venn (Lemonade Illustration).

Audio production by Leon Chambers and by Creative Listening.

Typeset by QBS Learning.

**Corpus**
Development of this publication has made use of the Cambridge English Corpus (CEC). The CEC is a computer database of contemporary spoken and written English, which currently stands at over one billion words. It includes British English, American English and other varieties of English. It also includes the Cambridge Learner Corpus, developed in collaboration with the University of Cambridge ESOL Examinations. Cambridge University Press has built up the CEC to provide evidence about language use that helps us to produce better language teaching materials.

**English Profile**
This product is informed by English Vocabulary Profile, built as part of English Profile, a collaborative programme designed to enhance the learning, teaching and assessment of English worldwide. Its main funding partners are Cambridge University Press and Cambridge Assessment English and its aim is to create a 'profile' for English, linked to the Common European Framework of Reference for Languages (CEFR). English Profile outcomes, such as the English Vocabulary Profile, will provide detailed information about the language that learners can be expected to demonstrate at each CEFR level, offering a clear benchmark for learners' proficiency. For more information, please visit www.englishprofile.org.

**CALD**
The Cambridge Advanced Learner's Dictionary is the world's most widely used dictionary for learners of English. Including all the words and phrases that learners are likely to come across, it also has easy-to-understand definitions and example sentences to show how the word is used in context. The Cambridge Advanced Learner's Dictionary is available online at dictionary.cambridge.org.

CAMBRIDGE
UNIVERSITY PRESS & ASSESSMENT

Shaftesbury Road, Cambridge CB2 8EA, United Kingdom

One Liberty Plaza, 20th Floor, New York, NY 10006, USA

477 Williamstown Road, Port Melbourne, VIC 3207, Australia

314–321, 3rd Floor, Plot 3, Splendor Forum, Jasola District Centre, New Delhi – 110025, India

103 Penang Road, #05–06/07, Visioncrest Commercial, Singapore 238467

Cambridge University Press & Assessment is a department of the University of Cambridge.

We share the University's mission to contribute to society through the pursuit of education, learning and research at the highest international levels of excellence.

www.cambridge.org
Information on this title: cambridge.org/9781108961691



First published 2022

20 19 18 17 16 15 14

Printed in Italy by L.E.G.O. S.p.A.

*A catalogue record for this publication is available from the British Library*

ISBN 978-1-108-95968-1 Starter Student's Book with eBook
ISBN 978-1-108-96169-1 Starter Student's Book with Digital Pack
ISBN 978-1-108-96172-1 Starter Workbook with Answers
ISBN 978-1-108-96173-8 Starter Workbook without Answers
ISBN 978-1-108-96170-7 Starter Combo A with Digital Pack
ISBN 978-1-108-96171-4 Starter Combo B with Digital Pack
ISBN 978-1-108-96174-5 Starter Teacher's Book with Digital Pack
ISBN 978-1-108-95969-8 Starter Presentation Plus

Additional resources for this publication at cambridge.org/empower